KEY TERMS IN POPULAR MUSIC AND CULTURE

Key Terms in Popular Music and Culture

Music and Culture

Edited by

Bruce Horner and Thomas Swiss

Copyright © Blackwell Publishers Ltd 1999; editorial introductions and arrangement copyright © Bruce Horner and Thomas Swiss 1999

First published 1999

2 4 6 8 10 9 7 5 3 1

Blackwell Publishers Inc.
350 Main Street
Malden, Massachusetts 02148
USA

Blackwell Publishers Ltd
108 Cowley Road
Oxford OX4 1JF
UK

Library of Congress Cataloging-in-Publication Data

Key terms in popular music and culture / edited by Bruce Horner and Thomas Swiss.
    p.   cm.
Includes bibliographical references and index.
ISBN 0-631-21263-9 (hdbk : alk. paper). — ISBN 0-631-21264-7 (pbk)
    1. Popular music—History and criticism.   2. Popular culture.
I. Horner, Bruce, 1957– .   II. Swiss, Thomas, 1952– .
ML3470.K49   1999
781.64—dc21   99-24348
                                                                 CIP

British Library Cataloguing in Publication Data

A CIP catalogue record for this book is available from the British Library.

Typeset in 10.5 on 13 pt Galliard
by Ace Filmsetting Ltd, Frome, Somerset
Printed in Great Britain by MPG Books, Bodmin, Cornwall

This book is printed on acid-free paper.

Contents

CONTENTS

Contributors

ROBIN BALLIGER wrote the lead chapter for the book *Sounding Off! Music as Subversion/Resistance/Revolution*. She has forthcoming essays on popular music and identity in Trinidad, and the cultural politics of intellectual property legislation. She also writes for the popular press and hosts a radio program in the San Francisco Bay area.

DAVID BRACKETT is a composer and guitarist who teaches in the Music Department at the State University of New York, Binghamton, and has written extensively about the analysis and aesthetics of a wide range of twentieth-century music. His book, *Interpreting Popular Music*, was published by Cambridge University Press in 1995, and he has published numerous articles and reviews. He is currently editing a *Rock and Roll Reader* for Oxford University Press, and writing a history of the phenomenon of crossover in popular music of the twentieth century.

SARA COHEN is lecturer at the Institute of Popular Music, University of Liverpool. She is author of *Rock Culture in Liverpool* (Oxford University Press, 1991), and has published articles on popular music and the music industry, place and local identity, gender and sexuality, kinship and ethnicity. She is currently conducting and writing up several research projects on popular music and the city.

MARK FENSTER has published numerous articles on popular music institutions and practices, and is the author of *Conspiracy Theories: Power and Secrecy in American Culture* (University of Minnesota Press, 1999). He earned a PhD at the Institute of Communications Research at the University of Illinois at Urbana-Champaign, and a JD at Yale Law School.

CYNTHIA FUCHS is Associate Professor of English, Film and Media Studies at George Mason University. Her work on popular music and youth culture has been widely published. She is co-editor, with Chris Holmlund, of *Between the Sheets, In the Streets: Queer/Lesbian/Gay Documentary* (University of Minnesota Press, 1997).

LUCY GREEN is Head of the Music and Drama Academic Group at the London University Institute of Education, where she lectures in music education and the aesthetics and sociology of music. Her publications include *Music on Deaf Ears: Musical Meaning, Ideology and Education* (Manchester University Press, 1988) and *Music, Gender, Education* (Cambridge University Press, 1997). Her current research concerns how popular musicians go about learning their skills, and what relationship this bears to music education in school and college classrooms.

BRUCE HORNER is Associate Professor of English at Drake University, where he teaches courses in song criticism, writing, and literature. His essays on song criticism have appeared in such journals as *Mosaic*, *Writing on the Edge*, and the *Journal of Musicology*. He has also published extensively on writing pedagogy, and is author of *Terms of Work for Composition* (forthcoming, State University of New York Press).

ANAHID KASSABIAN is Assistant Professor of Communication and Media Studies at Fordham University, and serves as editor of the *Journal of Popular Music Studies*. She has published widely in the field of popular and film music, most recently co-editing *Keeping Score: Music, Disciplinarity, Culture* (University Press of Virginia, 1997). A new book on film music is forthcoming from Duke University Press.

HOLLY KRUSE holds degrees in political science, history, and media studies. She is currently teaching communications at Villanova University, and her publications on popular music appear in the *Stanford Humanities Review*, *Tracking*, the *Journal of Communication*, *Popular Music*, and the collections *Mapping the Beat* and *On Record*.

RICHARD MIDDLETON is Professor of Music at the University of Newcastle Upon Tyne. He is the author of *Pop Music and the Blues, Studying Popular Music* (Open University Press, 1990), and numerous essays on popular music topics. He is a founder and editor of the journal *Popular Music*.

RUSSELL A. POTTER, who teaches at Rhode Island College, is the author of *Spectacular Vernaculars: Hip-Hop and the Politics of Postmodernism* (State University of New York Press, 1995), as well as a contributor to recent books on popular music, including *Mapping the Beat* (Blackwell, 1997) and the *Cambridge Companion to Rock and Pop* (forthcoming).

GILBERT B. RODMAN is Assistant Professor of Communication at the University of South Florida. He is the author of *Elvis after Elvis: the Posthumous Career of a Living Legend* (Routledge, 1996). His articles have been published in *Cultural Studies*, the *Journal of Communication Inquiry*, and elsewhere.

DAVID SANJEK is Director of the BMI Archives and was US Chair of the International Association for the Study of Popular Music from 1995 to 1998. He is co-author with Russell Sanjek of *Pennies from Heaven: the American Popular Music Business in the Twentieth Century* (DaCapo Press, 1996). His recent essays appear in the collections *Readin' Country: Steel Guitars, Opry Stars and Honky Tonk Bars*, *Mapping the Beat: Popular Music and Contemporary Theory*, and *Sexing the Groove*, in addition to many journals. He is at work on a study of the role of copyright in the history of American popular music.

JOHN SHEPHERD is Professor of Music and Sociology at Carleton University, Ottawa, where he is also director of the School for Studies in Art and Culture. His most recent books include *Music and Cultural Theory* (Polity Press, 1997, with Peter Wicke), and the co-authored *Rock and Popular Music: Politics, Policies, Institutions* (Routledge, 1993). He is Chair of the Editorial Board and Joint Managing Editor of the *Encyclopedia of Popular Music of the World*.

DAVID SHUMWAY is Associate Professor of English and Literary and Cultural Studies, Carnegie Mellon University. He is the author of *Michel Foucault* (1989) and *Creating American Civilization: a Genealogy of American Literature as an Academic Discipline* (1994), and co-editor of *Knowledges: Historical and Critical Studies in Disciplinarity* (1993). He is currently working on a book of interpretations of rock performers and a book on the discourses of romantic love in twentieth-century America.

WILL STRAW is Associate Professor in the Graduate Program in Communications at McGill University and Director of the Center for Research on Canadian Cultural Industries and Institutions. Straw is an editor of the book *Theory Rules: Art as Theory, Theory and Art* (University of Toronto Press, 1996) and, with Simon Frith, of the forthcoming *Cambridge Companion to Rock and Pop* (Cambridge University Press).

THOMAS SWISS'S books include *Measure* (Alabama University Press) and *Rough Cut* (Illinois University Press). He has also co-edited several collections, including *Mapping the Beat: Popular Music and Contemporary Theory* (Blackwell) and *Magic, Metaphor and Power: Cultural Theory and the World Wide Web* (Routledge, forthcoming). He is Center for the Humanities Professor of English at Drake University.

PAUL THÉBERGE is Associate Professor in the Faculty of Information and Media Studies at the University of Western Ontario. He has published articles on music, technology and culture and, as a composer, has created sound works for various media, including radio and film. He is author of *Any Sound You Can Imagine: Making Music/Consuming Technology*, published by Wesleyan University Press.

DEENA WEINSTEIN is Professor of Sociology specializing in social theory and mass media at DePaul University. Her writings on various facets of rock music, including studies of its audience, analysis of its detractors and assessment of interaction within bands, have been published in a variety of journals and edited collections. For the past decade she has written for a variety of magazines and newspapers as a rock journalist. She is the author of *Heavy Metal: a Cultural Sociology* (1991).

Acknowledgments

Thanks to Min-Zhan Lu and Cynthia Lewis for putting up with both the music and the noise. Thanks also to Sofia Turnbull and Nancy Smith for keeping us on schedule, Skye Giordano for the Web site, Jacob and Alley for music updates, Sean Cubitt, Suzanne Schnackenberg, Dan Alexander, Andrew Herman, Susan Rabinowitz and our friends at Blackwell, and all the contributors to this book. And for support: Ronald Troyer, Joseph Lenz, and Bruce Martin, the Drake University Center for the Humanities, and the University of Iowa Center for Advanced Study.

Putting It into Words: Key Terms for Studying Popular Music

Bruce Horner and Thomas Swiss

There is an inevitable tension between words and music. In songs, music gives life to the words. But change the words, and you change the meaning of the music. Moreover, in our conversations and writing about music, our words have power over music: the terms we use to describe music, or the terms used in describing it to us, shape how we think about the music, what we listen for, and the values by which we judge it. What are we to make of these effects? How do we respond to this tension?

This volume is a collective attempt to address these questions. Taking those terms that surface repeatedly in debates about popular music, the chapters explore the competing definitions given the terms, the effects of these different meanings for our understanding of the music, and the tension between the music and the meanings ascribed to it. In addition to presenting the history of debate on certain terms in the study of popular music, the writers further that ongoing debate. Approaching popular music from a variety of perspectives representing a range of professions, academic disciplines, and interests, they take up the task of not simply assessing but rethinking the relation between popular music and the terms used in studying it.

This task is taken up in two ways. Those chapters appearing in part I, "Locating popular music in culture," examine the ways in which popular music can be understood in relation to key terms in the general study of culture – ideology, discourse, history, politics, and so on. Taking popular music as a site through which cultural reproduction and change take place, the writers of these chapters consider the different yields that have resulted from the ways in which such terms of cultural analysis are applied to the study of popular music. In the chapters appearing in part II, "Locating culture in popular music," writers examine how the different meanings given terms common to the vocabulary of popular music – even the very terms "popular" and "music" – help shape the music and our experience of it. But rather than providing the "final word" on the meaning of these terms and on popular music itself, all the chapters are meant to provoke further debate on popular music and its study.

This book is intended in part to redress the poor treatment popular music has received from many scholars, even in fields otherwise committed to the study of "popular" culture, such as cultural and media studies. When not ignored altogether, popular music typically has been treated as a "special" case not susceptible to ordinary treatment because of what is seen as its forbiddingly "abstract" character as music, or it is "read" as if its meaning resided only in the conditions of its production as a mass market commodity, or it is approached in truncated form as some other genre (such as poetry). To put it another way, the study of popular music currently resides on the borders, or in the gaps, between a number of disciplines: musicology, literary study, communication studies, sociology, and anthropology. While each of these disciplines has contributed to the study of popular music, all have operated under specific disciplinary de-limitations producing specific "constructions" of what constitutes popular music and how to study and evaluate it.

Every one of the writers appearing here has worked to change that by crossing disciplinary borders, bringing their considerable training and experience to bear in new ways on the study of popular music to combat the limitations of specific disciplines, including their own. By focusing on the discourses surrounding key terms of popular music, the book asks both those familiar with popular music study and those new to its study: what are we talking about when we talk about popular music?

Each chapter ends with a brief list of resources for those interested in further pursuing the issues addressed. In addition, we have set up a Web site (www.multimedia.drake.edu/keyterms) that contains additional resources, including images, sounds, and other multimedia materials relevant to the chapters in this book, as well as keywords for each chapter with direct links to some of the best Internet resources available in the area of music and culture. We hope thereby to encourage readers to see popular music study as an ongoing project in which we all have a stake. Popular music and the language we use to talk about it shape the sense we have not only of each, but of ourselves.

Part I
Locating Popular Music in Culture

1
Ideology

Lucy Green

The emphasis of study upon a particular aspect of music is in itself ideological because it contains implications about the music's value.

Despite a great diversity of opinion, most scholars nonetheless share certain fundamental views about the term "ideology." These include the notion that ideology represents sets of ideas, values or assumptions which large numbers of people in a given society believe in at any one time. The ideas, values, and assumptions are not straightforward truths, nor are they deceitful or cynical falsehoods, but they grow out of social relations in such a way as to appear helpful and explanatory to people from various perspectives. This process occurs even though not everyone in a society necessarily agrees with or benefits from all the prevailing ideologies, and even though different ideologies within one society often come into conflict with each other.

Part of the reason why ideology is so influential is that it possesses a dual tendency toward reification and legitimation. Reification treats abstract concepts, such as "totalitarianism" or "individual freedom," as if they were real, concrete, unchangeable things or facts. Legitimation means justifying a belief in those reified concepts, and, more importantly, it justifies the social relations that are based on them. For example, in a given society, the ideology of "totalitarianism" might be used to justify the fact that people have no right to vote; or the ideology of "individual freedom" might be used to justify the right of the individual to carry weaponry. It is through processes of reification and legitimation that ideologies gain persuasive powers to either directly or indirectly influence the ways people live, how they behave, and how they relate to each other. In sum, ideology can be understood as sets of ideas, values, and assumptions that tend to reify and legitimate their objects, and through this, to perpetuate existing social relations.

The concept of ideology has two fundamental implications for an understanding of popular music. First, there is no such thing as popular music existing independently of the social world. The very term "popular music" itself indicates that we are talking about the use to which certain music is put by people, or about how many people like the music, or how many people dislike it, or whether we ourselves like, dislike, approve, or disapprove of it, or about how many records are sold, and so on. That is to say, as soon as we use the term "popular music," we are presuming to talk about the use and value of the music. For this reason, it is prone to becoming an ideological term, as I will illustrate below.

Second, any discussion of ideology in relation to popular music can proceed only by considering, or at least being aware of, the entire musical field, including popular, classical, folk, jazz, and other styles from all over the world. There would be no sense in having the category "popular music" unless there were also other categories from which it is distinguished, such as "classical music." Names for different types of music only come into existence, and only have any meaning, in contradistinction to each other. In this chapter, then, I consider ideologies about music in general before focusing on popular music as a specific example within that general field.

One of the most significant ideological practices concerning music in the twentieth century has been precisely to make distinctions between different musical styles, of which popular and classical, very broadly defined, have been particularly prominent. A major point of discussion here has been the question of value. During the twentieth century, various ideological positions have suggested that superior musical value emanates from certain properties, including universality, complexity, or originality. Such properties can be seen as central to ideological constructions about music, not because they are "false" or inaccurate reflections of musical value, but for the following two reasons.

First, they involve a "reification" of music. For example, the idea that a piece of music is universal assumes that the music must have an eternal, unchangeable, inevitable, and natural appeal to human beings regardless of who they are, where or when they live. Second, such notions legitimize the viewpoints of those people who make the claims in the first place. For example, the claim that a piece of music is valuable for being "universal" implies that the music's value must be independent of any interests of the people who value it. Indeed, the music must be so good that it would always be good for any people in any social situation at any historical period. This, in turn, means that the people valuing such music do so not out of self-interest. Rather than claiming to confer value on the music, they claim only to be recognizing value assumed to inhere in the music "objectively," imagined as reified object. This makes their views appear legitimate.

Some people have argued, or have assumed, that classical music, very broadly defined, is the only really valuable style of music and that it alone possesses such properties as universality, complexity, and originality. Other people have argued, contrastingly, that popular music, or certain subcategories of popular music, is also valuable. But rather than contradicting the evaluative claims of the classical supporters, this latter argument can readily be drawn in, so as to rest on very similar claims – such as the assertion that popular music has universal appeal, that some popular music is very complex, or that various popular musicians are highly original. Whichever way the argument goes, whether in support of classical music, popular music, or any other kind of music, it remains ideological insofar as it involves reification and legitimation of the music and its value.

In addition to the concepts of universality, complexity, and originality, the concept of autonomy has played a prominent role in discussions of musical value. In general, when people use the word "autonomy" in relation to music, they mean that the music is highly valuable, and that it has developed in ways that are logically connected to the forms and processes of the musical style as it existed at the time the music was composed, without any regard for contingencies such as making money or being popular. To this conceptualization of autonomy, theorist Theodor Adorno adds that the truly valuable, autonomous piece of music has a close relationship to the society from which it comes, because it in some way replicates and reveals the forms and processes of that society through its use of parallel musical forms and processes.

The concept of musical autonomy as a source of musical value has ideological resonances which are similar to those of the concepts of universality, complexity, or originality discussed above. But in some ways it has implications for valuing popular music, which can be rather different from the implications of those concepts. As I have already indicated, autonomy is particularly and explicitly opposed to social contingencies and social functions of music, such as money, fame, fashion, or enjoyment. Autonomous music is supposed to be good precisely because it disregards or even flies in the face of such social factors. Popular music, contrastingly, is usually overtly and even proudly dependent upon such social factors for its production and in its mode of consumption.

To Adorno, popular music was not universal, complex, or original; but not only that, it lacked autonomy. It encouraged people to regress to an earlier, infantile, stage of development. Instead of autonomously and progressively working through musical logic independently of commercial concerns, Adorno argued, popular music repeated the same, tired old patterns over and over again in order to sell itself to a listenership that craved familiarity. At the same time, so as to appear varied, it added superficial differences to these old patterns, deceiving people into thinking that these differences were new and fresh. Thus people were being fed a limited, repetitive diet while imagining they were receiving something varied. For Adorno, as well as for other of his contemporaries, a diet of this nature helped to perpetuate social relations by inducing a "mass consciousness" which prevented people from thinking independently and challenging the existing social organization. To put this another way, the music itself was actually a part of ideology.

Not surprisingly, there have been vociferous criticisms of Adorno from many people who do not think that popular music is necessarily so damaged by ties to the commercial market or is so simple or so unoriginal. Many do not see it as a harmful and repetitive drudge and do not consider that popular music fans (often including themselves!) have regressed to a state of infancy. These critics contend that Adorno measured the value of popular music in ways that were suitable only for evaluating classical music, and, furthermore, that the two types of music are really so different as to require completely different ways to evaluate them.

A number of scholars have recently grappled with the implications of this view by studying popular music from a musicological perspective. In doing so, they have observed that traditional musicology is not necessarily suitable for studying popular music. I would like to indicate how this unsuitability has been diagnosed, in relation to three areas identified by Richard Middleton (1990, pp. 103–7). First, musicology has developed a rich vocabulary and many sophisticated approaches for understanding musical qualities, such as harmony and form, which are particularly pertinent in classical music. But as David Brackett argues in chapter 10 of this volume, musicology lacks the same wealth of understanding in relation to qualities such as rhythm, timbre, texture, pitch inflection, rhythmic inflection, recorded sound-production (mix), or modality, which are more significant in popular music. Second, musicology has tended to view the notated score as the prime object of study; and many of the parameters on which it has focused, such as harmony and form, coincide with aspects that are relatively easy to notate. Here again, popular music requires a different approach, because it is fundamentally an aural type of music in

8

which the performance or the recording, as distinct from any notation, must be taken as the prime object of study. Third, in the past couple of centuries, musicology has identified a canon of "masterworks" which have come to be considered the greatest examples of musical value. These masterworks have certain characteristics in common. For example, they are all notated, they have all been published in printed form, they are thought to be innovative in relation to the era in which they were composed, and they have all been composed by an individual, Western male. Once again, these characteristics do not necessarily apply to a great deal of popular music. But if this lack of applicability is not recognized, musicologists will assume that the music is lacking in value.

While Adorno did not adopt a traditional musicological approach but a speculative, quasi-sociological or quasi-philosophical one, his critics have argued that his approach was fundamentally influenced by traditional musicological assumptions and by the norms and expectations associated with classical music, making his approach unsuitable as an avenue for understanding popular music. Furthermore, Adorno never conducted any serious analysis of any popular music.

It is helpful to remember that the traditional methods of studying classical music may not be altogether suitable for that music either. Clearly, all music, whether popular, classical, or any other sort, has rhythmic, timbral, textural and inflexive characteristics of one kind or another; most music is now available as a sound-recording and is therefore produced, or mixed; all music takes place in time and usually involves some sort of live performance at some juncture, whether or not it is ever notated; a great deal of music is "new" in certain senses; a great deal of music, including classical music, involves some improvisation; and all music is produced by people, whether male or female and whether individually or collectively. The fact that musicology has developed in ways that tend to ignore these aspects with relationship to classical music does not mean that classical music is completely devoid of these aspects. What it does mean is that musicology has contributed to the belief that classical music is based only on harmony, melody, and other notatable parameters; that it is always fixed in notated form; that it is always progressively innovatory and complex, individually composed by men, and so on. With reference to ideology, the relevant point about this belief is that even though it may not accurately represent classical music, it does not harm the reputation of classical music. In fact, it contributes to the reputation of classical music as highly valuable. It is therefore part and parcel with the ideological evaluation of classical music's superiority.

One further point worth noting is that just as some people have argued that popular music, like classical music, can be universal, complex or original, so too is it possible to argue that certain subcategories of popular music can be autonomous. These can only ever be subcategories of popular music, rather than popular music as a whole, because in order to argue for their autonomy, it is necessary to distinguish them from some other music that is seen to lack autonomy. For example, there have been points in history when a band has been seen by its followers to be "alternative" and against the commercial mainstream. In such cases, the music produced by the band would be considered to have some autonomy, although its fans would be unlikely to use that word. At other times the same band is seen as losing its autonomy when it "sells out" by changing its music to pursue commercial concerns. Occasionally, the music of some bands or individual musicians which is in the broadly "popular" field maintains relative degrees of autonomy for longer periods. But it is more difficult for such music to maintain autonomy than it is for classical music. This is partly because of the relative lack of government subsidies, university lectureships, fellowships, and other support mechanisms for non-classical music. Ironically, the apparent autonomy of classical music actually relies heavily on this sort of financial support. It is also partly because of the general ideological expectations and the existing social relations that surround the production and consumption of popular music.

As I suggested above, the argument that music can be universal, complex, or original is still ideological even if it is put forward in support of popular music and opposed to the superior value placed on classical music. So too with claims that certain "popular" music can be autonomous. It is not the style of the music itself, or even its economic position, but the content of the claims being made for its superiority that make the position ideological.

A constant difficulty in writing about ideology is that the writer must be operating from within some ideological position or other: we cannot entirely escape ideology. One way to deal with this difficulty is to ground ideology-critique by making it specific to concrete objects or concrete situations. Adorno's great contribution, and the reason why despite his many faults he is still read and respected by many people, is that unlike almost anyone before him, he grounded his ideology-critique of music in actual concrete pieces of music, in musical styles, or in the society in which the music was produced and/or consumed. Focusing largely on classical music, he tried to show how real pieces of music were, as I noted above, an autonomous, or an ideological expression of some truths about society.

However, although he often grounded his critiques in his own highly abstract notions of music and society, he never grounded them in ordinary people's notions about music or their uses of music. He made a lot of assumptions about what people "got out of" music, what they thought about it, what effects it had on them, and how they used it, without ever actually asking either listeners or musicians about their experiences, about what the music meant to them, and without ever observing them using music. He was disdainful of the idea that it was worth asking people such questions or observing their behavior, since, according to him, people were already so ideologically influenced that they did not know what they thought, and anything they did think or do would anyway be ideological. But, if looked at another way, we can see that in order to find out something about the content of ideology, it makes sense to ask people what they think or to observe what people do, before leaping to any conclusions about them.

Both the formal and the informal education systems of a society have a great deal to do with ideology. Most particularly, education perpetuates ideologies that are already well established, helping to assimilate (or "defuse") ideological challenges. Education can even help to produce new ideologies in line with changing economic and social conditions. In doing so, education imbues children with self-images, expectations and achievement orientations that fundamentally correspond to their existing social situations. In this way, education helps to perpetuate social relations by guiding pupils into an acceptance of their situation and the concomitant taking-up of roles that are adaptable to the current economic and social climate, and at the same time largely similar to those of their parents in social class terms. Education provides a clear, focused site on which to ground discussion of ideologies about music.

Some years ago I undertook research on music and ideology in education. At that time (1980–4), formal English music education had been overwhelmingly concerned with classical music, but a number of teachers were beginning to incorporate some popular music in their curricula. My research analyzed the common-sense views concerning musical value, and the classroom approaches to music, of teachers in 61 schools. I also analyzed the contents of the music curriculum, the national examination syllabi, and the books and other resources commonly used by teachers. The aim was to "get at" ideology, not by accepting the face value of the teachers' opinions or the overt forms of the curricula, syllabi, and books, but by uncovering the assumptions that lay behind these. I wish to highlight two areas that emerged.

Figure 1.1 Education imbues children with self-images, expectations and achievement orientations that fundamentally correspond to their existing social situations. (Photograph by Lucy Green.)

First, it was apparent that the minority of textbook writers and curriculum planners who did value popular music, and who did regard it as educationally relevant, nonetheless tended to assume that its value rested fundamentally on the very same claims as those upon which the value of classical music rested. That is to say, many opinions were put forward to suggest that, for example, popular music had "universal" appeal; that much popular music was "complex" or "original"; or that there was a distinction between different kinds of popular music, some of which was assumed to be "autonomous" (such as progressive rock), as distinct from other types which were assumed to be "commercial" (such as Top 40 pop). The ideological tendencies toward reification and legitimation already discussed were thus just as prevalent as they were in the views of those people who supported classical music in opposition to popular music.

Second, an analysis of the treatment of classical and popular music by teachers, curricula, syllabi, and books revealed differences in which aspects of the music were emphasized. Generally, the treatment of classical music focused on what, in ideological terms, would be called the "music itself," "intra-musical" processes, or in other words the notes and how they fit together. Contrastingly, the treatment of popular music concentrated largely on "extra-musical" associations related to the social circumstances of the music's production and reception, such as the dress of the performers or the subculture with which they were associated. The emphasis of study upon a particular aspect of music is in itself ideological because it contains implications about the music's value. As I have suggested, musical value has been seen to emanate from properties such as universality, complexity, originality, or autonomy. If teachers present music primarily in terms of its intra-musical contents (the "notes"), this implies that the significant aspects of the music are precisely those which are not tied to any specific social situation and are therefore universal, which involve complexity, and which make possible the development of originality and autonomy. Contrastingly, if teachers draw attention only or mainly to extra-musical associations, this suggests that the "music itself" is of less importance than its social context, that the music is a servant of its social context and, therefore, that it cannot be universal or autonomous. Also, since the "music itself" is apparently not worth analyzing, this suggests that it has no complexity, which in turn suggests the impossibility of it having any real originality. Overall, then, even when popular music was taught, it was approached in ways that implicitly rendered it as inferior to classical music.

The treatment of classical and popular music in schools was thus both contradictory and ideological. On the one hand, materials that were aimed at supporting the value of popular music tended to appeal to the very same qualities upon which the value of classical music rested. The invocation of these qualities, as has already been argued, reifies that music and legitimates the valuation of it. On the other hand, when instructors actually used popular music in the classroom, their treatment of it made it appear to lack those very characteristics purportedly possessed by classical music. The ultimate superiority of classical music was thus affirmed and legitimated. In short, the evaluation and the treatment of classical and popular music in schools reified musical value as universal, complex, eternal, and so on, and legitimized classical music's superiority by maintaining classical music as the only music really worthy of study.

These ideological tendencies helped to perpetuate existing social relations. In general, a small number of middle-class children benefited from the treatment of music in schools, to the detriment of some other middle-class, and of most working-class, children. As I suggested above, education helps to perpetuate existing social relations, and it does this partly through imbuing children with expectations and orientations toward taking up similar roles as their parents. At the same time, in the famous phrase of Bourdieu, the school "demands of everyone alike that they already have what it does not give." In other words, the education system is based on certain implicit values, and educational success depends on acceptance of and familiarity with those values. However, not all children come to school sharing these values: those who do stand more chance of succeeding.

At the time of the research, the ideology that classical music is the most valuable type of music for educational purposes was accepted by the majority of teachers, curriculum planners, and examination authorities, as being equally relevant for all children. This was the case even though it may not have corresponded with the musical tastes, values, and experiences of them all. For example, regardless of their parents' musical affiliations, many children from all social classes were quite clearly far more interested in various types of popular music than in classical music. Not only that, but some middle-class and many working-class children came from family backgrounds in which classical music was anyway not particularly highly valued. The ideology of classical music's superior value corresponded with the values of a minority of middle-class children, whereas it deviated from the musical tastes of some middle-class and many working-class children.

In order to achieve the highest possible educational success in the national music exam for 16-year-olds at that time, it was necessary to have undertaken at least two years and more usually five or six years of specialist instrumental tuition, outside and in excess of the normal school curriculum. This tuition was available free of charge to some extent, but the system survived mainly on the basis of a large number of teachers who were privately paid. In general, for financial as well as cultural reasons, working-class children did not have as much access to classical instrumental tuition as middle-class children. Concomitantly, they did not have as much opportunity to select music courses, nor did they display as much interest in doing so, as middle-class children; and even when they did select courses, they tended to be disadvantaged. They therefore achieved less overall educational success in music than middle-class children. Here, then, is one way in which ideologies about music serve to perpetuate existing social relations: in this case, relations between social classes concerning both the possession of certain musical values and the opportunity for music-educational success.

In this chapter I have suggested a view of ideology as a set of common-sense assumptions which, although complex and manifold, tend to reify and legitimate, and thus to perpetuate existing social relations. With reference to popular music, it is necessary to understand ideology within the terms of the whole musical field, because specific categories of music are manifested only in contradistinction to others. Some of the main distinguishing forces in creating different categories of music involve ideological constructions of value. These constructions often contain the idea that valuable music is imbued with qualities such as universality, complexity, originality, or autonomy. Whereas classical music readily lays claim to such qualities, popular music and other styles of music can do so less readily, and often only with qualification. In both cases, the claims of value are ideological insofar as they involve reification and legitimation. In other words, regarding reification, they tend to give music the appearance of inevitability, naturalness, and so on; and regarding legitimation, they tend to justify the pre-existing musical values of whichever social group employs them. This in turn contributes to the perpetuation of existing social relations by helping to regulate musical practices, expectations, and opportunities. The education system is one example of a social mechanism that aids in this perpetuation and regulation.

The concept of ideology in relation to music can be helpful to understanding how and why certain musical values come to be accepted as common sense; how these values are reproduced through history; how they contain propensities for reification and legitimation; and, moreover, how they perpetuate social relations. This perpetuation occurs partly because musical ideologies affect actual musical practices by regulating the availability of different musical expectations and opportunities to people from different social groups.

I have also indicated that it is never possible for a writer to sit outside of ideology. My own viewpoint must therefore contain some ideological aspects, and it is in this area that it becomes increasingly difficult to disentangle objective argument from evaluative assumption. The best I can do here is to highlight an apparent conundrum in my position. By suggesting that musical value is an ideological category, I have made it appear that music can "really" have no value in itself at all, but that its value is always derived from its social contexts. While I do believe that this must be so, I am not content to follow this through in such a way as to suggest that all music is equally valuable or equally valueless. On the contrary, I believe that both the ways in which intra-musical meanings are constructed and the social contexts lying behind music do form

15

important, relevant, and genuine claims for musical value. Ideology-critique can make us aware of some of the distinctions between different types of evaluative claims, help us understand how musical values affect musical practices, and, most significantly, indicate how our musical practices can act back to affect our musical values. What ideology-critique cannot and should not do is allow us to slip into a position of total relativism from which we are unable to even attempt to distinguish "good" from "bad" music. The process of making such distinctions, however, lies with other chapters in this book, and other pieces of writing.

Acknowledgments

I would like to thank Charlie Ford and Dave Laing for their comments on a draft of this chapter.

Resources

Adorno, Theodor W. (1976) *Introduction to the Sociology of Music*, trans. E. B. Asthon. New York: Seabury.
Brackett, David (1995) *Interpreting Popular Music*. Cambridge: Cambridge University Press.
Frith, Simon (1987) Towards an aesthetic of popular music. In Richard Leppert and Susan McClary (eds), *Music and Society: the Politics of Composition, Performance and Reception*. Cambridge: Cambridge University Press, pp. 133–49.
Frith, Simon (1996) *Performing Rites: On the Value of Popular Music*. Cambridge, MA: Harvard University Press.
Green, Lucy (1988) *Music on Deaf Ears: Musical Meaning, Ideology and Education*. Manchester: Manchester University Press.
Martin, Peter (1995) *Sounds and Society: Themes in the Sociology of Music*. Manchester: Manchester University Press.
Middleton, Richard (1990) *Studying Popular Music*. Milton Keynes: Open University Press.
Vulliamy, Graham (1977) Music and the mass culture debate; and Music as a case study in the "new sociology of education." In John Shepherd, Paul Virden, Trevor Wishart, and Graham Vulliamy, *Whose Music: a Sociology of Musical Language*. London: Latimer.
Walser, Robert (1993) *Running with the Devil: Power, Gender and Madness in Heavy Metal Music*. Hanover, NH: Wesleyan University Press.

Wolff, Janet (1987) The ideology of autonomous art. In Richard Leppert and Susan McClary (eds), *Music and Society: the Politics of Composition, Performance and Reception.* Cambridge: Cambridge University Press, pp. 1–12.

2
Discourse

Bruce Horner

We can no longer maintain any distinction between music and discourse about music, between the supposed object of analysis and the terms of analysis.

Any discussion of the relation of popular music to discourse must confront two questions. First, are we talking about the discourse *of* what is sometimes called "the music itself," or are we talking about the discourse *about* the music – how we talk about music? Second, by "discourse" do we mean discourse in the abstract, as invoked in such highfalutin' phrases as "the discourse of traditional musicology"? Or do we want to use discourse as linguists often use the term, to refer to any instance of actual language use larger than the sentence, such as when analyzing transcriptions of talk among fans at a rock concert?

How we answer both these questions depends on our view of the relationship of language to material experience. For example, if by the discourse of popular music we mean discourse *about* popular music, does that mean that how we talk about popular music has, or at least may have, material effects on that music and our experience of it? Or, on the other hand, should we understand popular music to be a discrete entity operating autonomously with effects unrelated to how any individual or group of people may describe it, with the question then becoming whether discourse about popular music accurately represents it? To put it more simply, to what extent does music lead to the (verbal) discourse about it? Or to what extent does verbal discourse produce the music?

The argument of this book as a whole is that the discourse used to describe popular music has material consequences for how that music is produced, the forms it takes, how it is experienced, and its meanings. That is, this book is informed by a poststructuralist view of the relationship of language to knowledge and material life. To understand this poststructuralist perspective, however, we need to place it in the context of both the history of discourse on music – as a response to and engagement with that history – and the material instances of discursive practice. The poststructuralist perspective represents a departure from, and a critical response to, traditional views of the relation of discourse to music. However, as I will argue, in emphasizing the importance of discourse, some critics paradoxically neglect to consider their own discourse as itself a practice of negotiating competing ideas and beliefs to produce knowledge, in response to contingencies of purpose and circumstance. To counteract such neglect requires refocusing our attention from discourse, viewed in the abstract, to discursive practice: the specific instances and circumstances in which the terms of any discourse are used. I use the clash between academic study and popular music as each of these is commonly conceived to illustrate how the popular music classroom can be a useful site for challenging and revising both academic and popular music discourse.

As Lucy Green argues in chapter 1 in this volume, and as a number of critics of the discourse of traditional musicology have observed, by far the most dominant discourse about music in the nineteenth and twentieth centuries has treated music and discourse about that music as discrete entities. It is within this discourse that, as Carl Dahlhaus (1989) has shown, there has been an elevation of "absolute" music – that is, music for instruments alone, excluding both the singing of verbal texts and the association of music with specific verbal meanings or narratives – over all other musical genres. This elevation of "absolute" music has the effect of dismissing as less "pure" and less worthy such common (and, in one sense, "popular") forms as operas, "program" music – which is linked with a specific narrative, and links certain sounds with narrative events (as in Dukas's *Sorcerer's Apprentice*) – much liturgical music, and that most statistically dominant and popular of musical forms, song. Within this dominant discourse, music must be kept separate from (verbal) discourse. One sign of the dominance of this perspective is the almost exclusive focus in much traditional musicological analysis on relations of pitch and duration, and a remarkable neglect of what are commonly termed "extramusical" factors in the construction of its meaning(s) – such as the political economy of musical patronage, publishing, and performance, the staging of music events, and the specific social significance listeners have attached to musical scores, instruments, lyrics and librettos, and performances. While from other perspectives all these may be seen as central aspects of the music, in the dominant discourse I am describing, the "internal" musical elements of pitch and duration are studied with an aim of codifying how these "musical" elements themselves constitute a specific discourse, or language, *of* music, irrespective of and discrete from such "extra"-musical factors.

The common designation of this approach to music as "analysis" rather than "criticism" reveals the ideological assumption that the approach taken is value-free. In other words, it is assumed that the persons involved are performing, or attempting to perform, objective representations of what is described, rather than offering judgments as to its value, aesthetic or otherwise. The musical score is taken as the music's "foundation," and the patterns of pitch and duration notated in the score are "analyzed" for the formal structures they are thought to evince. However, as Joseph Kerman has observed, in the practice of this sort of music analysis, the question of value in fact "is at the same time absolutely basic and begged," since the choice to analyze a given piece of music presumes that it merits such attention, and the analysis almost inevitably demonstrates the formal features of the music to possess some admired complex "inner coherence" (Kerman, 1980, p. 14). In other words, we might say that the discourse of music analysis, rather than identifying a coherent formal structure already residing "in" the music, *produces* such coherence and structure, and the valuation of it, for those participating in the discourse.

As other chapters in this volume argue, much popular music does not appear to lend itself to such analysis. Whatever complexities there may be in the sonic materials it employs rarely lay in its pitch relations: much popular music employs quite routine harmonies and harmonic structures. (It is in this respect that, for some music analysts, some jazz, because of its complex harmonies, occupies a middle ground in status between "classical" and "popular" music.) Those sonic features of popular music that might be regarded as complex are not those well represented in traditional Western musical notation, and so receive little recognition. Moreover, much of the appeal of popular music seems to reside in extra-musical features: the bravado displayed by the musicians in performance, their apparel and images as star personalities, the paraphernalia of the commodities identified with them (CD covers, T-shirts, stickers and buttons, posters), and, of course, the words of their songs. Finally, to many pop music fans, the few attempts to locate comparable formal features in the "music itself" of popular music miss the point of the music. A study of Van Halen guitar solos that analyzes a notated "score" of them can seem as out of place, as foreign to the popular music discourse of fans, as a focus on the iconographic significance of Beethoven's hairstyle would seem to the discourse of traditional musicology. Within that specific discourse, knowledge about such matters does not count as knowledge at all, or not as knowledge worth knowing.

Over and above these conflicts, analysis of "the music itself" is for many problematic in a more fundamental way: the notion that music is an entity susceptible of analysis is itself discursive. As evidenced by cultures which have no concept equivalent to "music," the designation "music," rather than being simply a name given to an existing object – like naming a newly discovered planet or star – is for poststructuralists a term that brings such an object into being. As Lucy Green (1988, p. 32) puts it, "We are able to distinguish music as such, only when it conforms to pre-established collective definitions of what counts as music." The very notion of "music" is itself not only value-laden (see chapter 10 in this volume) but constructive of musical knowledge and experience: in other words, naming something "music" confers a particular value, a way of understanding, and an experience on that which it so designates. By the same token, further designations – such as the various categories for music (e.g. "popular," "classical," "folk," "world," "blues") – are also constructive of our knowledge and experience of these as such. To name a set of phenomena "rock music" is to contribute to our sense of it and our experience of it. It gives us a sense of its relation to other phenomena (non-music, other types of music) and the ways in which we should think about, experience, and respond to it.

If we grant the poststructuralist argument on the power of discursive terms to construct knowledge and experience, then we can no longer maintain any distinction between music and discourse about music, between the supposed object of analysis and the terms of analysis representing that object. Music is what we call music, and our discourse about it would seem to shape what it becomes for us. This is an argument with particular appeal to those of us interested in challenging the dominance of traditional musicological discourse, for it undermines any basis for claims to the objectivity of traditional musical analysis and its disdain for musics outside the traditional Western canon of classical music. The putative objectivity of musical analysis, and the inherent complexity and coherence of the music analyzed, are from this perspective the effects of the discourse: the "analysis," far from *revealing* musical structure, instead can be seen as *constructing* it, and listeners' sense of it, just as the discourse of disdain for popular musics is no longer seen as a response to the lack of value those musics possess but an active construction of them as lacking in value. Moreover, the assumption that only those with training in the discourse of such analysis can reveal the true nature of the music is seen as producing the effect of mystification: the music, which would otherwise be available for all to make meaning out of, is removed from immediate access, its meaning policed by those few "in the know" through training in the discourse of musicological analysis. Thus the discourse not only constructs our experience and understanding of the music but creates hierarchical social relations to it as something people can understand only through the expertise of the music analysts (as illustrated by the "program notes" distributed to classical music audiences to tell them what it is they will be hearing, or should listen for, in performance).

Against this imposed hierarchical relation to music and its meaning, poststructuralism insists that such mystifying discourse is only one way of constructing music, one which we may dismiss for its politically noxious effects. Once this perspective is adopted, the meaning and very nature of all musics, popular and otherwise, would now appear to be up for grabs, subject to the desires and skills of those discoursing about it, for their discourse appears to have the power to construct and shape its meaning and nature. In my experience, many students are especially drawn to this perspective, as it seems to grant them far greater power to determine for themselves the nature and meaning of popular music. And given the long history of the disparagement of popular music and those peoples producing and enjoying it, and given the history of the political oppression suffered by many of those same peoples, poststructuralism's challenge to the authority of those disparaging such music is very welcome indeed. For example, to the insistence that, say, heavy metal music is not, in fact, "music" at all (a claim once made by a music department faculty member at my institution), poststructuralism seems to enable us to reply, "Sez who?" Or even, "Maybe not for you, but that's *your* problem for not knowing any better." More profoundly, naming something "noise" can be challenged as a politically interested attempt to devalue the culture of a subordinate social group, as has happened with rap (see chapter 10 in this volume).

This recognition of music as discursive construct can itself quickly falter, however, and in two ways. First, the rejection of the discourse of traditional musicology and its construction of "popular music" as a term of opprobrium can quickly lead to the rejection of discourse in general. That is, if the dominance of discourse seems to have had ill effects on attitudes toward, knowledge about, and our experience of popular music, then we might conclude that we should abandon discourse altogether, and step outside it. This is especially tempting once we recognize the limitations of dominant discursive representations of popular music and the power these often have over our experience of it. For example, commercial bin categories are clearly inadequate as representations of the constant crossover of specific music. Is Bruce Springsteen "rock" or "pop" or "folk"? How about Ani DiFranco or Jewel? Into how many categories might U2 fit? ("rock"? "popular"? "world"?) Where, if anywhere, should we put Lyle Lovett, Tom Waits, or k.d. lang? Are Shania Twain or Wilco "country," "popular" or "rock"? And what happens to our experience of such music when we think of it in terms of only one of these categories? Yet despite the clear limitations of such categories, when I have asked students in a course I teach on writing about songs to make a list of the categories they use to think about music, initially they nearly always draw up lists that echo the bin categories into which music stores arrange their displays of CDs and cassettes: "rhythm and blues," "rock," "easy listening," "women's music," "country," "folk," "new age," "classical," "world," and so on. I have also found that when I ask students to describe a song they have already read about, their descriptions usually echo what they have read.

At the very least, this shows the power of the discourse we encounter – in this case, the discourse not of traditional musicology but of commercial institutions – to affect how we think about and experience music. And in response to this power, some adopt the perspective that any discourse, whether the discourse of traditional musicology or the discourse of commercial music, simply "gets in the way" of understanding what the music really is. People adopting this view try to expose how common terms for music misrepresent it, how such terms distort or draw our attention away from aspects of the music they are meant to describe.

An attack on the corrupting influence of the language we use on our experience of music is particularly appealing because it preserves the conceptual possibility of an uncorrupted experience of music. It offers the possibility of having one's cake and eating it too, of admitting that the terms we use to describe music can affect our experience of music, while also claiming that if we are simply careful enough to sweep aside all that language, to purge ourselves of its influence, to step outside discourse, we can escape those effects to really know the music and have an "authentic" experience of it. And it puts those making this argument in the enviable position of apparent enlightenment; others may have fallen prey to such corruption, they say, but we are too wise to have been trapped – we know better than to let CD bins, music reviews, or anything else get in the way of truly knowing music. And so those making such arguments offer to help others transcend such corruption and join them as one of the elite "in the know." This argument is buttressed by the common, and much more longstanding, belief in music as a universal language (of "harmony") with the power to heal social divisions and bridge differences, rehearsed not only in centuries of innumerable song lyrics and poems but also in such present-day practices as "We Are the World" type charity events, congregational singing, Coca-Cola TV commercials, and musicians' international tours. My students, along with many others, sometimes express this idea in terms of just listening to the music, of letting the music "speak for itself."

Note how this parallels the same argument that hails "absolute" music as somehow purer than other forms of music. For invoking the possibility of music speaking "for itself" slips right back to the idea of music as separate from discourse, an idea which, as we have seen, is itself a discursive construct. In other words, the attempt to escape the effects of discourse on music simply substitutes a different discourse about music: in place of the commercial bin categories, it names music as "transcendent," or as "ineffable," or a "mystery."

A version of this attempt to escape the power of discourse is to appeal to experience as a self-evident, static force countering discursive constructions of that experience. Rather than distinguishing between "the music itself" and discourse about it, this response acknowledges the power of discourse to construct "the music," but clings to the idea of experience as outside discourse about that experience and its corruption of it. Those adopting this approach herald one's experience of the music as an antidote to prevailing interpretations of it. Experience, rather than the musical score, is seen as providing access to what is authentic about the music, against which one may measure discursive distortions of it. Susan McClary (1991), for example, makes this argument in countering traditional discourse on both Western classical and popular music. Appealing to the physical bodily experience of all types of music, she calls for recognition of music's ties to the physical, including the erotic, which she sees traditional, supposedly "objective" musical analyses delegitimizing through attempts to render music a purely "masculine" – i.e. cerebral, "rational" – entity, devoid of physicality.

This invocation of the bodily experience of music as providing a more reliable foundation for understanding it is itself quite appealing. First, it appeals to the annoyance many have felt about traditional taboos preventing audiences at classical music performances from moving about as they listen, the ways in which the traditional garb of classical music performers cloaks their bodies from view, and, conversely, the pleasure experienced at

24

performances of popular music in clapping, dancing, and admiring the bodies of performers. In place of defining music as a purely cerebral form divorced from sensuous bodily pleasure, we have here a seemingly much healthier, liberating view of music as pre-verbal expression of a natural physicality suppressed by dominant discourse on music. Moreover, identifying one's personal experience of music as the foundation on which to rely in understanding music elevates all listeners to positions of authority to speak about the music: almost everyone, after all, can experience and has experienced music, so we no longer need to rely on purported "experts" to tell us what we are to think and feel about it. This elevation thus appears to allow for a democratic distribution of authority over music.

However, as in appeals to let the "music itself" speak, arguments like this are vulnerable to the charge of simply substituting an alternative discursive construction of music for the discourse they reject. In place of music as cerebration, we have music as sensuous experience, or as an avenue to such experience and to what is imagined to be our primal nature as sensual, physical beings with bodies responding naturally, through dance, to music's rhythms. And so, in place of the taboos classical music discourse places on experiencing music as physical, we have a discursive insistence on experiencing music as physical. What such arguments neglect is the degree to which this picture of "individual" or "personal" experience of music is itself a social, discursive construct. This is not to deny the appeal for many of imagining music as sensual, nor the validity of testimonies to experiencing it as sensual. But it is to deny the claim that this representation of music is somehow more "authentic," "natural," or outside social historical specificities than claims that music is inherently cerebral, or pure form. (Indeed, the appeal of this argument is suspect in its implicit invocation of what Russell Potter, in chapter 6 in this volume, identifies as a common, racist cultural narrative of some musics, and the peoples producing them, as more primitive, earthy, in touch with physical "nature" than Western classical music and the people associated with that music.) Appeals to experience as the foundation for understanding music are inadequate, as they neglect the dialectical relationship between experience and discourse as shaping one another. Most obviously, they accept discursive representations of experience as "natural" and of individuals and their experience as autonomous rather than embodiments of social material forces. While it may be true that many individuals experience at least some forms of music as physically powerful and sensuous in ways unacknowledged in *some* discourses, their testimony to their experience does not validate representations of the music as sensuous and as about sensuality; rather, their testimony demonstrates the power of a *different* discursive construction of music as sensuous to mold their experience.

We can account for the desire to escape the power of discourse in our attempts to grasp music as, on the one hand, a manifestation of more powerful discourses of American individualism and consumer capitalism, and, on the other, a response to the discourse of social determinism associated with orthodox Marxism. In the discourses of American individualism and consumer capitalism, individuals are posited as autonomous consumers, possessed of their own inherent, individual needs, desires, and experiences, which are then either met or denied by social institutions and which act as an independent force shaping the "market," which in turn responds (when not impeded by social institutions) to meet those needs and desires. The opposed discourse of orthodox Marxism posits individuals as the passive carriers of a consciousness wholly determined by social structures – by one's class position, most obviously. Given the choice these discourses present between seeing oneself as independent, autonomous, and free or as wholly the product of impersonal social structures, many quite understandably opt for the former view, despite its readily apparent limitations in denying the historical, class-, gender-, and race-specificity of the needs, desires, and experiences by naming them as purely "individual."

However, both alternatives fall short in how they imagine discourse and, concomitantly, individuals and "the social." This leads to the second of the questions any consideration of the relation of discourse to music must confront: whether by discourse we mean an abstract, unified set of precepts, terms, and beliefs, or a material site for specific discursive practices. The concern about either resisting discourse or, alternatively, being wholly in its sway in responding to music arises not only from the dominance of beliefs in individualism and the pervasive ideology of consumer capitalism but also from the assumption that discourse is total, uniform, and static in its forms and effects. The attempt to invoke "music itself," or one's "individual experience," as a resource to draw upon in countering the effects of discourse makes sense only if we assume: (a) that we can escape discourse; (b) that the discourse we confront is itself a uniform monolith; (c) that we are not engaged in discourse in invoking such categories. Alternatively, if we recognize discourse as not a static monolith – "Discourse" – but as "discourse," a site for and means of negotiating conflicting and shifting representations and constructions of experience, the individual, and music, then the question becomes not how to evade the impact of Discourse on music, nor how to reconcile ourselves to the

26

determination of music and our experience of it by Discourse, but how to engage in competing discursive practices constructing, and reconstructing, music, ourselves, and our experience of it as we discourse, and to what ends. Taking up that question shifts our focus from the effort to fix "music" or "experience" to examining the materiality of discursive practices: the uses, for whom and for what purposes, under what conditions, of discoursing in particular ways about music.

This shift from a focus on Discourse to discourse and the politics of discoursing in particular ways also addresses a common criticism lodged against the poststructuralist position. That criticism is that those arguing for a poststructuralist insistence on the inescapability of discourse are simply substituting yet another unchallenged foundation for those it attacks. In place of assuming that music is discrete from discourse, or assuming that our individual experience of music gives us access to music's true essence, poststructuralists seem to assume discourse (or, rather, Discourse) as the foundation and essence of music. Turning poststructuralist arguments against poststructuralism, some of its critics have pointed out that calling music a "discursive construct" is itself simply yet another way of representing/constructing music discursively. And not only that, it can have just as "mystifying" an effect on our understanding of music as calling music a transcendent, ineffable essence, pure form, or an experience of primal physicality. There is a contradiction, then, in some poststructuralist arguments, between insisting on the lack of originating truth as foundation for any representation of music and proclaiming music to be a discursive construct.

The resolution of this contradiction does not, however, lie in simply shrugging and pretending to allow everyone entitlement to his or her own view of music, poststructuralist or otherwise. As suggested by my students' experience, one's views and experience of music are never really "one's own" but come from existing language and material conditions. The point of critiquing such language is not to try to escape it but to learn better how to draw on the various competing ways of constructing music so that we can participate actively in constructing and reconstructing, or revising, music and its meanings, in order to work toward certain ends. Key to this project is recognizing that, while some discourses hold greater sway than others at a given moment for given populations, there are always a range of discourses and discursive positions on which we may draw, including those clearly current and those, dominant in the past, which have since faded from prominence. That range is limited, of course. Nonetheless, it offers real possibilities for active participation in constructing music's meanings. Rather than inculcating particular views of popular music, we might engage actively in drawing on the range of possible ways of talking about popular music, and participate in constructing its meanings for particular ends.

There are two dangers that accompany such efforts. First, people sometimes take the position that if music is simply a discursive construct, and if all we have are battles among representations with no musical "thing" against which to test the validity of those representations, then people are free to make music mean whatever they like. There is, then, a kind of spurious "freedom" that seems to be available, all the more dangerous for its appeal. What those adopting this position forget is that the language we use to describe music, and our own desires, does not exist apart from history or material realities; all these constantly reshape one another. The terms we use to describe music may affect our desires for and experiences of it, but these then affect our (subsequent) language. In the class I have described, students sometimes argue that in fact they are free to categorize songs and singers as they please. And of course, as far as their argument goes, they have a point. We are not bound to think of music only in terms of given commercial bin categories, for example, powerful as they are. However, insofar as we are nonetheless bound to language and history, we cannot invent categories out of thin air that have no basis in existing language. So, for example, students can invent new categories, but they do so out of existing discursive material: linking up one or more commercial terms, for example, like country-folk or women's pop or (more energetically) hip-hop metal punk, grunge-world-classical, neo-big-band rhythm and blues. All these examples suggest simultaneously both listeners' reliance on existing terms to make sense of their experience of music and the pliability and limitations of those terms, the ability of listeners to play with and create novel experiences out of existing language to capture what that language is by itself inadequate to represent.

Further, all these examples of students manipulating existing terms also illustrate how historical material conditions can shape our overall response to music: all the students' counter-categories mentioned above sustain, rather than challenge, the idea of music as an object of consumption for pleasure. That is, their knowledge and experience of music is shaped not simply by the terms they use in talking about music but by the institutionalized practices by which the music is produced and encountered as a consumer commodity. Music, for most of us in the late twentieth-century West, is something that comes in packages we buy, collect, and listen or dance to for emotional pleasure, rather than being something we perform

28

for a job (in the discourse of some musicians) or compose to get closer to the mysteries of divine creation (as it has been for some composers) or study to maintain a tradition of excellence (as it continues to be within many conservatories). We have to remember that accepting music as a discursive construct does not mean that it has no "real" material presence. Rather, its presence is everywhere in the technology we possess (CD players, music printing, microphones), in the social practices and institutions in which we engage (shopping at music stores, attending concerts, dancing at clubs), in our social locations – our gender, class, race, generation, geographic region, sexual orientation – and our specific histories, as, say, a cab driver, the younger sister of a reader of *Stereo Review*, an avid exercise club aficionado, or the child of country music stars. To paraphrase Marx, we may be able to "make" music, or at least our knowledge and experience of music, ourselves, but not in conditions of our own choosing.

This does not, however, condemn us to the role of passive carriers of meanings determined by set social historical conditions. For at any given historical moment, the present included, there exist not only a range of discursive constructions of music but a range of practices with it. Further, while one's individual experience may be socially historically determined, those determinations are not uniform but diverse and conflicting. Thus, our individual experience is neither fixed nor uniform but shifting and contradictory – in the language of post-Marxists, not "determined" but "overdetermined." One can, after all, be not only a "scholar" of popular music but an amateur classical pianist, ballroom dancer, singer of nursery songs, and jazz fanatic. And while for analytical purposes we can identify each of these as separate categories of music and musical meaning, in the actual process of lived practice the values and meanings and experience of them spill from one category to the next: we may sing jazz tunes to our children, analyze the melodic structure of "Jack and Jill," swing to classical piano music (much of it, after all, explicitly identified with dance forms), and use our fanatical devotion to a pop star to fuel a scholarly project on her. In considering any specific instance of our discourse about any of these musics, as when someone asserts that a given song is "good," it is likely that we are negotiating a range of conflicting beliefs and practices, discourses and social forces, about what constitutes "good" music.

To illustrate what such negotiation might look like, I return to the example of students in my class. It is true that when asked to describe music, they have tended initially to echo categorizations of music in commercial discourse, not surprising given the dominance of that discourse in present-day US culture, and have had difficulty imagining other ways of categorizing music. But some of them, recalling how they organized their private collections of CDs and tapes, have also realized they have, in fact, other ways of categorizing music that cut across those provided by commercial discourse, categories that distinguish music by when, where, or with whom it is heard: "home" music, "long car ride" music, "private morning" music, "friend" music, "roommate" music, music for getting ready to go out in the evening, and so on. Others have recalled ways of categorizing that lump all the commercial categories of music into one – "bought" or "consumed" music – and have added types of music unacknowledged by such categories: music like nursery songs, jumping rope songs, church hymns, sports pep songs, and the like, distinguished by being sung oneself and the occasion at which it is sung.

None of these alternative ways of categorizing, nor the others they have come up with, is "better" in some absolute sense than the commercial categories they originally came up with, but they are better for certain purposes with which they have aligned themselves, at least for a time, just as the commercial categories have specific uses for some people some of the time, uses defensible or not according to particular principles and values. And no student, any more than the rest of us, could claim to have adhered to only one discourse. We are all aware of, susceptible to, or in any case shaped by, a range of discourses that produce different experiences of music for us, individually and collectively. We are all, to put it simply, products of our culture. But we are also producers of our culture, capable of moving among various elements of culture and changing those elements, as we position ourselves differently, in response to different pressures in our lives. We need to abandon the ideal of resolving conflicts among ways of talking about popular music and accept our role in participating in those conflicts, a role we are already playing, consciously or not, as individuals as well as in contest with others, as we continuously reposition ourselves in our ongoing involvements with music, inflecting and reinflecting it for ourselves and others, and with consequences for the experiences of both others and ourselves.

To return to the larger question posed by this chapter and this volume, this means that the terms we use in discoursing about popular music, and our inflections of these terms, matter: they can help to maintain or alter the experience and construction of popular music, as our discourse interacts with competing discourse, from other sites, also working to maintain or alter it. This difference the practice of discourse makes for popular music has particular resonance for people at academic sites: those who "study" popular music, whether as students or professors. Of course, it often seems downright perverse to *study* a form which in so many of its manifestations seems diametrically opposed to the very idea of studying – think of Alice Cooper's "School's Out," Paul Simon's "Kodachrome," Springsteen's "No Surrender," or Pink Floyd's "The Wall." While the academic study of popular music may garner it a bit of respect, academic respect would seem to be one of the last things popular music would seem to either want or need (see chapter 4 in this volume). It seems at best irrelevant to popular music, at worst a threat to its vitality.

Consequently, many students and professors who do study popular music seem nervous about it. "Crank up Springsteen on the box," Joseph Harris (1991, p. 1) observes of his teaching, "and what you'll see is most of your students sitting a little too straight and too quietly, with the others slumped down in their chairs looking intently at the lyric sheets before them – as if they were wondering if they ought to be taking notes." Mirroring such nervousness, Andrew Goodwin (1997, pp. 43, 45) confesses to feeling "strange" about the cool status he enjoys among students as a "professor of pop" and, conversely, "sheepish" on campus about his own activities as a pop musician (see also chapter 9 in this volume). To have such "pop" knowledge is not seen as appropriate for professional academics. But what Goodwin concludes from these feelings is not that we should banish the study of pop because of the conflicts between the enterprises of academic study and popular music; instead, he argues that pop music gives us "an opportunity to ask questions about what we could say with it, and what we can – and do – learn from it" (Goodwin, 1997, p. 50). What is wrong, for Goodwin, is our limited conceptions of what it means to be a "professor." In terms of my argument, what is wrong is imagining both academic discourse and the discourse of popular music as discrete, static, monolithic entities rather than as competing, fluid, and often intersecting ways of inflecting the meanings of *both* academic study and popular music. Imagined in terms of roles, the issue is often seen as a competition between, on the one hand, the professors, with their traditional academic knowledge about popular music, and, on the other, students, assumed to know popular music strictly as fans, with the question being which knowledge will dominate. But from the perspective I have been advancing, neither students nor professors occupy such singular roles or speak in such uniform ways: they are not each subsumed within a single, monolithic, static discourse. Were students only fans, they would not be enrolled as students in courses in popular music. Similarly, if professors were possessed only of some purely "academic" interests, they would not be teaching pop music. Nor are the ways either have of talking about popular music so uniform. As suggested above, even those pursuing traditional musicological approaches to canonized works of Western classical music bring to those works valuations of them. Similarly, both students and professors bring a range of conflicting discursive resources – interests, beliefs, terms – to popular music. Rather than being a symptom to be eased, the nervousness both may feel can be tapped for its potential to encourage students and teachers to reflect on the politics of studying popular music, and to forge different identities for themselves and for popular music in the new relations they establish to it in light of such reflection.

In other words, this felt conflict between popular music and academic study comes from thinking that discourse ought to be unified, static, and monolithic rather than the site of conflict among a range of beliefs and ideas, subject to varying inflections. The assumption producing this nervousness about studying popular music seems to be that we must keep each discourse separate, that only one must rule, and that we ourselves must adhere in our identities to the beliefs and ways of talking of only one of these: one must be either a fan or a scholar, an archivist or a musician, and the interests of one not only cannot change, they must not "spill over" to contaminate the other. Everything, and everyone, must stay within designated borders. Popular music must be strictly "fun" (an imperative impossible to enact), or it must be examined "objectively" (also, if less obviously, impossible), or it must be understood in terms of stylistic traditions or the history of the recording industry (that is, only music historians or sociologists with significant expertise should be allowed to speak about it), or it must be "experienced" (but how?), or it must always be seen as a discursive construct (well, just try). What such absolutes attempt is to take popular music, including the discourse that constructs it, outside the contingencies of immediate circumstance, purpose, desire, and belief, to substitute Popular Music and Discourse for instances of popular music and discourse. Reversing Marx's dictum, those advancing such absolutes assume that the purpose of popular music study is to interpret popular music, not to change it, and so, when they recognize the possibility that academic discourse might indeed change it, they get nervous.

However, instead of either trying to legislate popular music and discourse about it by naming what it is and how it should be discussed, or lapsing into the *laissez-faire* pluralism of "allowing" everyone to do as they please – which would leave unchallenged the discourses already in place to shape our sense of what pleases – we can ask of any discursive acts (that of others and our own) what difference that way of talking about a particular instance of popular music might make, for whom, under what conditions, and how, and why we might want to perpetuate such effects or not. Addressing ourselves to such questions will require sensitivity to, if not nervousness about, the range of existing dominant, alternative, and residual ways of talking about, and knowing, popular music, and the effects of these on its construction and our experience of it. But it will also lead to both critical and creative reconstruction of our desires for the discourse that we produce in response.

Rather than responding to conflicts between the different discourses on popular music by trying to keep them separate, or by pledging allegiance to one and suppressing others, we can and should seek out such discursive conflicts as sites for their potential to revise our sense of popular music, and our ways of discoursing about it. For like the creation of popular music "itself," in our discourse we can combine and revise our experience, enabling ourselves to hear, as if for the first time, the songs we thought we already knew.

Resources

Cook, Nicholas (1990) *Music, Imagination, and Culture*. Oxford: Clarendon Press.

Cooke, Deryck (1959) *The Language of Music*. Oxford: Oxford University Press.

Dahlhaus, Carl (1989). *The Idea of Absolute Music*, trans. Roger Lustig. Chicago: University of Chicago Press.

Foucault, Michel (1972) *The Archaeology of Knowledge and the Discourse on Language*, trans. A. M. Sheridan Smith. New York: Pantheon.

Frith, Simon (1996) *Performing Rites: On the Value of Popular Music*. Cambridge, MA: Harvard University Press.

Goodwin, Andrew (1997) On being a professor of pop. *Popular Music and Society*, 21, 43–52.

Green, Lucy (1988) *Music on Deaf Ears: Musical Ideology, Meaning, and Education*. Manchester: Manchester University Press.

Harris, Joseph (1991) Misreading movies. *Iowa English Bulletin*, 39, 1.

Horner, Bruce (1998) On the study of music as material social practice. *Journal of Musicology*, 16, 159–99.

Kerman, Joseph (1980) How we got into analysis, and how to get out. *Critical Inquiry*, 7, 311–31. (Reprinted in *Write All These Down: Essays on Music*. Berkeley: University of California Press, 1994, pp. 12–32.)

McClary, Susan (1991) *Feminine Endings: Music, Gender, and Sexuality*. Minneapolis: University of Minnesota Press.

33

Middleton, Richard (1990) *Studying Popular Music.* Milton Keynes and Philadelphia: Open University Press.

Nattiez, Jean-Jacques (1990) *Music and Discourse: toward a Semiology of Music,* trans. Carolyn Abbate. Princeton, NJ: Princeton University Press.

Shepherd, John (1991) *Music as Social Text.* Cambridge: Polity Press.

3

Histories

Gilbert B. Rodman

People like to separate storytelling which is not fact from history which is fact. They do this so that they know what to believe and what not to believe. This is very curious. How is it that no one will believe that the whale swallowed Jonah, when every day Jonah is swallowing the whale? I can see them now, stuffing down the fishiest of fish tales, and why? Because it is history.

Jeanette Winterson, *Oranges Are Not the Only Fruit*

On the first page of the syllabus for my undergraduate class on popular music, I warn my students that what they are enrolled in is not a history course. That is, my class doesn't look much like what my students expect a history course to be: a chronological survey of names and dates that they will need to memorize and regurgitate. While I do spend a week at the start of the semester mapping out a sketchy overview of some of the major shifts in US popular music since the turn of the century, the bulk of the course is devoted to more contemporary issues and questions – the ethics of sampling, the gender politics of the Spice Girls, the rise of multinational entertainment conglomerates, and so on – most of which are too current to strike my students as even vaguely historical in nature.

Nevertheless, throughout the semester, our discussions of even the most current of topics will hinge upon our understanding of popular music history. For example, explaining how the music industry works today requires us to have some knowledge of the sheet music business at the turn of the century, the heyday of Tin Pan Alley, the rise of radio and BMI, and so on. Our debates about contemporary moral panics over allegedly "dangerous" (e.g. Marilyn Manson) and/or "vacuous" (e.g. the Spice Girls) forms of popular music require us to compare them to previous moral panics around such popular music figures as Elvis and

Madonna. Making sense of the various arguments about the ethics of sampling will require us to situate those issues within the context of previous shifts in the technology of music-making and historical patterns of musical "borrowing"/"theft." And so on. In short, every issue we address is one that we will wind up examining in light of historical contexts.

In this chapter, I want to make explicit the argument that is more of a hidden agenda in my classroom: namely, that studying popular music *always* requires us to take questions of history into account. Our efforts to study popular music (or virtually anything else, for that matter) ultimately boil down to a form of storytelling. We start with a set of unanswered questions. What does this song mean? Why did this genre develop the way it did? What effects does this shift in the industry have on musical creativity? From there, we go on to do research that hopefully allows us to tell a story that answers those questions in persuasive fashion. Yet the beginnings of the stories that we tell about popular music, whether they are about today's hitmakers or turn-of-the-century minstrels, are always the endings of other stories that we have not told. And it is here – in the gap between the stories we are most interested in telling and the stories that precede them in time – that questions of history come into play in crucial ways.

I should emphasize up front that the impulse to tell stories – and the need to historicize that always goes along with it – plays an important role across the entire spectrum of popular music studies, regardless of discipline, methodology, or subject matter. A political economy approach, for instance, requires us to tell stories about the flow of money through a profit-driven industry; subcultural analysis produces stories about the relationship between particular styles of music, the communities of fans and artists that form around them, and the larger cultural formations in which those sounds and practices circulate; musicological analysis leads to stories about what the music in question means and how that meaning is produced; and so on.

To illustrate my argument in more concrete fashion, I draw on the example of my own research on Elvis Presley, although, in many respects, the phenomenon at the heart of my research is not historical at all. On the contrary, when I started working on Elvis in the early 1990s, the mystery I hoped to solve was centered on contemporary aspects of music and culture. Why, so many years after his death, was Elvis appearing across such an astonishingly broad swath of the US cultural terrain in so many strange and unpredictable ways? Why, to borrow a line from Mojo Nixon and Skid Roper, was Elvis everywhere? Why wasn't he behaving the way that dead stars are supposed to? It wasn't surprising that Elvis could regularly be found on oldies radio stations or as the focal point of fan gatherings and newsletters. Nor was it particularly shocking that his estate, his former record label, and the various studios for whom he had made films were milking his continuing popularity for everything they could. But it was difficult to explain why Elvis was such a pervasive presence on less obviously relevant corners of the cultural terrain. For example, what was he doing in mainstream news reports on such "hard news" topics as the fall of communism in the Soviet Union, Operation Rescue's blockades of women's health clinics, or the 1992 presidential election? Why was he being invoked in advertisements for such far-flung enterprises as CD-ROM databases, copy shops, and luxury automobiles? Why was he suddenly a frequent figure in science fiction novels and short stories? What made him into a punchline for virtually every major syndicated comic strip in the USA? And – perhaps most curiously – why were so many people who openly despised Elvis and all that he stood for working so hard to keep him in the public eye?

While these are all questions about what was then the present, and while the phenomenon of "Elvis sightings" was (and still is) very much a contemporary one, it became evident to me very early in my research that any convincing explanation for Elvis's lingering cultural presence needed to address the question of how past events had helped to create a context in which that contemporary phenomenon could come about. For example, one of the more striking ways in which Elvis cropped up on the cultural terrain between 1989 and 1992 was as a powerful symbol of contemporary US racial politics. Probably the most notorious example of this was Public Enemy's 1989 song "Fight the Power" (prominently featured in Spike Lee's film *Do the Right Thing*), which pulled no punches in calling Elvis a "straight-up racist." But Chuck D and company were hardly the only people invoking Elvis as part of a larger public conversation on racism in the USA. A year later, in Living Colour's "Elvis Is Dead," a song from the hard rock foursome's second album, *Time's Up*, the group continued the discussion by explicitly quoting – and then extending – Public Enemy's jab at Elvis. In 1991, Joe Wood wrote an article for *The Village Voice* that was ostensibly about the Young Black Teenagers (a *white* rap act), though it actually devoted more space to Wood's argument about Elvis and racial politics than it did to the YBTs. In 1992, the US Postal Service's announcement that it would be issuing a series of stamps featuring Elvis and rock 'n' roll other legends was met with public statements of concern in *The Washington Post* about the Postal Service's need to make sure that their final roster of rock 'n' roll legends was not all white (Nicholson, 1992). That same year, when Dave Marsh's 1982 Elvis biography was reprinted, these fresh charges of racism leveled at Elvis had become so numerous and widespread that Marsh took almost half of the book's new introduction to try and explain why it was wrong to see Elvis as a racist and what such a misconception meant for the future state of race relations in the USA.

Still, none of these texts were intended to be history lessons as much as they were attempts to engage with and intervene in one of the more pressing and divisive political questions of the moment. Which left me with a thorny question to answer: why on earth was Elvis, who had been dead for more than a decade, such a significant and oft-invoked figure in debates over racism in the 1990s? To answer that question, I had to do more than simply make sense of the contemporary moment in which these artists and writers were working; I also had to understand the specific histories that they were invoking, and I had to be able to make meaningful connections between those histories and the present. In this particular case, that meant I had to tell a story that encompassed both the state of contemporary race relations (on the one hand) and competing visions of the role that race and racism had played in the rise of rock 'n' roll from the 1950s onward (on the other). For what Elvis meant in these particular contemporary texts was inextricably bound up with arguments about what Elvis had represented in the past and whether the birth of rock 'n' roll was best envisioned as a progressive moment of racial integration or as yet another in a long line of racist appropriations of black music by white musicians, audiences, and businesses.

Historicizing, however, is about more than simply recognizing and understanding references to past events: it is also about providing a valuable sense of perspective on contemporary phenomena – even when those phenomena make no apparent allusions to the past. For example, one of the most common claims that my popular music students make early on in the semester is that "things" are far more extreme now than they have ever been. Most often, this line of argument revolves around the claim that the current breed of "scandalous" musicians (from Madonna to Marilyn Manson, from Prince to Snoop Doggy Dogg) has crossed lines of good taste and propriety that even the most outrageous artists of yesteryear would never even have considered crossing. Sure, my students will argue, Elvis was a rebel back in the fifties, but all he really did was sneer and shake his hips a bit. Today, on the other hand, it is common for musicians to release songs

38

filled with four-letter words and graphic descriptions of wild sexual acts, to make videos that are just barely this side of soft-core pornography, and to do things on stage even raunchier than that.

The problem with such claims is that they are rooted in what are essentially ahistorical historical comparisons. That is, while my students are ostensibly working to explain the differences between two points in time, their assumption seems to be that those differences are superficial ones at best. In trying to judge Elvis's 1950s performances by contemporary standards and finding him decidedly tame, my students assume that the culture in which Elvis first wiggled his pelvis is similar enough to US culture today that identical standards of what counts as outrageous public behavior can be applied to both eras. The historical question that needs to be addressed here, however, is not whether Elvis would be seen as controversial today (or, conversely, how controversial Marilyn Manson would have been in 1956), but whether Elvis was more outrageous by the standards of his era than Marilyn Manson is by today's.

Viewed through *this* historical lens, it is not clear that even the most "extreme" contemporary musical acts are as transgressive as Elvis was forty years ago. While my students are certainly right to suggest that Elvis's hip thrusts would barely raise an eyebrow were they to be broadcast on national television today, we need to remember that the culture in which Elvis rose to stardom was far more strait-laced about "suggestive" public displays than "the same" culture is today. The mid-1950s, after all, were an era when even the most socially and morally acceptable form of sexual activity (i.e. procreative intercourse between a married couple) was too risqué for prime time television: for instance, even though their real-life marriage was public knowledge, Lucille Ball and Desi Arnez still slept in separate beds on *I Love Lucy*, and even when Lucy's real-life pregnancy was too obvious to hide from the camera, the word "pregnant" was still too scandalous to actually utter on the air. In that tightly buttoned-up cultural environment, then, Elvis's hip-shaking was nothing less than revolutionary. By contrast, even the most radical of contemporary popular musicians are working in a cultural context where frank depictions and discussions of human sexuality are common features of *non*-controversial forms of popular culture (e.g. soap operas and PG-rated films) – which ultimately makes even the carefully calculated button-pushing of artists like Madonna or Prince less "over the top" than what Elvis did when he first came along.

Having argued that we always need to take questions of history into account in studying popular music, I want to anticipate four potential misconceptions about what that actually entails. Specifically, I want to suggest that:

- doing history is about interpreting facts, not just reporting them;
- historical contexts are things that we have to construct in our story-telling;
- people make history, but never in conditions of their own making;
- historical events appear to be inevitable only after they have happened.

First, it is important to recognize that placing research on popular music in historical context is more than simply a matter of citing names and dates, or inserting the "proper" facts about past events into the stories that we are telling. For while it is certainly important not to get verifiable historical facts wrong (one cannot, for example, get away with claiming that Elvis was a Korean woman or that his first hit single was "Louie Louie"), we also have to remember that even the most widely agreed-upon historical facts are subject to competing – and potentially equally valid – interpretations. That there are demonstrably wrong answers to the historical questions we may ask *does not* always mean that there are clear-cut and indisputably right answers for us to use in telling our own stories.

Thus the ongoing debate over Elvis's racial politics ultimately does not revolve around establishing the true facts of Elvis's story as much as it hinges on competing claims about which facts matter most, how best to interpret those facts, and what is the proper story to be told using those facts. For example, Greil Marcus's much-celebrated review of Albert Goldman's much-reviled Elvis biography takes specific issue with Goldman's misquote of Sam Phillips's famous claim, "If I could find a white man who had the Negro sound and the Negro feel, I could make a billion dollars." In particular, Marcus objects to Goldman's substitution of "could sing like a nigger" for "had the Negro sound and the Negro feel," and argues that Goldman brutally distorts the history of rock 'n' roll by placing a racist slur at its heart. But while Marcus presents a devastatingly convincing argument as to why Goldman's version of this historical moment is flawed, significantly enough, his case does not rest on establishing the verifiable truth about what Phillips really said (especially since Phillips denies ever making any version of the statement in question). Rather, it depends on using other verifiable facts (e.g. Phillips's open willingness to go against the segregated norms of early 1950s Memphis by recording black musicians) to tell a different version of the story, one in which the slur attributed to Phillips by Goldman is simply too implausible to let stand.

Closely related to this last point is the fact that, ultimately, there is more to doing historical work than simply fitting our discussion of contemporary issues into already established historical contexts. Instead, we actually need to *create* historical contexts to fit the questions that lie at the heart of our work. To put a slightly different spin on a point I made earlier, the beginnings of the stories we tell are actually the endpoints of *multiple* other stories that we don't have time or space to tell in full. Thus, historicizing can be thought of as an act of stitching together new stories out of scraps taken from several earlier tales. The key questions here, then, are *which* historical facts to choose out of those available to us, and then *how* to interpret those facts and weave them together to form a persuasive narrative.

For example, we can tell very different versions of "the same" story – say, the tale of Elvis's rise to national prominence in 1956 – depending on which historical facts we decide to use in framing and supporting our narrative. To be sure, not all the facts we could draw on are going to be equally relevant to our story, and the facts that are available to us place unavoidable limits on what stories we can plausibly tell. But there is also no single right answer to the question of which facts are the most important here. If we are especially concerned with the racial politics of the rise of rock 'n' roll, as in chapter 6 in this book, then it might be especially important for us to pay attention to who originally wrote and recorded the various songs on which Elvis built his career, how faithful his versions of those songs were to the spirit of the originals, what the racial demographics of the audiences who bought those records were, who did and did not receive royalty payments on sales of those records, whether Elvis's success helped boost the popularity of the black artists whose music he performed, and so on. On the other hand, if we are more interested in the rise of youth culture that rock 'n' roll helped to bring about (see, for example, chapter 8 in this book), then we are more likely to ask questions about the age of Elvis's audiences, how links were forged between rock 'n' roll and other youth-friendly aspects of the leisure and entertainment industries (soda shops, drive-ins, etc.), the rise in disposable income among post-war teens, and so on. Each of these sets of historical questions will put a very different spin on the story that results.

One can find this same principle at work in broader "histories" as well. Looking at three different volumes dedicated primarily to the history of post-Second World War Anglo-American popular music, one can see "the same" story being told in strikingly different ways. DeCurtis and White's *The Rolling Stone Illustrated History of Rock and Roll,* for example, consists of nearly 100 essays, most of which focus exclusively on a specific artist (Elvis, the Beatles, Madonna), scene (Chicago, Memphis, San Francisco), or musical style (doo-wop, folk rock, funk, rap). The story resulting from these essays is one that emphasizes musicians over moguls, albums over audiences, and songs over social forces: in this version of rock 'n' roll history, the major theme is that of rock 'n' roll as a creative, artistic endeavor, and the story's major figures are the Great Artists responsible for making such Great Music. Charlie Gillett's *The Sound of the City,* on the other hand, maps roughly the same period of musical history, but concentrates far more intently on the recording industry and the role played by specific labels in the music's rise to prominence. Here, rock 'n' roll becomes more of a terrain created and fought over by shrewd entrepreneurs and media empires than a revolutionary artistic oeuvre, and industry figures such as Motown's Berry Gordy and Atlantic's Ahmet Ertegun become central to the tale. Meanwhile, Reebee Garofalo's *Rockin' Out* takes yet a third approach to the story at hand. While Garofalo writes a great deal about both artists and the industry, his main focus is on rock 'n' roll as a powerful social, cultural, and political force. As a result, non-musical events (for example, the civil rights movement) play a larger role in the story, and Garofalo makes a deliberate effort to explain how popular music both shaped and was shaped by the culture around it.

Another common misconception about questions of history stems from the tendency to oversimplify the way history actually unfolds. This oversimplification typically takes one of two forms: either it dramatically overemphasizes the role played by broad, impersonal forces in the making of history, or it grants too much credit for historical change to "great" individuals. An example of the former tendency can be found in the relatively common claim that the rise of rock 'n' roll in the 1950s was simply the inevitable result of social, economic, and cultural forces that had been at work for years beforehand. One version of this argument would have us believe that it was a combination of the economic prosperity of post-war life, the entertainment industry's drive to create a new and highly profitable market centered on youth culture, and the growing desire for black music by white audiences (among other factors) that ultimately made rock 'n' roll happen. According to this vision of rock 'n' roll history, no particular individual was somehow essential to the way the story unfolded: if there had been no Elvis Presley, someone else would have played the role he did just as well. Albert Goldman's aforementioned

Elvis biography is a textbook example here – Goldman bends over backwards to portray Elvis's success as a consequence of anything (luck, timing, slick packaging, other people's talent, etc.) besides Elvis himself – but he is far from alone in this regard. As Simon Frith points out in "The academic Elvis," academic work on popular music – including, Frith admits, his own early writings (e.g. *Sound Effects*) – has all too often echoed the more facile versions of non-scholarly histories and biographies.

On the flip side of the coin – and often offered as a deliberate response to the vision of history where people are interchangeable parts bound up in the works of some larger machine – we find an approach to history that celebrates Great Men (and it is almost always men who are lauded this way) as the principal agents of historical change. Here, for example, Elvis might readily be touted as a profound visionary who recognized what was wrong with US culture in ways that no one else had before him, and who singlehandedly set out to change that culture. Instead of broader forces leading inexorably to the triumph of rock 'n' roll, this vision of history is likely to see Elvis as a lone hero fighting *against* an overwhelming array of broader forces – busting down the barriers between black and white, shattering the stifling sexual morality of the era, teaching youth to think for themselves and question authority, and so on – in order to bring into existence his personal vision of a better life for us all. Some of the sharpest and most insightful commentators on Elvis's life and music have made such overstated claims (see Guralnick, 1979; Marsh, 1982; Marcus, 1991, pp. 26–39). To be fair, they have undoubtedly done so out of a passionately felt need to rebut the widespread vision of musical history as nothing more than impersonal social forces. Nevertheless, such claims *are* overstated. One doesn't have to portray Elvis as having some sort of master plan to transform US culture in order to make a strong case that he played a unique role in bringing dramatic changes about in that culture.

In the end, the main problem with each of these competing visions of rock 'n' roll history is not that they make untenable claims as much as that each manages to ignore the important insights of the other. There really were a host of structural and institutional forces that combined to make rock 'n' roll possible – and, without these, rock 'n' roll might never have come into existence at all. But it is also true that without the unique talents of figures like Elvis and Chuck Berry, the ultimate shape and impact of rock 'n' roll would have been very different: take Presley and Berry out of the picture, and rock 'n' roll might very easily have become a primarily piano-based music after the example of figures like Fats Domino,

Jerry Lee Lewis, and Little Richard. The difficult balance that we need to strike in our historical work lies in the recognition that historical change is the byproduct of unique individual achievements in the context of social, cultural, economic, and political circumstances that are beyond the ability of those individuals to create or control on their own.

Finally, it is vital for us to recognize that history never looks as neat or predictable while it is unfolding as it does after the fact. One of the most difficult tricks in doing historical work is recapturing the sense of uncertainty that existed at some prior moment about what would happen next. In hindsight, for instance, it is quite easy (and common) to view July 6, 1954 as "that fateful day" when Elvis cut his first single for Sun Records and started off on the road to international stardom – and even easier for us to frame the stories we tell in such a way that Elvis's subsequent fame and fortune are seen as the natural and inevitable consequence of wheels set in motion that summer afternoon in a little studio on Union Street. At the time, however, there was nothing at all inevitable about the future of Elvis's career. Even two years later, after he had signed a contract with RCA-Victor and had two singles go to the top of *Billboard*'s pop charts, Elvis could still be heard to speculate about what he was going to do *when* – not "if" – the rock 'n' roll fad faded away. Today, of course, we know precisely how Elvis's story turned out. Back then, however, no such knowledge was possible – just as today we cannot speak with absolute certainty about what next year's (or even next week's) headlines will be. In telling our own stories, then, and in doing the historical work that we need to in order to have our stories make sense, we have to be careful about seeing predictable cause-and-effect relationships between events where no such certainty actually existed.

Perhaps the best example to use to illustrate this point is *Last Train to Memphis*, the first volume of Peter Guralnick's biographical opus on Elvis. What is remarkable about Guralnick's book is that he tells a story that most of his readers already know in intimate detail (or think they do), yet he manages to present it in such a way that the reader is still surprised time and time again by what happens next. Guralnick pulls off this seemingly impossible task, not by uncovering a vast storehouse of previously unknown facts that fundamentally alter the story we have heard countless times before, but by the way in which he tells his tale: specifically, how he allows it to unfold before us in much the way it unfolded at the time for those who lived it. Which means that Elvis's own surprise at his rise to stardom becomes a surprise for us as well.

And this, in the end, may be the most important reason why "doing history" matters for the study of popular music: not because it will allow us to answer all our questions, but precisely because it won't. If done well, history will surprise us, challenge us, and lead us to new – and hopefully better – questions. Which, in turn, will lead us to tell better stories.

Resources

DeCurtis, Anthony and White, James Henke (eds) (1992) *The Rolling Stone Illustrated History of Rock and Roll*, rev. edn. New York: Random House.
Frith, Simon (1981) *Sound Effects: Youth, Leisure, and the Politics of Rock 'n' Roll*. New York: Pantheon.
Frith, Simon (1996) The academic Elvis. In Richard H. King and Helen Taylor (eds), *Dixie Debates: Perspectives on Southern Culture*. London: Pluto.
Garofalo, Reebee (1997) *Rockin' Out: Popular Music in the USA*. Boston: Allyn and Bacon.
Gillett, Charlie (1983) *The Sound of the City: the Rise of Rock and Roll*, rev. edn. New York: Pantheon.
Goldman, Albert (1981) *Elvis*. New York: Avon.
Guralnick, Peter (1979) *Lost Highway: Journeys and Arrivals of American Musicians*. New York: Vintage.
Guralnick, Peter (1994) *Last Train to Memphis: the Rise of Elvis Presley*. Boston: Little, Brown.
Marcus, Greil (1981) Lies about Elvis, lies about us: the myth behind the truth behind the legend. *Voice Literary Quarterly*, December, pp. 16–17.
Marcus, Greil (1991) *Dead Elvis: a Chronicle of a Cultural Obsession*. New York: Doubleday.
Marsh, Dave (1982) *Elvis*. New York: Thunder's Mouth (reprinted 1992).
Marsh, Dave (1985) How great thou art [1977]. In *Fortunate Son: Criticism and Journalism by America's Best-Known Rock Writer*. New York: Random House, pp. 303–6.
Nicholson, Bill (1992) Please Mr. Postman . . . : if Elvis deserves a stamp, so do America's black rockers. *The Washington Post*, 26 January, p. C5.
Rodman, Gilbert B. (1996) *Elvis after Elvis: the Posthumous Career of a Living Legend*. New York and London: Routledge.
Winterson, Jeanette (1985) *Oranges Are Not the Only Fruit*. New York: Grove Press, p. 93.
Wood, Joe (1991) Who says a white band can't play rap? Cultural consumption, from Elvis Presley to the Young Black Teenagers. *Voice Rock & Roll Quarterly*, March, pp. 10–11.

4
Institutions

David Sanjek

I don't care to belong to any club that will accept me as a member.

Groucho Marx

Everything that pleases one has a reason for pleasing, and pouring scorn on
the crowds that mistakenly gather here or there is not the way to bring them
back to where they ought to be.

Charles Baudelaire

I

Occasions arise in life where a collision of incompatible circumstances
produces a profound sense of dislocation. Sometimes, this results in new
ways of thinking; at other times, nothing more than the confirmation of
hidebound prejudices. I have found myself caught in such a quandary more
than once during certain public events, particularly during formal award
ceremonies for those involved in popular music – such as the Grammies.
My alienation on these occasions results not so much from the cut of my
rented clothes or the fact that I know virtually no one seated about me as
from the collision between the formality of the setting and the frivolous,
pleasure-seeking nature of the phenomenon or figures being honored. In
the case of popular music award ceremonies, nothing in my experience of
listening to it conforms with the wearing of tuxedos, rubber chicken din-
ners, or a sequence of sincere tributes to the rewards of a lifetime dedicated
to promoting other people's pleasure. The sedentary rituals of an awards
ceremony seem more compatible with affairs of state than with those connected to the honky-tonk, house party, stadium or one night stand.

I imagine that the individuals honored for a career in popular music
must experience a comparable sense of dislocation. Finding themselves
the object of such a structured ceremony invariably calls to mind all the

forces of routine and regimentation they have systematically endeavored to avoid. I imagine, for example, that Robert Plant, lead singer of Led Zeppelin, was galvanized by such a flood of sentiments when he interrupted his 1994 induction into the Rock and Roll Hall of Fame to observe, "I never wanted to do this. I always thought we'd always be rebels." Under the circumstances, the possibility of continuing his life as a liberated hedonist must have come across to him, and others, as unseemly or simply adolescent. How could he trash a hotel room or topple an array of speakers on-stage now that he had been officially memorialized? After such respectability, what opportunities remain for disruption or dissipation? On the other hand, these ceremonies can also confirm that however many awards one receives, a sense of ostracism never wholly evaporates. During the 1992 Rock and Roll Hall of Fame ceremony, the New York City-based African American producer Bobby Robinson spoke of his relationship with the newly inducted and long deceased Elmore James, the slide guitarist who penned and played "Dust My Broom" and "The Sky Is Crying." When Robinson paused during his reminiscences of their collaboration on the latter song, he received the kind of dismissive applause that seemed to send him to the dustbin of history. This sorry episode illustrates that awards can just as easily confirm the vitality of popular music or condemn it to the past. One person's received truth can become another's recycled, and rejected, memories.

It was not supposed to be this way. Popular music – particularly the many variants that arose in the aftermath of the Second World War – was conceived for the sake of the moment at hand, not the decades to come. We were good rockin' *tonight*, without a thought to the future, whose outcome was abandoned to the attractions of immediacy and improvisation. But whether the makers, consumers, or even the manufacturers of popular music intended or desired it to be so, the institutions that have arisen over the course of the past half-century and attached themselves to the enterprise we associate with popular music cannot any longer be felt to inhibit our experience of the culture they accompany. Instead, they form an inalienable element of that phenomenon. Of course, we might succumb – and we do, time and again – to the attractive alternative of individualistic connoisseurship. Our likes and dislikes thereby remain a matter of solitary sensibility, unsullied by any distasteful association with other people or alien organizations. By doing so, we inhabit that space the art critic Harold Rosenberg memorably characterized as a "herd of independent minds." Yet that body of institutions remains a procrustean bed in which we cannot help but lie, all the while remembering that if popular music cannot be identifiable with or reducible to its representations, those representations nonetheless remain a portion of the musical experience. In the end, the normalization of our experience of popular music by those institutions that process musical culture must not prohibit us from pursuing the novel and the unexpected.

To develop more fully the definition of the institutions attendant to popular music, I first illustrate how their function is clarified by a set of conceptual frameworks elaborated by Howard S. Becker, Simon Frith, Pierre Bourdieu and Sarah Thornton. I then illustrate the function and history of those institutions by drawing upon two of the most influential in popular music: the organ of popular opinion (*Rolling Stone* magazine) and the industry support organization (the National Academy of Recording Arts and Sciences, the presenter of the Grammy Award). By briefly examining their history and the complex and contradictory role they play, we will more fully understand how institutions collide with but do not altogether override prevalent anti-authoritarian assumptions about popular music. Much as we would like to do so, we cannot separate ourselves from the forms of representation that constitute the public face of the cultural materials that drive the affective dimension of our lives. We do so not so much at our peril but driven by the pretension that we remain superior to them.

II

Institutions attendant to the domain of popular music include the weekly *Billboard* charts, the playlists of mass market radio; MTV, the distribution system, the musicians' union, and the managerial framework that takes artists from rehearsal studios to the performance stage, among others. These varied and consequential domains can be collectively grouped by a term sociologist Howard S. Becker coined – the "art world," which he defines as "the network of people whose cooperative activity, organized via their joint knowledge of conventional means of doing things, produce(s) the kind of art works that art world is noted for" (Becker, 1982, p. x). Becker's notion is particularly valuable, for our understanding of popular music remains predominantly artist-centered, neglecting those ancillary individuals and organizations that make the music come to life. Becker reminds us that all artifacts are made by means of cooperative networks of affiliated individuals or groups, not isolated geniuses. At the same time, those ceremonies and activities I discussed at the start of this essay perpetuate the individualistic perspective that the notion of an "art world" critiques. Even if the Rock and Roll Hall of Fame, for example, honors producers, arrangers, and executives, the focus of its activities remains the individuals and groups that the star-making machinery circulates.

The notion of an "art world" is further clarified by the phenomenon of "gatekeepers" that Simon Frith develops in *Sound Effects*. A variety of individuals and organizations exist in between musicians, writers and the consumers of their work. Frith argues that these gatekeepers by and large determine what sounds will be made available to the general public and what will not, leading to the condition that all people can "want" is what they are able to get. Frith's comments suggest that there is a musical equivalent to the Philosophy 101 conundrum: namely, "If a recording is made or a group performs and one is unable to hear them, do they really exist?" The answer is, of course not. The various gatekeepers insure that our knowledge of popular music remains forever partial. It is often erroneously assumed that these gatekeepers act in a coordinated fashion. Corporate entities in particular are commonly thought to constitute a united front, whereas the research of Keith Negus, and others, illustrates with ethnographic specificity that corporate offices can be a hotbed of conflict and confrontation.

For most of us, however, these entities exist at a distance, their daily contributions to the production of popular music invisible and unrecognized, except in a negative sense. They are viewed as barriers to our pleasure, not the source of its encouragement. Furthermore, the substance of our interaction with popular music is felt to be incompatible with the discourse of sales figures, awards ceremonies, and halls of fame. A person's investment in popular music may be initially monetary, and ever more expensive as the price of recordings rises, but remains felt as predominantly emotional and individualistic. For many people, their interest in music constitutes, to a significant degree, one of the primary means by which their life possesses meaning, a way of alleviating, however temporarily, the daily grind of passionless subsistence. Popular music is, in effect, serious fun, and we feel our pleasure deflated when institutions transform that fun into statistics or the fashion of the moment.

At the same time, our investment in that fun not only helps define our place in the world but also distinguishes us from those incapable of understanding or participating in our chosen sources of pleasure. In other words, our investment in popular music represents a form of the "cultural capital" Pierre Bourdieu identifies as conferring status and significance on people's lives. Our knowledge and appreciation of popular musical culture remains an evocative marker of our social status. The degree to which we are able to absorb or reject certain forms of music depends upon our position in the social system in a number of ways, including: the amount of available fiscal capital we can spend in order to have access to music; the accumulation of educational resources that permit us to understand music as a formal text; and the influence our location in a particular social class has on which forms of music we will appreciate and which we will deny.

How much "cultural capital" we possess and how we dispense it determine which popular music institutions will matter to us and which will not. As we will see, those who define music as a "serious" enterprise and its performance as a sign of certain forms of technical competence consider the bulk of institutions connected to popular music banal in the extreme. In addition, for many of us, the importance of "cultural capital" pales before that of what Sarah Thornton calls "subcultural capital" – an index of "hipness" that illustrates a form of status connected more to one's calculated investment in the kind of distinctions that separate fun from falsehood. The possession of "subcultural capital" results from its own system of criteria, with a distinct premium placed upon being "in the know" or possessed of certain forms of awareness not mediated by those institutions considered alienating or "uncool."

III

I turn now to a consideration of a set of institutions connected to popular music that illustrate this body of distinctions, beginning with the organ of popular opinion, as epitomized by *Rolling Stone* magazine. For some individuals, to be pictured on this publication's cover or to be emotionally invested in who does appear there constitutes one of the primary sources of subcultural capital in their lives. The group Dr. Hook's 1972 hit song "The Cover of the *Rolling Stone*" sarcastically addresses the cultural, and economic, cachet that arises from being featured so prominently in the public arena. For others, that manner of publicity serves only a negative function. To individuals or groups whose sense of cultural cachet has nothing to do with mass popularity – elements of the punk or hard core communities, for example – the possibility of being plastered across the nation's newsstands amounts to one of the most egregious instances of "selling out." Notwithstanding that dichotomy, *Rolling Stone* has served as the principal journalistic gatekeeper of popular music for longer than any other publication. When it began in 1967, its only immediate competitor was Paul Williams's *Crawdaddy*, begun the year before. While

50

Williams focused principally on recordings, *Rolling Stone* from the start not only designated a wider editorial compass but also endeavored to present a professional appearance to the general mass media. As founder and editor Jann Wenner said at the time, *"Rolling Stone* is not just about music, but also about the things and attitudes that music embraces. . . . To describe it any further would be difficult without sounding like bullshit, and bullshit is like gathering moss" (Draper, 1990, p. 69).

In order to satisfy immediate financial needs and maintain access to the publication's subjects, Wenner simultaneously manipulated the music industry and maintained a necessary distance from it. For a time, *Rolling Stone* achieved an artful balance between objectivity and publicity. The coverage of cultural phenomena like the early music festivals at Monterey, Altamont, and Woodstock and the Charles Manson murders was particularly noteworthy by virtue of the publication's ability to combine obeisance to the dominant social mythology with a sarcastic tweaking of the clichés of youth culture ideology. For a considerable period of time, the range of musical forms and social formations encompassed by *Rolling Stone* was sufficiently broad that the periodical routinely enlarged rather than merely confirmed one's cultural horizons.

However, as youthful fanaticism fell prey to social inertia and the original audience began to age into adult responsibility, the missionary zeal of *Rolling Stone* gave way to a less adventurous, mainstream perspective. This transformation was signaled in part by the change in editorial format in 1973 to a general interest publication that combined a particular interest in music with attention to other expressions of modern American culture, politics, and the arts. The metamorphosis continued in 1977, when the editorial offices moved from San Francisco to New York City, and was cemented with the notorious "Perception/Reality" advertising campaign of 1985. In order to shore up falling advertising revenues, this strategy drew upon the transformation of *Rolling Stone*'s readership in what came across as a calculatedly cynical maneuver. No longer the epitome of countercultural insurgency, the audience was now assumed to be affiliated uncritically with mainstream social values. The ad copy that accompanied the image of a bar of soap read:

> If you think *Rolling Stone* readers are the great unwashed, this should send that thinking down the drain. In the last 7 days alone, *Rolling Stone* readers worked up a lather with soap and shampoo 40 million times. If you've got health and beauty aids to sell, you can clean up in the pages of *Rolling Stone*. (Quoted in Draper, 1990, p. 345)

51

The longstanding success of this campaign and the increasing influence of its assumptions about *Rolling Stone*'s readership is confirmed by the present-day dominance of fashion-connected advertising and seasonal clothing supplements in its pages. Rather than the features of the "great unwashed," it is more often than not the visages of physical perfection found upon the runways of the contemporary fashion industry that appear as one turns the cover page. By implication, music now comes across not as the expression of a cultural vanguard but as one more revenue stream among many others for the mass media. The transformation of the publication was, perhaps, even more effectively signaled by the "100 Best Singles" issue released in 1988. Here was not only the erection of a popular music canon but also the expression of the perspective of one individual on that canon: Jann Wenner. Assuming editorial prerogative, he manipulated the list so that it conformed with his tastes, not those of his editorial staff or even his eventual audience. For the average reader, the subcultural capital encompassed by the results was rendered virtually worthless. The self-satisfied promotion of a narrow point of view epitomized the collision between the two song titles employed in the Perception/Reality campaign: "All You Need Is Love" and "What's Love Got to Do with It?"

At the same time, criticizing the transformation of *Rolling Stone* amounts, in part, to a failure to acknowledge the parallel transformation of the society which it both helps create and covers. Rather than assuming that the publication acts as an impediment to some idealized notion of the community of individuals devoted to rock 'n' roll, it would be wiser to investigate the ways in which certain allegiances and emotions have changed over the course of time. A number of readers, young and old, continue to attach an abundance of cultural and subcultural capital to *Rolling Stone*, and denying them their desires amounts to the promulgation of a kind of loyalty test imposed to reinforce one rigidly defined set of ideological and aesthetic parameters over another. The persistent attraction to the notion of "selling out" among those who value popular music often serves to exclude rather than include other people. If one task popular music is meant to perform is to construct a more egalitarian sense of community, that community can be defined in an extremely narrow fashion. Our contradictory fascination with and loathing of the institutions affiliated with popular music illustrates the complexity of this investment in the importance of music in our lives. Only something that matters this much could raise such ferocity over a matter of what may otherwise be seen as nothing more than individual taste.

The history of the National Academy of Performing Arts and Sciences

(NARAS) and the annual Grammy Awards affords another opportunity to consider the complex and contradictory presence of institutions in the domain of popular music. Conceived in 1957 by prominent members of the music community in Los Angeles, the initial motivation of NARAS was to obtain respect for an industry that felt itself to be driven excessively by commercial considerations and prey to the passions of the moment. As Henry Schipper suggests, a combination of idealism and intolerance motivated the organization, convinced that the sudden success of rock 'n' roll signaled the abandonment of any standards of artistry or sophistication. To guide NARAS's decisions, a credo was written by the satirist Stan Freberg, some of whose material treated rock 'n' roll specifically as abominable tripe:

> We, the National Academy of Record Arts and Sciences, being dedicated to the advancement of the phonograph record do pledge ourselves as follows: We shall judge a record on the basis of sheer artistry, and artistry alone – artistry in writing, performance, musicianship and engineering. A record shall, in the opinion of the Academy either attain the highest degree of excellence possible in the category entered, or it shall not receive an Academy Award. Sales and mass popularity are the yardsticks of the record business. They are not the yardsticks of the Academy. We are concerned here with the phonograph record as an art form. If the record industry is to grow, not decline in stature, if it is to foster a greater striving for excellence in its own field, if it is to discourage mediocrity and encourage greatness, we, as its spokesmen, can accept no other credo.

The assumptions underlying this proclamation clearly amount to a fence constructed by a body of gatekeepers, for the individual who drafted it and those whose interests it represented felt much of the popular music of the time was decidedly mediocre and devoid of artistry. Ironically, from that day forward, the material produced by the record industry has grown in stature, but NARAS has usually lagged behind, committed to maintaining an outmoded canon and a dubious aesthetic agenda.

Until 1961, the Grammy Awards failed to include any recognition of rock 'n' roll. Thereafter the number of awards, originally only 28, increased each year, a sign not only of generic proliferation and market segmentation but also of the Academy's reluctant but inevitable decision to enlarge their notion of the musical canon. Most of the pioneers of rock 'n' roll failed to receive honors during the height of their success and had to wait for a Lifetime Achievement Award or were commended for a minor portion of their repertoire – Bob Dylan, for example, received his first award in 1979 for "Gotta Serve Somebody," an expression of his short-lived affiliation with religious fundamentalism.

Rock 'n' roll was not the only genre denied a substantive role in the musical canon defined by NARAS. Even if awards were given for rhythm and blues from the first year, a number of the major exponents of the genre were overlooked, time and again. Motown was awarded only one Grammy during the course of the 1960s, and not until Stevie Wonder acquired award after award in the 1970s did the label receive the kind of attention it deserved. The lag time between the public success of a musical genre and the introduction of a category honoring its practitioners has became longer and longer. Heavy metal was first recognized in 1987, some two decades late, and its initial recipient was Jethro Tull – a group whose leader was a flautist and whose music bore a pale resemblance to the genre it was supposed to illustrate. Rap was admitted into the Grammy fold in 1988, a decade after it first appeared on the commercial charts.

Part of the reason for this apparent institutional obliviousness has been the phenomenon of bloc voting. Individual chapters have more than once agreed en masse to support their local performers, as was the case with Nashville in the mid-1960s. This led to the Anita Kerr Singers receiving the "best performance by a vocal group" award in 1965 rather than The Beatles for "Help." Members of NARAS recognized the inappropriate-ness of the decision, but acknowledged the propensity for the member-ship to act in a lockstep manner and shun outsiders. Stan Coryn of Warner Communications observes, "When you're in your own club, you don't expect a lot of homeless to be there to make you feel tense. There was about as much tension [in NARAS] as in a country club" (quoted in Schipper, 1992, p. 43).

Popular music, it can be argued, thrives on contention, not concilia-tion, and it therefore comes as no surprise that NARAS and the Grammy Awards amount to institutions that most individuals either denounce as an impediment or disregard as inconsequential. However, as is the case with *Rolling Stone*, the organization itself and the body of achievements the NARAS has recognized perform a vital role in the affective and ideo-logical relationship most people hold to popular music. Specifically they embody what Sarah Thornton refers to as the "chimera of a negative mainstream." They offer building-blocks or a yardstick that can be re-jected out-of-hand less for what they are than for what they represent. By assuming the fundamental rigidity of the Grammies and the NARAS, we can commend ourselves for possessing a more fluid perspective devoid of any rigid objection to change. Admittedly, the history of the awards is rife with missed opportunities and misguided decisions. Nonetheless, it has to be understood that the Grammies illustrate *a* notion of the canon of popular music, not *the* notion of an acceptable canon. Our purportedly fluid alternative is no less idiosyncratic or restrictive.

In the end, if we choose to reject what either the Recording Academy or *Rolling Stone* stand for, we ought not to confuse their assumed distortions of popular music with any alleged dishonesty. Rather, the anger and agitation that they, and other institutions connected to popular music, elicit in us collides with the fact that nothing about the subject is fixed or final. Popular music exists because bodies of individuals have collectively affirmed their admiration for a particular group or artist. Fans may not feel their emotional investment possesses any institutional character. Nonetheless, when two or three are gathered together, some manner of institution has come into existence, whether the members like it or not. At the same time, this need not threaten the fluidity of fans' allegiances, nothwithstanding the degree of fixity it lends to popular music. Whether a whim or deep set conviction, the forces that lead to the institutionalization of fun remain predicated upon facts that no list of awards or issues of a magazine can exhaustively measure.

In the end, as Greil Marcus reminds us, our critical engagement with history of whatever sort depends upon our "willingness to be fooled: to take an idea too far, to bet too much on too small an object or occasion, to be caught up and even swept away." What he advocates, therefore, is "an objective platform for a subjective revision of our relations to the past, present, and the future" (Marcus, 1995, pp. 6–7). Taking his agenda to heart, each of us possesses an idiosyncratic notion of how a Hall of Fame, canon of deserving recordings or journalistic record of popular music ought to be constructed. Therefore, my willingness to entertain the need for a wing in the Hall of Fame devoted to Captain Beefheart or the designation of Johnny "Guitar" Watson's "Space Guitar" (1952) as a primal instance of rock 'n' roll allows me to create an emotional road map in order to make sense of my experience. Others would find themselves helplessly lost if they pursued the directions these choices imply.

As my epigraphs to this chapter are meant to illustrate, our relationships to the institutions of popular music are and will remain complex and contradictory. Much as we, like Groucho Marx, reject any sense of commonality that would erode our individuality, at the same time we should not ignore, as Charles Baudelaire asserts, the fact that each form of pleasure has its meaning, however misguided those appetites appear to be. All of us dance to the rhythms of the funky drummer, but our steps invariably differ.

Resources

Becker, Howard S. (1982) *Art Worlds*. Berkeley: University of California Press.

Bourdieu, Pierre (1984) *Distinction: a Social Critique of the Judgment of Taste*, trans. Richard Nice. Cambridge, MA: Harvard University Press.

Christgau, Robert (1995) Institutionalized. *Village Voice*, 24 January, pp. 63, 66.

Draper, Robert (1990) *Rolling Stone Magazine: the Uncensored Story*. New York: Doubleday.

Frith, Simon (1991) *Sound Effects: Youth, Leisure, and the Politics of Rock 'n' Roll*. New York: Pantheon.

Marcus, Greil (1995) *The Dustbin of History*. Cambridge: Harvard University Press.

Negus, Keith (1992) *Producing Pop: Culture and Conflict in the Popular Music Industry*. London: Arnold.

Schipper, Henry (1992) *Broken Record: the Inside Story of the Grammy Awards*. New York: Birch Lane.

Thornton, Sarah (1996) *Club Cultures: Music Media and Subcultural Capital*. Middletown, CT: Wesleyan University Press.

5
Politics

Robin Balliger

In what ways, I wondered, did the popularity of reggae and hip-hop music signal a diasporic identification for Afro-Trinidadians or relate to poverty in Trinidad's economic downturn?

"Politics" in popular music is commonly understood to mean "political songs" – songs which either serve or struggle against dominant institutions like the state and economic system. For example, the national anthem or songs in many advertisements use music to reinforce nationalism and normative consumption, while political songs that "rage against the machine" suggest forms of resistance. In this chapter, I consider certain assumptions about what constitutes both political struggle and political meaning in popular music by tracing a definition of politics that moves from formal political structures to power relations in everyday activities.

One view of politics in society contends that political processes occur mainly through state political institutions and practices (such as voting). This view often leads to a certain approach to political struggle aimed at either reinforcing or changing those structures. For example, major labels are part of an entertainment industry that controls global music production and circulation, and many would argue that in addition to benefiting monetarily, it is in the political interest of these corporations to produce music content that reinforces their dominant market position. Independent labels and non-commercial radio, on the other hand, arose in opposition to corporate control of music – by controlling the means of production, some felt, artists would have greater control over political meaning. Recently, at the college radio station where I work, a young politically minded DJ was pulling CDs out of the current rotation file and mentioned that he wasn't playing anything with a barcode! But whether one appreciates his uncompromising anti-industry stance or finds it frighteningly rigid, there is more to the politics of popular music than structures of cultural production.

For example, many recent arguments regarding cultural imperialism assume that the structure of cultural production determines meaning. Cultural imperialism is understood as the domination of the world by the USA and Europe, not only through overt military, political, and economic means, but also by promoting Eurocentric norms through education, language, and cultural products (like music and MTV). But if the centralized control of cultural production supports "First World" domination, some theorists argue, the development of inexpensive recording equipment and cassette technology in the 1980s made the means of production widely available – and therefore democratized expression. While it is generally salutary that more people can produce music, the proliferation of recording also reproduces ideologies which have little relation to a progressive agenda.

Cultural imperialism and the entertainment industry represent forms of politics exercised through the market; state intervention constitutes another form of structural control over cultural production. States legislate cultural policy to maintain social relations by fostering national identity and common values, but cultural policy is often highly contested because nation-states usually lack homogeneity on the basis of race, class, religion, or political ideology. Many countries use the state apparatus to ban music because of its political content, and US-based groups like the Parents Music Resource Center (PMRC) lobby for labeling or banning music for ostensibly moral reasons. In an extreme case, Nazi Germany's promotion of Aryan culture was as important in state cultural policy as in genetic engineering. While theorists tend to focus on either the state or the market, the two reinforce each other in the modern era.

In contrast to these structural views, some theorists argue that politics occurs not only in formal institutions but also in everyday practices not specifically labeled "political." Antonio Gramsci's concept of hegemony, for example, breaks with the idea of rule as enacted through purely state political forms because, in his view, domination saturates the whole social process. Opening the terrain of "the political" in this way means that the arenas of "art" or "the private" are not outside the political. Contestation occurs in and through these arenas. Hegemony, while saturating all arenas, is, however, never complete because oppositional practices affect and shape the hegemonic process. Gramsci thus counters the determinism of structuralist approaches by arguing that new technologies and structures of control by the state and entertainment industries also *generate* new forms of cultural and political opposition – this is a dialectical view of cultural struggle.

Michel Foucault's notion of "governmentality" elaborates on these concepts. In contrast to earlier forms of power exercised directly by a sovereign over his subjects, in modern society "governance" occurs through informal "management" (including the disciplining of bodies in education and the workplace). Rather than coercion, participation in modern capitalist society is garnered through consent and the internal exercise of "free will." Foucault also focused on the politics of representation, and argued that aspects of daily life that are *not* considered political are often the *most* politicized – because what counts as political or not is already a strategy of domination. For instance, in some societies popular music is considered a powerful social force, whereas in the West the division between high and low culture represents popular music as meaningless entertainment in order to devalue popular expression and its political content. This is also referred to as *naturalization,* as it is in the interest of dominant forces in society to present certain concepts as universal and unchanging, rather than produced by a political system in a particular historical moment and therefore vulnerable to change.

If we accept the expansion of "politics" to include not only state and economic structures but also power relations in everyday life, then in approaching the politics of popular music we need to address not only the structural position of its production, and not only the content of its lyrics, but also its sound and reception in particular contexts. Instead of political songs, we might best think about music and politics by approaching music as an activity embedded in relations of power. This is not to shift entirely away from analyzing structures or to valorize reception. Such a shift can be politically dangerous because it nullifies structural inequalities: if we all interpret texts freely, then why would the control of production matter at all? In my view, to thoroughly address the politics of music in society, one should consider the structure of cultural production *and* how music is received in particular situations and moments. The following sections provide more historical details and examples, before addressing the politics of music in relation to contemporary globalization.

Mass Culture

The arrival of "mass media" in the twentieth century brought about significant changes in music, politics and society. With the advent of

recording technology, and control over the production of most recordings by a centralized entertainment industry, many political theorists feared
that mass-produced entertainment would be the state's ultimate ideological weapon – think of George Orwell's vision in *1984*. Others believed
that mass forms also had the potential to communicate radical messages
and be powerful tools for promoting social justice. The issue of whether
mass-produced music can only serve dominant interests, or whether it is
possible that this music can have radical content, is highly contested even
today. Below I consider a few important moments in the debate over mass
culture and its relationship to popular music.

Walter Benjamin's essay "The work of art in the age of mechanical
reproduction" (originally published in 1936) describes how the development of photography, film, and recorded sound impacts culture, knowledge, and power. He argues that the mass reproduction of art disrupts
the sense of fixity and the "aura" of the original. Because multiple copies
allow for the altering of images in the process of reproduction, a person's
relationship to these objects is displaced spatially and temporally. For
example, by the time Benjamin was writing, many people no longer had
to go the symphony to hear classical music – they could listen to it on a
phonograph in the living room at any time. People began to know the
world less by direct experience and increasingly through mechanically
reproduced representations of reality.

Like Benjamin, Max Horkheimer and Theodor Adorno of the Frankfurt School made important observations about the meaning of these
changes for society. They argued, however, that mass culture could only
serve reactionary politics and dominant economic interests. Their writings
in the early 1940s were heavily influenced by their experiences in Germany and the instrumental use of mass media (and especially the "loud-
speaker") in Nazi cultural policy. After relocating to Los Angeles, these
writers witnessed the emerging entertainment industry and its power to
shape consciousness on a mass scale. Adorno argued that standardized
rhythms in popular music served capitalism by shaping the proletariat into
a "mechanized collectivity" of worker/consumers. Ironically, even though
Adorno was politically radical, his contempt for popular music led him to
favor classical music and elite forms of art.

In contrast, Benjamin believed that the reproducibility of art could
intervene in bourgeois conceptions of high art and develop the social
function of art for the masses. Moreover, he argued that while music can
manipulate its audience, it also places the audience in the position of
critic. Benjamin's dialectical position counters the determinism of

Horkheimer and Adorno's argument and foreshadows reception theory. Reception-oriented approaches to mass culture argue that audiences do not passively absorb messages. Instead, cultural texts (like music) are actively "decoded" and will always have multiple meanings. In addition, because people exist in many different relationships to the dominant culture (e.g. by race, class, gender), people will interpret messages differently, sometimes even in opposition to the "intended" messages. Often, critics who emphasize production are labeled "cultural pessimists" because the industry dominates the audience, while reception theorists are thought of as "cultural optimists" because audiences control meaning.

The fact that popular music has been a powerful force in radical causes worldwide seems to underscore Benjamin's belief that mass art can be a form of resistance. Popular music played an important role in anti-colonial struggles and in civil rights and counterculture movements in the 1960s and early 1970s. Among many possible examples, Gil Scott Heron's "The Revolution Will Not Be Televised" and Bob Marley's "Stand Up for Your Rights" galvanized sentiment along broad political lines and across divided geographies. While forms of rhythm poetry are part of a long history of struggle in African-American music, in the 1980s rap emerged as a mass form. Overtly political songs like Public Enemy's "Fight the Power" sold millions as their anti-racist stance resonated with people worldwide. More than providing a "voice," mass political music reinforces solidarity because the music becomes a vehicle through which the oppressed recognize each other and become more aware of their subordination.

The songs mentioned above had political force not because they have political lyrics, but because the music was understood in particular contexts of struggle. To illustrate how political meanings change according to context, consider that songs which once marked the radical impulse of a generation, like John Lennon's "Imagine," have recently been employed by Britain's Conservative Party; Allen Ginsberg's image lends counterculture chic to Gap ads; and mass entertainment like MTV markets itself as "underground." Moreover, while the power of mass political music appears undeniable, some would argue that when radical artists achieve mass popularity, it actually means they have been co-opted or brought under control by the very institutions they are fighting. The entertainment industry makes money when artists sell, no matter what the message, so even radical artists participate in a broader system of exploitation. These negative views about mass culture have led some to conclude that the only possible site for cultural resistance exists at the margins of society.

SUBCULTURES AND IDENTITY POLITICS

Following on the work of Gramsci (and culturally informed Marxists like E. P. Thompson and Raymond Williams), British cultural studies began in the early 1970s to analyze processes of political control. Simply put, a number of scholars were motivated by the following questions. If capitalism exploits the majority of the population, why don't people rebel? Has the dominant system developed techniques to generate allegiance to it even when it is not in a person's "objective" interest? Or, perhaps people *are* resisting the system, but not through overt political means. These questions led Stuart Hall and others to look more carefully at cultural practices in the reproduction or disruption of class relations. Many of these same questions were taken up around issues of race and gender, especially in the USA, as scholars focused on cultural resistance through identity politics.

British cultural studies focused on media as an important ideological tool of the state in post-war Britain, and took a serious interest in emergent music subcultures like the Teds, Mods, and Skinheads. Researchers found that the scenes created by these groups often provided an avenue through which to carve out social space and practice forms of conduct in opposition to dominant values. While some youth subcultures resisted working-class culture, in other cases the rejection of middle-class norms actually reinforced working-class values, thus perpetuating their working-class subordination. Later work on music subcultures such as punk or Riot Grrrl emphasizes counter-hegemonic practice through style – a "do it yourself" refusal of dominant values and gender norms supported by scenes, zines, and underground networks. Critics of subcultural analysis, however, argue that these cultures reproduce dominant values through the accumulation of "subcultural capital" and are not oppositional simply by virtue of their structural position in society.

Black, Chicano, and Asian cultural critics have shown that music and expressive culture are ways in which oppressed groups construct community, preserve collective memory, and narrate diaspora. Beyond political lyrics, musically defined spaces temporarily suspend the dominant temporal and spatial order. An important contribution to this line of thought, supplied by feminist critics, is the argument that culturally affirming social practices provide sites in which alternative subjectivities are embodied. At the same time, oppositional genres (like rap or punk) require a nuanced, contextualized analysis, because "genres" often resist some forms of domination and reinforce others (e.g. male dominance).

Since I have been involved in subcultural music activities for my entire adult life, let me elaborate some of these issues through a personal narrative. In music school I was involved in improvised music (contemporary classical and free jazz), and thoroughly believed that radical music existed only at the edges of society, in music that was "noise" by dominant definitions and had clearly not "sold out." After hearing the Sex Pistols in 1978 and being inspired by their energy and in-your-face politics, I left school and dropped the flute to play electric bass in the "alternative" music scene. But I soon observed the process by which this subculture was marginalized even as elements of its dress and language were repackaged and sold as post-apocalyptic high fashion and cyberpunk entertainment. For me, the creativity of this scene waned as early as 1982. In college radio, I also witnessed the transformation of "alternative" as *oppositional* to "alternative" as a marketing category. College radio became a farm-school for major label A&R (artists and repertoire) reps.

About this time, the two-tone movement and "world music" were emerging, emphasizing anti-racism as a response to the reactionary political climate of the 1980s. I formed an original, racially mixed band that was influenced by the Afro-beat music and radical politics of Nigerian musician Fela Kuti. The "world beat" movement had an idealistic, but politically naive, strategy of targeting mass culture in order to subvert racist and reactionary discourses. World beat was attacked for reasons ranging from "cultural imperialism" to "Madison Avenue Marxism" (because we were doing radical politics in a pop format). While some of this criticism was deserved, I would argue for a more sympathetic reading as world beat overtly confronted the reactionary politics of the Thatcher and Reagan era, the "culture wars," homophobia surrounding the AIDS crisis, and the covert war in Central America.

Learning from these experiences, I became one of a diverse group of artists and musicians who embarked upon a new strategy of engagement. Remaining committed to an anti-capitalist stance and a subcultural, "do-it-yourself" attitude, we created Komotion, an alternative cultural center in San Francisco. I was the director of programming for Komotion activities, which included a performance space, art gallery, and "sound magazine" with international distribution. Komotion's events included Middle Eastern, African, and "alternative" music nights (including touring artists like Chumbawamba, Zvuki Mu, John Trudell, Hakim Bey, and many others). We produced hundreds of benefits that raised awareness and money in support of soup kitchens, environmental groups, battered women's shelters, and US political prisoners like Leonard Peltier. Komotion also housed a recording studio for educational projects, such as middle-school students performing an "eco-rap" about environmental racism. As a collective, we took it upon ourselves to create a lively, safe environment for performers and audiences, but Komotion was finally shut down after ten years for minor permit violations. Building and fire codes are designed to protect the public, but they are also a means for controlling cultural and political expression. I returned to graduate school in the early 1990s to develop my understanding of music as a political force, especially in the changed conditions of global capitalism.

GLOBALIZATION

As I have discussed, much criticism on popular music ascribes a stable political content to music based on the point of production. Put bluntly, in this criticism "big is bad, small is good," because "big" supposedly represents domination while "small" represents resistance. Similar arguments that the West dominates the cultures of less powerful nations give a spatial dimension to cultural domination and resistance. But it is precisely these spatial dimensions that critics have now begun to question because of the increasing globalization of the political economy and media.

Like Walter Benjamin writing on the effects of media technologies in the first half of the twentieth century, scholars from diverse disciplines have recently argued that technological advances are having a profound impact on our relationship to the world. While there are many competing definitions of globalization, the general argument is that since the 1970s, changes in capitalist production and media technologies are disrupting center–periphery power relations associated with European hegemony of the past five hundred years. For example, rather than the West being the fixed center of wealth, power, and ideas, transnational corporations span the globe in networks; non-Western nations increasingly challenge the economic, political, and cultural power of the West; the deindustrialization of the "First World" creates "Third World" conditions in some areas of the West; the new international division of labor fuels mass migrations of people, disrupting culture and place; and rapid transnational media flows affect our sense of distance, time, and space.

The effects of globalization compel us to rethink cultural imperialism and definitions of "national" or "local" culture. In the West, it is commonly asserted that, even if "our" culture has been corrupted by mass culture industries, authentic native culture still exists in the "Third World."

However, in globalization, "local" cultural production becomes more commodified and increasingly benefits a particular class (even in less industrialized states). When a large segment of the population becomes excluded from "its" culture's expressions and profits, what then constitutes community?

George Lipsitz has suggested that with similar kinds of austerity and inequality occurring worldwide, transnational cultural production may facilitate "poly-lateral dialogue" among aggrieved communities – raising interesting questions about the relationship of culture to changed material and political conditions. Rather than the politics of music being strongly associated with a place, racial identity, or national origin, music once associated with distinct places is being taken up by musicians and audiences in many locations – and for many different reasons. New technologies of music circulation and dialogue, like the Internet, create virtual music communities among listeners dispersed in space. (But because digital technology is easy to copy, nations are being coerced by international law to enforce copyright; e.g. China recently shut down twelve pirate CD factories.)

At the same time, mass migrations of labor also place diverse peoples in closer proximity than ever before, and music often functions as a meta-language for people from different backgrounds. In these conditions, popular music as a meaningful transnational discourse has much to tell us about the changed conditions of people's lives in particular locations. New alliances are based not only on feelings of affiliation through music, but on the fact that people are literally being repositioned by global capitalism and its changing socio-economic landscape. Finally, while some are quick to celebrate the decline of homogeneity in nations (e.g. British culture as wholly white), hybrid identities may efface actual racial violence, and hybridity in music provides another site of consumption for a market requiring continual novelty.

CASE STUDY: THE POLITICS OF LOVE SONGS

Expressive culture was a crucial site of struggle against slavery and colonialism in the Caribbean, but how is globalization affecting the politics of music? I did research in Trinidad and Tobago, a post-colonial, multiethnic, media-saturated state, looking at how genres of popular music (both local and foreign) mapped onto different race and class positions. By analyzing social fragmentation through popular music consumption, I hoped to gain

an understanding of how communities and contestation were being transformed. Foreign musics like dancehall reggae and hip-hop are immensely
popular in Trinidad. In what ways, I wondered, did these musics signal a
diasporic identification for Afro-Trinidadians or relate to poverty in Trinidad's economic downturn? Was an avoidance of national cultural forms like
calypso music evidence of the influence of US cultural imperialism and the
recent introduction of MTV, or was the adoption of foreign music (including aspects of its speech, gesture, ideology, and dress) a way to protest the
dominant culture and policies blamed for increased suffering?

Below, I discuss a small part of this research which focuses on the
popularity of American rhythm and blues ballads (or "slows" as they are
called in Trinidad) among young women. While ballads are also popular
with African-Americans and women generally in the USA, very little
criticism has focused on this music. Ballads are usually ignored, seen as a
form of mass distraction, or condemned as pabulum. As Anahid Kassabian
suggests in chapter 9 of this volume, this neglect may result from critics
looking for political content in song lyrics alone, rather than situating
music like love songs in the lives of listeners. My approach was to analyze
mass music in a specific social context and critically engage its popularity.

Music consumption is highly divided by race and class in Trinidad, but
I learned that slows were popular among working-class and poor young
women across racial lines. Importantly, these songs were meaningful to
women in relation to social disintegration and domestic violence. Youth
and women have been hit hardest by Trinidad's economic downturn since
the mid-1980s, and form the "new poor" identified in World Bank reports. Macroeconomic forces produce increased suffering expressed in the
domestic sphere of the household – the abstract violence of a system
translated into immediate domestic relationships with incredible brutality
– especially as men experience job loss as emasculation. In the supposed
sanctity of the "private" sphere, where can women turn for safety and
comfort? The comments below are from four young women, discussing
how slows help them get through bad times:

Sometimes music is the only thing to hold onto . . . it can't talk back.

When I feelin' down I listen to slows. Music is very important and at certain
times in my life, keeps me going, it helps to lift your spirits.

Slows are my favorite music, I love Celine Dion, Mariah Carey, Whitney
Houston. I like the meaning, it's very touching, it makes you think, it helps

66

you to relax. I like R. Kelly, "I Believe I Can Fly," Celine Dion latest "All By Myself." I try to understand these lyrics by writing them down, going through them slowly, playing the cassette over and over. . . . Most women listen to slows, some men do to.

Sometimes I would be in a sort of mood, like down-spirited, and I turn on the radio and a certain song would cheer me up. I like R. Kelly, Boyz II Men. Most of these artists sing songs based on reality and things that actually happen to them, and the same thing that might be happening to you as well. . . . They have a line that would say things will be better.

For these young women, slows cannot be reduced to foreign commercial products; they are a lifeline. With increased crime and social instability, these songs represent a constant, reliable source of security. From audience interviews, I learned that women relate to female vocalists as peers and trusted voices for counsel, sometimes more trustworthy than family or friends. Much of the soothing effect occurs in the sonic qualities of the music, in soft tones and rhythms, emotional tension release achieved through complex chord progressions, soaring vocal lines, and the "grain of the voice." Drawing on the language of geography and music, slows also produce a "soothing space," as the bedroom becomes a temporary refuge against a larger social assault.

While it is possible to argue that these songs are a form of acquiescence, victimization, and defeat, a situated textual analysis suggests that slows are rarely about defeat, and instead foster female empowerment at a time of heightened socio-economic and gender oppression for women. In contrast to the aggressive bravado of male singers in many popular music genres, for example, in slows the position of power is reversed: men are vulnerable in love, a woman's love becomes necessary for the man's completeness, women hold the power to bestow love, to forgive, or to produce emotional anguish in men. In slows, sexual boasting by male vocalists usually takes the form of claims about the man's ability to please a woman, as opposed to rap and hard rock, where women exist as objects for male pleasure.

Not all times are revolutionary, even if they should be. And the ways of "speaking struggle" depend on the social and historical context. For me, slows are indicative of a fundamental contradiction of globalization – as sources of oppression become more complex, diffuse, and unlocatable – people experience oppression in more immediate material, emotional, and intimate spaces. In response, slows construct a soothing world in which personal relationships embody caring, lasting support and love, something to hold onto beyond any individual or society, a quiet way of surviving the everyday "state of emergency" experienced by many.

My brief discussion of slows illustrates how popular music marks new sites of meaning, identification, and struggle for audiences in relation to globalization. We can link the violence of structural adjustment policies administered at the international level with specifically gendered, personal experiences of violence in the "private sphere" by situating the politics and meaning of popular music consumption among a community of participants. While foreign mass music has become meaningful for women in this particular place and moment, meanings in popular music are always multiple and contested. And even with the disruption of social, cultural, and political space in global capitalism, it is important to remain mindful of continued metropolitan dominance in cultural production. Rather than forcing popular music into a predefined politics of resistance or domination, a situated analysis of popular music consumption aids in defining "politics" in this historical moment.

CONCLUSIONS

From the exhilaration of attending a concert with thousands of screaming fans to the intimacy of slow dancing in a dimly lit nightclub or listening alone in one's bedroom, popular music is a complex practice that gains meaning in specific social landscapes. Understanding the politics of popular music through decontextualized readings of lyrics may be misleading, since the "politics" in music frequently works through the clash of words and sound, or when the noise in music *is* the message – social noise, for example, employed as confrontation or interference, as David Brackett suggests in chapter 10 of this volume. Popular music may operate in the reproduction of dominant social relations, or it may be resignified or appropriated by different communities of listeners. For example, as club music travels within social spaces marked by class, race, or sexuality, it may be understood as vapid, commodified entertainment by some and as dance floor euphoric liberation for others. And as it travels internationally, it may signify Western decadence and/or freedom against oppressive regimes.

In short, musical activity as political activity is embedded in historically constituted relations of power. Politics doesn't occur simply through coercion, consciousness, or formal political mechanisms, but in informal processes of socialization. Therefore, domination can also be resisted through informal means, including cultural practices like music. Meaning does not reside in music texts themselves but in their articulation with society. Context is crucial, as music consumption by different social groups and in different locations and times may completely change music's political meaning. Since the politics of music involves struggles over subject-producing practices which gain meaning in specific contexts and moments, rhythms, sounds, and collective spaces may affirm ways of being and produce embodiment in opposition to dominant society. Finally, it is important to consider the politics of music in a changed world system – one marked by increased transnational labor and cultural flows, the disruption of stable spatialized inequalities, and the heightened commodification and politicization of everyday life.

Acknowledgments

I would like to thank Thomas Swiss, Andrew Goodwin, Donald S. Moore, and Mathew Callahan for their invaluable contributions to the remix. This essay drew on dissertation research in Trinidad and Tobago, funded by a Fulbright Scholarship, the National Science Foundation, Wenner-Gren Foundation, Mellon Foundation, and the Center for Latin American Studies at Stanford University.

Resources

Attali, Jacques (1977) *Noise: the Political Economy of Music*. Minneapolis: University of Minnesota Press.

Benjamin, Walter (1969) The work of art in the age of mechanical reproduction. In *Illuminations*, trans. Harry Zohn. New York: Schocken, pp. 217–51.

Garofalo, Reebee (eds) (1992) *Rockin' the Boat: Mass Music and Mass Movements*. Boston: South End.

Gilroy, Paul (1994) "After the love has gone": bio-politics and etho-poetics in the black public sphere. *Public Culture*, 7, 49–76.

Hall, Stuart and Jefferson, Tony (eds) (1976) *Resistance through Rituals: Youth Subcultures in Post-war Britain*. London: Harper.

Lipsitz, George (1994) *Dangerous Crossroads: Popular Music, Postmodernism and the Poetics of Place*. London: Verso.

Martin, Linda and Segrave, Kerry (1993) *Anti-Rock: the Opposition to Rock 'n' Roll*. New York: Da Capo.

Ross, Andrew and Rose, Tricia (eds) (1994) *Microphone Fiends: Youth Music and Youth Culture*. New York: Routledge.

Sakolsky, Ron and Wei-Han Ho, Fred (eds) (1995) *Sounding Off! Music as Subversion/Resistance/Revolution*. New York: Autonomedia.

Sharma, Sanjay, Hutnyk, John, and Sharma, Ashwani (eds) (1996) *Dis-orienting Rhythms: the Politics of the New Asian Dance Music*. London: Zed Books.

Valentine, Gill (1995) Creating transgressive space: the music of kd lang. *Transactions of the Institute of British Geographers*, 20(4), 475–85.

6
Race

Russell A. Potter

Hip-hop backbeats have supported vocalists as far-flung as Bruce Springsteen and Sinéad O'Connor, and digital samples have crossed over still more unexpected territory.

INTRODUCTION

In the history of popular music, perhaps no concept has been as vexed as that of race. From the "race" records of the 1920s to the political reception of rap music in the 1980s, race has been both calling card and wild card, draw and repulsion, essence and pose. No history of popular music or study of its contemporary formations can afford to neglect the issue of race, yet "race" as such has been continually elided, both within the music industry's discourse on its own modes of production and consumption, and by many of music's self-appointed critics. For even as popular music embodies and evokes a mosaic of racial identities and histories, its relationship with identity has never been as deterministic as those who see race as an essence have tried to construe it. "Black" music has always drawn "white" audiences, and indeed often drawn from "white" musical traditions.

Thus, there is no absolute test of authenticity to which either musicians or critics can turn – yet this has never prevented people from trying. Whether in the Afrocentric jazz genealogies of Amiri Baraka or Andrew Ross's postmodern celebrations of cultural indeterminacy, the question of the cultural authenticity of music has survived numerous attempts to reduce it to either bluntly racial fundamentalism or an ironic politics of pastiche. The reasons for this are caught up in the specific histories of the music business, the cultural politics of consumption, and the shifting technologies by which audiences have been interpellated. In the process of entering into the subjectivities of musical space, each listener must construct her or his own eclectic map of these histories, and it is with my own first map, and the questions it raises, that I begin.

DIGGING IN THE CRATES

In 1977, when I was seventeen, one of my friends told me that the best blues guitarist he had ever heard was someone named Blind Blake. He suggested that I pick up some of his records. Running off a strangely syncopated rolling bass line, he grimaced and remarked, "It's kinda like that, but better." I tried to copy the riff, but I couldn't quite get the timing right. Not long afterwards, I set out to the local record stores in search of this apparently unheralded guitar genius. No one, it soon appeared, had ever heard of him, at least not at the chain record stores, or even at the funkier independent record shops where Jethro Tull and Jeff Beck shared the shelves with bongs, pipes, and black-light posters. I finally found a store that said it had some of his recordings, a store on the other side of town, one of the first big music mega-stores. I went there – it took two bus rides lasting over an hour – and in one corner of its warehouse-like spaces I found a whole rack full of music by performers I'd never heard of before. Who was Georgia Tom? Victoria Spivey? Big Maybelle? Son House? Their recordings, for the most part, consisted of reissues of scratchy old 78 r.p.m. records, compiled by equally obscure labels with names like Biograph, Yazoo, and Document. The covers of these albums featured grainy old black-and-white publicity photographs, sepia-toned images of young black men and women in dark suits, laced up leather shoes, and felt hats with downturned brims. There often seemed to be only one known photograph of any given artist, since the same photo would be used on every album. Some of them, like Bo Carter (author of the irresistible "Banana in your Fruit Basket"), were eternally grainy and out of focus – their only surviving photograph must have been a small one, taken maybe in an early version of those take-your-own-picture photo booths. Almost all of these recordings had been made in the 1920s, 1930s, and 1940s, and the eerie surface noise of the originals ran over each of the albums like a Brillo Pad over Teflon, etching away the smooth musical surfaces and sticking their riffs to my mind. I picked up a couple of Blind Blake discs and was soon sitting at home with the eerie strains of songs such as "Black Dog Blues," "Dry Bone Shuffle," "Hard Pushin' Papa," and "Too Tight Blues #2" emanating from my Realistic speakers.

Reading over the closely printed liner notes, written evidently by a small

72

group of aficionados and cognoscenti who actually possessed these old discs, I learned of something known as "race records," which seemed to me at the time to represent some ancient chapter in musical history when records and their audiences had a race. After all, this was the 1970s; my friends and I listened to a complicated mix of artists that didn't appear to line up along segregated racial lines. Music by the artists we listened to most – Joni Mitchell, Stevie Wonder, Jethro Tull, Aretha Franklin – seemed to appeal to everyone, and while race was certainly seen as an ingredient in their styles and personalities, it didn't produce anything approaching a one-to-one correspondence with audience. No doubt this had something to do with radio at that time, since you could still hear all these artists and more – everyone from Eric Clapton to Isaac Hayes, from the Pointer Sisters to Jackson Browne – on a single radio station, even in the course of a random half-hour listen. But it also had to do with a sense that my friends and I shared, a sense that the promise of increasing racial equality and social justice was in some sense being fulfilled by the intensely intertwined musical cross-influences that shaped our ears and excited our minds. There was a train a'comin, and whether it was sung on its way by Curtis Mayfield or Rod Stewart, we were ready to climb aboard. "Race" records, like segregated schools and the Negro Leagues, seemed a strange reminder of a worldview we thought had surely passed, or was soon to pass away.

RACE AND THE MARKETING OF POPULAR MUSIC

Alan Freed the waves just like Lincoln freed the slaves.
> Chuck D of Public Enemy

It was not that long ago when things were quite otherwise. The history of the relationship between the recording industry and race is a long and convoluted one, and not susceptible to a brief summary. Nonetheless, its pivotal points are hardly secrets. It is the stuff of legend that when, on August 10, 1920, Mamie Smith and her Jazz Hounds recorded "Crazy Blues," her record company did not anticipate substantial sales. After all, it was reasoned, how many black folks could afford to own Victrolas? When the record went on to become the industry's first million seller, that logic was refuted, but its fundamental assumptions went unquestioned. The recording companies did not consider the possibility that white folks were buying blues recordings (though they certainly were); they simply figured that black listeners were more numerous than they had imagined. All the major labels of the day – RCA, Paramount, Columbia – set up separate "race" labels with different names and catalog numbers. They then sought out publications, such as the *Cleveland Call*, the *Pullman Porters' Review*, and the *Chicago Defender*, where they could reach and "target" black consumers. When, a few years later, a similar market was discovered for the music of the Southeast and West, the record companies took the same route, establishing separate "Hillbilly" and "Mexican" labels, and advertising these titles in places where their presumptive audiences would see them.

And so it remained for the next thirty years and more. Even as white artists became immensely successful with their versions of "swing" and "jazz" music, the major labels kept separate catalogs and series numbers, a musical apartheid that reflected and amplified the historic divisions in theater and vaudeville. It was undeniable that black musical forms had given birth to the biggest sales boom in the history of commercial recordings, but this perception was safely sealed behind a wall of heavy black bakelite, and wrapped in a brown paper sleeve festooned with images that evoked a world divided by stereotypes. How did the intended consumers react to record labels featuring darktown strutters in a panoply of latter-day minstrelsy, or straw-hatted hillbillies sipping moonshine from jugs? The record companies neither knew nor cared; it was the fiction of the audience that counted, and the music business still functioned with a largely top-down marketing attitude. The fantasy of the consumer took the place of actual market research, and there was little reason for anyone to question the assumptions that had so far brought in such substantial profits.

This system did not come to a crisis until the 1950s. In the postwar boom years, many things were changing. A bumper crop of young kids both black and white were craving something new and had little vested interest in the sounds of their parents' generation (see chapter 8 in this volume). New neighborhoods and new industries, along with the GI Bill, were raising standards of living and creating a dynamic, rapidly growing audience of increasingly affluent listeners. More mobile in both class and regional terms, this generation was ready to cross over boundaries and tune its dial to wherever the musical action was found to be. The growing black middle class could tune to superstations of its own, such as Memphis's WDIA, where Martha Jean the Queen and Rufus Thomas ruled the waves. Yet, at the same time, ostensibly "white" radio began to flirt with

Figure 6.1 This was the infamous "Moondog Coronation Ball," advertised on its handbills as "The Most Terrible Ball of Them All." (Photograph by Peter Hastings.)

DJs who, though white, consciously sought to talk "black." Radio (and later television) was a mass marketing tool that no one quite understood, and its potential for crossing over neighborhood lines was immense. One such DJ who discovered (belatedly) that he had tripped over a live wire was Cleveland's Alan Freed.

Freed, a DJ at Cleveland's WJW, played rhythm and blues (R&B) records for a largely black listening public. Unlike Memphis's WDIA, WJW did not, however, specifically *target* black listeners or advertisers, and only programmed R&B in the late night hours. This tacit acknowledgment of both black and white listenership was increasingly common as the 1950s rolled along, but in 1952 few people realized that such part-time fare was drawing a substantial audience, quite possibly more substantial than the regular daytime programming. Freed himself, known by his on-air moniker of Moondog, had little idea of the size of his audience, and when in March 1952 he decided to organize an R&B concert at the Cleveland Arena, his main concern was that he might not sell enough tickets to make back the cost of renting the hall. This was the infamous "Moondog Coronation Ball," advertised on its handbills as "The Most Terrible Ball of Them All." When the first fans began showing up around 8 p.m. on March 21, Freed was relieved that most of the tickets had sold in advance. The crowd was mostly black (though some music historians have promulgated the fiction that it was almost all *white*), and most of them had heard about the concert on Freed's radio show (aside from the handbills, the radio plugs were the show's only advertising). An hour later, as several hundred fans without tickets began to gather around the entrance, Freed realized there was going to be trouble. In Cleveland, a segregated city whose black population had grown substantially in the wake of the "Great Migration," a crowd of black folks made the all-white police on the scene nervous. Was this going to be some kind of riot? Around 9:30, when the crowd (now grown to more than six thousand) pushed in four of the arena's doors and walked right past the startled ticket-takers, the police called for reinforcements. After a tense period when the arena was filled far beyond its capacity (and with only the first song of the first act having been performed), the police shut down the concert and ordered everyone out, a process which took several more hours.

This is the show often hailed as the "first rock 'n' roll concert," usually because Freed was the one to introduce the term "rock 'n' roll" to describe the uptempo R&B discs he played. Yet in many ways it was just another R&B concert, with the distinction that it was not advertised on a "black" radio station and did not appear at a "black" venue. In later years, Freed would be accused by some Afrocentric music critics of being instrumental in stealing black music and repackaging it for white consumers, but in 1952 Freed's audience was still mostly black, and he did nothing to consciously attract white listeners. In later years, Freed certainly tried to cash in on the huge crossover craze for rock 'n' roll, but he was far from alone. By then, the record companies themselves (belatedly, as usual) realized that R&B recordings were no longer being sold only (or even primarily) to black consumers, and, having tried a variety of tactics to siphon off the profits made by the small labels that released most R&B records, began to sign R&B artists themselves, or acquire exclusive distribution deals. The industry magazine *Billboard* reflected this change, at first altering the chart listing of "Race Recordings" to "Rhythm and Blues," and finally (in 1963) eliminating the R&B chart altogether on the theory that R&B was then fully a part of pop.

Yet, two years later, the R&B charts were back, part of a trend that has continued to this day of listing individual charts for each genre and category of music. It turned out that the labels that were releasing R&B *wanted* to have a separate chart so that their sales figures could be sorted out from the burgeoning music marketplace, which was just then undergoing a "British Invasion" that denied most R&B recordings their top chart status. The double irony – that this supposed "British Invasion" was led by bands who imitated and followed in the footsteps of Little Richard, Bo Diddley, and Muddy Waters – was not lost on these originators of R&B, though most Americans today, with characteristic cultural amnesia, think of "rock" as a music without a race. Yet "R&B" is still an industry category, with "Urban Contemporary" as its sister label for radio-station formatting, and most major record companies still divide their marketing and A&R departments along these lines.

POSTMODERNITY IN THE MARKETPLACE

But now it's the late 1990s. The new national *Zeitgeist* declares that *because* race as a category is now supposed to have been largely transcended, we don't need to acknowledge race as a meaningful question – in fact, to do so somehow marks us as cynical old leftists who can't get with the new post-racial reality. Yet, strangely enough, this is also the era when even more intensely racialized musical categories – "urban contemporary," "R&B," or "Latino" – dominate radio and music stores, and audience targeting and "formatting" guarantee that the listeners to one kind of music, however much they may overlap in reality, will be perceived and marketed as distinct groups. If there is one tacit point of agreement, however, between the micro-marketing and racialized genre terms of the industry (an industry now almost entirely controlled by three or four companies) and cultural critics, it is that all categories are slippery.

This was made eminently clear when SoundScan, introduced in order to replace the industry's quasi-fictional sales estimates with actual figures from cash registers at a representative series of stores, revealed that sales figures for R&B and hip-hop CDs were far greater than had been previously assumed, and that the great bulk of sales occurred in suburban malls and chain stores whose clientele was presumed to be mostly white. Furthermore, with artists as well as audiences more and more heteroglot in their configurations, it became increasingly difficult to predict success (or failure) by using categorical notions of difference. What to do with Apache

Indian, who blended Pakistani bhangra with Jamaican dancehall and American R&B while living in England? What about constructed sounds such as that of Enigma, which blended Gregorian chants and South American tribal religious songs with machine-generated drumbeats, or Liu Sola's "Blues in the East," which mixed blues and jazz with Chinese zither and bang zi vocal styles? As the array of such generically heterolectic artists grew, no category seemed broad enough to be accurate or narrow enough to be predictably marketed. The recording industry, which had always in the past divided its audiences in order to conquer them, seemed lost in the crosstalk between the tracks, nervously gobbling up small independent labels whose A&R staff could serve, at least temporarily, as prosthetic taste buds.

Within music criticism, a similar tension over race and genre has long been manifest. In the early criticism of jazz, the bulk of published critics were white men who venerated the sound of New Orleans in much the same way they lauded Michelangelo's David or Mozart's Requiem, as a cultural artifact in need of curatorial attention and meticulous cataloging. As Amiri Baraka (1967, p. 18) noted, this kind of care was in fact a kind of assassination, a reduction of a living tradition to "that junk pile of admirable objects and data that the West knows as culture." There was a strong sense that black music demanded its own critics, who would understand the music in its full cultural context. Such critics need not be black, but they needed a whole lot more than a degree from Harvard or Julliard. Baraka himself and the musician-critic Ben Sidran were two early writers who met these criteria. In the years since the bop revolution, jazz finally won the critical and institutional recognition it long sought, but at a price very much like the one Baraka feared – it has become a cultural *object*, an institutional *subject*, but only in isolated cases the living breathing improvisational *practice* it once was.

The blues, a close second to jazz in terms of recording history, endured a much different critical reception. The first "critics" of the blues were not aestheticians but folklorists, who were far more interested in classifying narrative tropes and variants than in looking at cultural politics. These early folklorists worked with the assumption that the blues was a characteristic – perhaps quintessential – *folk* art. Thus, they treated its performers as necessarily naive and untutored practitioners of an oral tradition. This need to see musicians as untutored was so deeply rooted that when Big Bill Broonzy recorded an album for Mose Asch's Folkways label in the 1950s, the liner notes were written to suggest that Broonzy had scarcely left the plantation where his forefathers sharecropped. No mention was

78

made of his twenty years' recording experience as an urban Chicago bluesman. Other folklorists, such as the indefatigable Harry Smith (editor of the landmark collection *American Folk Music*), deliberately interwove recordings by black and white artists, annotating them chiefly in order to note their common relationship to well known themes and traditions, thereby effectively erasing the issue of race altogether.

Rock, the stepchild of the blues and R&B, received the most belated attention from critics who liked to think of themselves as "serious." Its critical beacons, from Lester Bangs to Greil Marcus, have tended to be eclectic and impressionistic in their approaches, as most of them cut their teeth writing for small independent rock magazines. Marcus, for one, has always preferred to celebrate the quirky and at times absurdist juxtapositions of pop music and pop culture. In *Dead Elvis*, he celebrates the postmortem postmodernism of Elvis kitsch, while in *Invisible Republic* he plays gleefully idiosyncratic riffs around Dylan's folkloric roots. In *Lipstick Traces*, his most ambitious work to date, he finds threads with which to connect everything from Johnny Rotten to the Situationist International, suggesting without necessarily documenting the shattered holograms of mass culture and its discontents. Yet Marcus has seldom addressed the question of race *per se*. For this, readers must turn to more politically committed critics, such as Nelson George. George's *The Death of Rhythm and Blues* is quite possibly the most direct and cogent account of the cultural politics of race and music, as well as of the music industry's unsuccessful attempts to render such issues predictable.

Along with *Village Voice* page-mate Greg Tate, George was also one of the first critics to take a serious look at hip-hop culture. Hip-hop, more than previous musical forms, had a very specific cultural origin: the South Bronx. One could, in fact, make a map of its spread from the Bronx to Queensbridge to Brooklyn and beyond (Tricia Rose offers one such map in her book *Black Noise*). Thus it was New York writers who first took notice, just as it was small New York-based record labels that first recorded it. Black-owned enterprises such as Enjoy, Winley, and Sugar Hill released the earliest hip-hop recordings in the late 1970s. Yet, as documented by Nelson George, once hip-hop became viable enough for the major recording companies to sit up and take notice, its path was frustratingly similar to that paved for R&B: appropriation, commodification, and an end to innovation. Small labels were absorbed, artists were dropped after their sophomore efforts had disappointing sales, artists were signed but left to rot on the shelf when the marketing breezes blew another way, and trends were relentlessly reproduced until they died.

A full critical discourse about hip-hop has emerged only in the late 1980s and 1990s, a good twenty years after the first artists broke through. The first few books read more like bluffers' guides than actual criticism, though some, such as David Toop's classic *Rap Attack*, are masterpieces of documentary musical reportage. In recent years, fuller treatments by Brian Cross (1993), Tricia Rose (1994), and Russell Potter (1995) have added to the critical weight of hip-hop, and rappers such as KRS-One and Chuck D have put their own books up on the shelf. Because of its focus on lyrical content, hip-hop is also the first music to contain its own critically aware and dynamic dialogue (although in recent years this dialogue has been increasingly lost in a sea of gangsta-rap sloganeering).

REDRAWING THE MAP

My own route into hip-hop was a circuitous one which caused me to question many of my earlier figurations of the musical universe. In the wake of the self-immolation of punk in the early 1980s, rock seemed eviscerated and all-too-predictable. At the same time, R&B still bore the scars of its own disco inferno, and there was a sense that popular music in general no longer had the kind of raw, rebellious energy that had once, to quote Dylan Thomas, through the green fuse driven the flower. It was at this time that I remember my first dim inclinations toward musical nostalgia, the sense that what had come before was better than what was or what was likely to emerge in the near future. I spent hours listening to old protest songs by Bob Dylan and Phil Ochs, which seemed somehow far more urgent and pertinent than the blasé, ironic meanderings of Culture Club or OMD. MTV was on the air and commercial-free, but most of the videos were so predictably aimless that they were scarcely more stimulating than a test signal. Such occasional flourishes of musical activism as there were sounded disappointingly smug and treacly to my ears. "USA for Africa"? "We are the World, We are the Children"? "No Nukes"?

In the midst of these musical doldrums, hip-hop was gradually emerging from the streets of New York as one of the brashest and most rebellious sounds of the century. Grandmaster Flash and the Furious Five released "The Message" in 1983, and the year after, Run-DMC broke out with their riff on "Walk This Way," but I never heard either song until years later. Why? Was it because the new generation of AOR (album-oriented rock) superstations rarely played hip-hop, and mainline R&B stations shunned it as well? Was it because college kids were still noodling around with their own post-punk experiments and never looked at the wall to see what time it was? Was it because I was still assuming that revolutionary music could only be played on a guitar? What had really happened, I belatedly realized, was that the ostensibly egalitarian and eclectic notions of race fostered in the musical environment of the 1970s had never really run that deep. At best, they were tenuous alliances; at worst, a kind of willed illusion, a dreamy *Zeitgeist* that temporarily papered over deep and persistent cultural and economic rifts. In seeming to move beyond race by imagining music as a transcendent force, my generation of suburban white boys had in fact abandoned the possibility of cultural crosstalk. In this we were aided and abetted by a music industry which studiously avoided risks, didn't put much stock in hip-hop and other emerging musical forms until well into the 1980s, and plugged into the popularity of hip-hop only after it felt it could market such dangerous music in a safety-sealed package.

The first time I actually stopped and listened to hip-hop, it was a strange and uncanny experience, something like the emergence of Chauncey Gardener from his late employer's mansion in the book and film *Being There*. Chauncey, a middle-aged gardener who has remained indoors for decades while the neighborhood outside slowly turned into a ghetto, attempts to deflect the threats of some local street kids by pointing his television remote at them and pushing the button. In a similar way, I found myself both enthralled and repelled when a friend sat me down and played the first few tracks of *Straight Outta Compton*. This was strong stuff, stronger than anything I'd imagined, and it cut across all my deep-seated liberal mores. "Fuck the Police," now that sounded fine, but Eazy-E's and Ice Cube's luridly violent threats, many of which seemed aimed directly at the listener, overflowed the vessel of rebellion. Unlike leftist anthems such as Phil Ochs's "Cops of the World," this music did not allow its listeners the comfort of feeling good about themselves. These cops weren't in Cambodia or Santo Domingo. They were parked around the corner carrying badges and guns paid for by taxpayers like you and me. Police sirens, gunshots, and screeching tires were aurally imported into the mix, creating a tense environment within which white listeners were both vulnerable and culpable. There was no room for righteous empathy, at least not before confronting a few of the skeletons in the white liberal closet.

My early encounter with N.W.A. was only a very timid beginning, and it was only after many hours of listening that I could really hear it in the context of hip-hop as a whole. To endorse hip-hop was not necessarily to endorse N.W.A., any more than listening to rock meant that you had to become an apologist for Alice Cooper, but it took me a long time to be able to separate the issues. The subjective experience of any musical form or genre is such that no listener can take in the whole before understanding the formal codes of difference – which perhaps is part of the reason why hip-hop's long absence from radio made it so difficult for baby-boomer ears to grasp. It was not until a younger generation came of age that hip-hop gained a significant following among white teenagers. Unfortunately, this also meant that white listeners, who were generally more affluent, exercised a disproportionate influence over what the industry perceived as market-place trends. So it was that, as the more militant black nationalism of late 1980s and early 1990s rappers began to fade, a new school of West Coast "gangsta" rappers took their place. One irony in all this is that the popularity of gangsta rappers among white listeners has sustained a large part of their sales (though that certainly does not much support the conspiracy theories of black anti-rap crusaders like C. Delores Tucker, who claims that rap records are a plot foisted on black communities by white-owned record companies). Another irony is that, as Chuck D has noted, the music industry only "let this shit succeed" when they were ready. The arrival of hip-hop on the stage at the Grammy Awards has in many ways been its death.

The most significant legacy of the past few years may ultimately be that the problematics of race must be acknowledged, and that we need to be suspicious of hazy constructions of a musical utopia (especially when they take place on televised award shows). Even beyond that, we must be no less suspicious of the old pieties of liberal championing of black art forms. In fact, the traditional bifurcation between black and white can no longer be said to constitute the question of race, not in a United States where the Latino population will shortly outnumber African-Americans, and the number of Asian-Americans has steadily increased. This is still more evident in popular music, where the recombinant influences of multiple generic and cultural threads have long since made it impossible to draw clear-cut ethnic or racial genealogies. Hip-hop backbeats have supported vocalists as far-flung as Bruce Springsteen and Sinéad O'Connor, and digital samples have crossed over still more unexpected territory. Hip-hop producers have recently sampled everyone from Sting to Joni Mitchell to Stephen Stills, and multimedia transcriptionists such as Beck have created aural textures so dense that, like James Joyce, they might well keep scholars busy for three hundred years and more.

In the end, we are back to the problematic articulated so many years ago by Walter Benjamin in his essay "The work of art in the age of mechanical reproduction." When audiences and artists can meet without meeting, sample without accompanying, and mix without mixing, the old sense of a music's cultural "aura" is one that cannot be maintained. The issue of race, and issues of identity politics in general, will certainly not, however, disappear as a result. For what brings us into contact with music is an *affective* politics, a *subjective* sense that the music speaks somehow to us, personally. Postmodern theorists have long asserted that subjectivity is fragmented, but upon these fragments all kinds of animated ruins have been, and will continue to be, shored. T. S. Eliot (whose image this is) was in one sense a prescient literary "sampler," and it is possible to see in hip-hop, rave, and other aural recycling aesthetics something both before and *beyond* postmodernism. These art forms may mark the (re)emergence of what Paul Gilroy (1993) regards as "oppositional modernisms," of movements which have avowedly *not* thrown out the baby of art with the bathwater of romantic notions of originality and irreproducibility. (Eliot's "The Waste Land" (1922), particularly in its original draft ("He Do the Police in Different Voices"), is filled with dense intertextual collages, allusions, and borrowings, which Eliot felt strongly enough about to annotate with his own footnotes.) Put in other terms, the fact that identity is "complex and contradictory" does not mean the affective ties and social bonds secured by music (or any other art form) are false.

Complex subjectivity demands complex art, and the contradictions of one may well find their expression (if not necessarily their resolution) in the other. If, as Jean Baudrillard has claimed, the recombinant simulations of late twentieth-century technology and culture have blurred or even reversed our notions of the "copy" and the "original," perhaps art in fact gains in power, as we need no longer apologize for the idea of art as collage, and can learn to be comfortable with the impure mixtures which mark both our social and aesthetic experiences. Popular music may indeed provide the quintessential instance of this process, even as – and for the same reasons – it remains the most elusive matter for theoretical analysis. There can be no erasure of race, but that is not because it lies under everything like a seamless stone foundation, but because its conflicted histories are still the quarry and the quagmire in which all stones are born, heaved up, and lost.

Resources

Addicted to Noise (an online music zine featuring the writings of Greil Marcus, Dave Marsh, and other contemporary pop critics): http://www.addict.com/

Baker, Houston A. (1984) *Blues, Ideology, and Afro-American Literature: a Vernacular Theory.* Chicago: University of Chicago Press.

Baraka, Amiri (Jones, Leroi) (1967) *Black Music.* New York: Morrow.

Benjamin, Walter (1969) The work of art in the age of mechanical reproduction. In *Illuminations,* trans. Harry Zohn. New York: Schocken, pp. 217–51.

Cross, Brian (1993) *It's Not About the Salary: Rap, Race, and Resistance in Los Angeles.* New York and London: Verso.

Hebdige, Dick (1987) *Cut 'n' Mix: Culture, Identity and Caribbean Music.* London: Methuen.

George, Nelson (1988) *The Death of Rhythm and Blues.* New York: Pantheon.

Gilroy, Paul (1993) *The Black Atlantic: Modernity and Double Consciousness.* Cambridge, MA: Harvard University Press.

Isbell, Charles (the "Homeboy from Hell"), with links to his New Jack Hip-Hop Reviews: http://www.ai.mit.edu/~isbell/isbell.html

Potter, Russell (1995) *Spectacular Vernaculars: Hip-Hop and the Politics of Postmodernism.* Albany: State University of New York Press.

Red Hot Jazz Archive: http://www.redhotjazz.com

Rose, Tricia (1994) *Black Noise: Rap Music and Black Culture in Contemporary America.* Middletown, CT: University Press of New England.

Tomlinson, Gary (1992) Cultural dialogics and jazz. In Katherine Bergeron and Philip V. Bohlman (eds), *Disciplining Music: Musicology and Its Canons.* University of Chicago Press, pp. 64–94.

Toop, David (1992) *Rap Attack No. 2: African Rap to Global Hip-Hop.* London: Serpent's Tail.

7
Gender

Holly Kruse

I would argue that two crucial elements have been painfully lacking from most feminist critiques of popular music: analyses of popular music institutions and economics, and analyses of practice.

The relationship between women and popular music, and especially women and rock, has become a popular site of academic analysis, particularly in the past fifteen years. Prior to the advent of MTV, feminists who studied rock and pop focused largely on whether lyrics were sexist. More recently, however, feminist analyses grounded in poststructuralist and postmodern theories have problematized issues of gender and meaning, and they have questioned whether the most obvious readings of popular music texts need be monolithic. In this chapter I discuss the relationship between women, signifying systems, and popular music, and I raise questions about the most popular approaches to the study of this relationship. Although questions of gender encompass a range of issues related to constructions of both masculinity and femininity (and the spaces beyond and between), I focus primarily on women because of the power relationships in the production and consumption of rock and pop music that have attempted to limit the roles and meanings available to women in the pop and rock worlds.

IS ROCK 'N' ROLL A "MALE" MUSIC?

Until recently, the question of whether types of music are "gendered" was not an issue widely debated in either academic or popular criticism. But in the past two decades, popular music scholarship has taken up the notion of gender as the social and cultural construction of difference coded as male or female, and as something understood in relation to, but not necessarily tied to, biology. Increasingly, music scholars argue that various kinds of music commonly regarded as gender-neutral are in fact gendered. In particular, in recent years popular and academic discourse about whether rock (as opposed to pop) is an almost exclusively "male" music became relatively widespread. At this point, it is necessary to make an important definitional distinction. For the purposes of this chapter, "pop" can be thought of as a form of popular music in which certain conventions of time (two to four minutes long), sound (emphasizing melody and hooks), and structure (verses and choruses) are followed. Rock, on the other hand, is a harder-edged, usually electric guitar-driven form of popular music, one that tends to be less interested in adhering to traditional pop conventions but instead has generated its own conventions, like the sprawling heavy metal guitar solo.

The increased visibility of women as rock musicians – in the past they had usually been restricted to the role of pop singer – has undoubtedly helped to account for increased interest in the relationship between gender and popular music. Yet even in the late 1990s, despite headway gained by female rock musicians like Patti Smith, Joan Jett, Melissa Etheridge, and Courtney Love, rock 'n' roll remains a primarily male domain. In fact, if one looks at rock history, one finds that many of rock's "revolutionary" moments, such as Woodstock, have marginalized women. The hippie culture that Woodstock exemplified and celebrated relegated women largely to the traditional roles of sex object and (earth) mother. More recent popular music "movements" have been similarly criticized for their male bias. Hardcore, a North American form of punk rock, with its mosh pits and stage diving, has been notable for the relative absence of female bands and fans.

However, no popular music in recent years has been as explicitly coded as male in popular discourse as rap. Not only are the majority of bestselling rappers male, but rap lyrics are perennially cited as among the most misogynist. Lyrics, as I will discuss later, are a focal point of gender-based analyses of popular music and are therefore crucial to an understanding of the relationship between women and various forms of popular music. In the late 1980s and early 1990s, rap lyrics like Ice Cube's "Nine months later . . . why did I bang her? / Now I'm in the closet looking for the hanger" from "You Can't Fade Me" present a sentiment still heard in rap music: that women are objects and even legitimate targets of sexual violence.

Of course, rap music did not invent misogynist lyrics. Feminist critics often point to songs of the 1960s like the Rolling Stones' "Under My

Thumb" and "Stupid Girl" and Bob Dylan's "Like a Rolling Stone" as prime examples of songs with lyrics that show contempt for women. It is important to note here, however, that songs' meanings cannot be analyzed simply by scanning their lyrics. Issues of meaning are highly problematic, so rather than merely dismissing rock as an exclusively male musical form, I shall turn instead to more complex questions of music and meaning.

GENDER, MUSIC, AND LYRICAL SIGNIFICATION

Music signifies in many ways – through the music itself, through associations between songs/artists and certain places/spaces and times, through intertextual relationships with other cultural artifacts – but at the most obvious level, it signifies through lyrics. While in recent years there has been something of a shift away from analyses of lyrics in popular music scholarship, lyrics must be understood as an integral part of most popular music texts. Not only do lyrics provide the "narrative" for a song, but lyrics help determine how artists are perceived by audiences, what they seem to "stand for." Lyrics are meaningful because they appear to give listeners insights into an artist's thoughts and feelings, and they allow listeners the pleasure of textual interpretation, of trying to determine the ever-elusive, ever-shifting "true meaning" of a song. Through this process of interpretation, listeners place their own feelings, beliefs and perceptions in relation to those they believe are expressed in the song. Thus, lyrics can provide a powerful point of identification for listening subjects.

Lyrics are obviously of profound importance to the songwriters themselves, allowing songwriters to exercise the power to create and play with meanings and identities. Indeed, lyrics, and the act of writing itself, can be thought of as political interventions at the level of culture. As part of what makes popular music "mean," lyrics are an element in the process of signification, helping to create cultural understandings and locate subjects within a framework of relationships of power. Subjects' identities are formed in part through their interactions with cultural texts, and because pop music lyrics are such an important point of reference for listeners and an important mode of expression for musicians, the contribution made by pop and rock music lyrics to meaning merits examination.

Lyrics are thus of importance in any analysis of gender and popular music. Rock music in particular has been characterized by male-voiced lyrics that articulate gendered structures of power that tend to mirror social relations in the real world. However, it is important to interject at this point that lyrics of even the most seemingly misogynist songs cannot be understood as merely woman-hating; other readings *are* possible. It is possible, for example, to read the Rolling Stones' "Under My Thumb" as a celebration of the act of revenge, something appreciated by men *and* women, rather than as a misogynist diatribe (a common feminist interpretation). However, this reading forces female listeners to identify with a male subject position in order to experience a celebratory and assertive sexuality. Still, it remains the case that even apparently sexist lyrics can be read in multiple, and often surprising, ways. This is a key point to keep in mind as I shift my focus to lyrics written and/or sung by female artists.

In fact, a female-penned song can be used to illustrate the same point. "Stand By Your Man," a country song which reached Number 1 on the pop charts when it was released in 1969, was co-written by its singer, Tammy Wynette, and is often used as an example of how female artists have helped perpetuate traditional notions of gender roles and thus their own oppression. Lines like "Give him two arms to cling to / And something warm to come to" have been widely interpreted as a reactionary espousal of a prefeminist point of view. However, other lines in the song make such a simplistic reading problematic. For instance, lines like "Sometimes it's hard to be a woman / Giving all your love to just one man" have been understood by some critics to be an expression of dissatisfaction with women's traditional roles within monogamous relationships.

However one reads "Stand By Your Man," there can be little doubt that it, like most popular songs sung by women, deals with issues of romantic love. In recent years, interest in women's lyrics has turned to the growing number of exceptions to this phenomenon. For instance, British musician Kate Bush can be seen as a pioneering figure who, beginning in the late 1970s, opened up new lyrical possibilities for female singers, taking on a variety of male and female roles in songs that dealt with topics like the destruction of aboriginal cultures, guerrilla warfare, witchcraft, and drug smuggling. By the early 1990s, aggressive female sexuality was being expressed quite openly by alternative rock and pop artists, with lyrics like "Lick my legs, I'm on fire" (Polly Harvey of P. J. Harvey) and "I'll fuck you 'til your dick is blue" (Liz Phair). Other women explored sexual power relations in songs about rape (Tori Amos's "Me and a Gun"; Juliana Hatfield's "A Dame with a Rod") and power inequity in romantic relationships (Lush's "The Childcatcher"). In addition to songs with sexual themes, other songs' lyrics conveyed a general sense of female assertiveness, as when alternative rock band L7 sings "Get out of my way or I might shove / Get out of my way or I'm gonna shove."

We must remember, though, that lyrics do not "mean" in a vacuum; they have meanings for all kinds of people in all kinds of audiences in all kinds of contexts. Often these meanings are intensely personal and/or transgressive: for instance, a favorite song at a gay male dance club at which I spent a fair amount of time in the 1980s was the Kenny Rogers/ Dolly Parton duet "Islands in the Stream." It may be hard to understand the attraction for a gay male audience of what on the surface appears to be a standard heterosexual romantic pop duet, but one can imagine how the lyrical theme of love triumphing over isolation (and the good-natured, self-conscious campiness of an artist like Parton) would have an appeal for individuals in this audience. Such examples illustrate how lyrics can have different meanings for different listeners in different contexts, meanings that cannot simply be read directly off the text.

Moreover, the contexts in which lyrics are heard can have a significant effect on how they mean. Listening to music on the stereo or radio in the privacy of a quiet room may draw inordinate attention to the lyrics of songs, and therefore to the personal mode of address used in pop and rock music lyrics. Yet in settings like dance clubs, concert venues, and parties, music is experienced primarily through its beat, its melody, and its presentation.

If lyrics are to be analyzed in relation to gender, then, it must be understood that they can have different meanings to different audiences in different contexts. No single meaning can be pinned down, though certain readings may be more obvious than others. Furthermore, musical meanings are made not only on the level of lyric content. What many academic analyses of popular music, and in particular of gender and popular music, overlook is the degree to which music itself signifies.

MUSICAL MEANINGS

In her book *Feminine Endings*, Susan McClary makes a powerful argument for the need to study not just lyrics, or, as will be discussed below, image, when investigating issues of gender and popular music. For centuries, Western music composition of all kinds has coded harmonic and rhythmic structures in terms of gender: for example, "masculine" ("strong") versus "feminine" ("weak") cadences. McClary contends that the failure to take such important musical points into consideration in many academic analyses is largely attributable not only to the inability of non-musicians to talk about music and its effects, but also to academics' refusal to acknowledge the gender significance of such technical musical devices.

One need not be a musicologist to combine analyses of music and lyrics in an attempt to address questions of gender and meaning. One might observe, for instance, that Kate Bush's use of ancient musical instruments like the dijeridu and the bouzouki, with their earthy tones, alongside modern instruments like the electric guitar and the Fairlight, resonates with her recurring lyrical theme of the interconnectedness of past, present, and future, as well as reflecting the masculine/feminine dichotomy and interplay she cultivates in her lyrics. Although structural components of Bush's music need not be studied in detail, the importance of instrumentation and sound is central to discussions of her work.

In addition to instrumentation and musical structure, another often overlooked site at which meaning is produced in popular music is the voice. When examining lyrics, many scholars fail to take into account how those lyrics are vocalized, yet this is a key terrain upon which the gendered struggle over signification in popular music takes place. Kate Bush, for example, with her ability to integrate shrieks, guttural noises, and other unconventional vocalizations into songs, was among the first artists to stand in defiance of traditional female pop and rock singing conventions. Men in pop and rock music historically have been allowed greater latitude to use a range of vocal sounds: the falsettos of all-male groups – from the Four Seasons and their doo-wop predecessors to the Bee Gees – have been accepted, as have the shrieks of rock stylists like Robert Plant and the vocal antics of early rock and roll artists like Little Richard.

Such a range of sounds has not been open to women in mainstream music. In fact, female singers who transgress the boundaries of what is considered "nice" singing often encounter hostility from the male-dominated music industry and music press. A *Details* magazine review of Babes in Toyland's major label debut album, *Fontanelle*, labeled singer Kat Bjelland's vocals as "out-of-control," the band's live show as "an hour of primal scream therapy," and concluded that the band's music is "Midol rock." Bjelland's response to the review was, "Midol rock – that's so fucking sexist I can't believe it" (Karlen, 1994, pp. 211–12). Powerful, unconventional female voices evoke profoundly negative and, not incidentally, gendered reactions because of what they signify, both to the singers and to the audience: the visceral expression of female pain, rage, and frustration.

This scream of female anger poses a direct threat to patriarchy, which attempts to cover over both the existence of such anger and the structures which engender it. Yet screaming is not the only way in which female vocalists convey anger and frustration. Rappers like Salt 'N' Pepa use the aggressive, straightforward form of speaking characteristic of rap to deliver their brutally honest pronouncements about gender relations. Singer Miki Berenyi, formerly of Lush, on the other hand, delivers powerful lines about topics like child sexual abuse in a high, thin voice that is overwhelmed by the wall of guitar sound created by the band. The combination of loud instrumentals and difficult-to-hear vocals is problematic. Yet while the difficulty of deciphering all of Lush's lyrics upon listening can be frustrating, the juxtaposition of powerful lyrics and underplayed vocals makes the songs' revelations far more startling. In this case, as in many others, analyzing lyrics reveals just a small part of the story.

FEMALE IMAGES IN POPULAR MUSIC

When we consider questions of gender and popular music, it is not enough to examine lyrics and such aspects of music as cadence formulas, instrumentation, and vocal style; one must also take image into account. Although the advent of music video has accentuated questions of image, images of women in popular music have been sites of scrutiny for decades. Pejorative critiques of female performers based on their images have been par for the course in popular music. Overlooked in these critiques of various prominent female artists was the *range* of artists discussed: Aretha Franklin, Grace Slick, Joni Mitchell, Carole King, Helen Reddy, Patti Smith, Ronnie Spector, and Janis Joplin represent a variety of musical styles and female images. Female musicians who grew up following the careers of one or more of these artists certainly could have had worse role models.

In recent years, alternative rock has presented young women with several particularly vociferous role models. Courtney Love of Hole is perhaps the most prominent of this group of aggressive, outgoing rock musicians, and she believes she has blazed a trail for younger women, allowing them to better fantasize about becoming female rock stars themselves. And, indeed, some writers have used Love as an example of the growing feminist consciousness of women in rock. Yet Love is still largely an exception to the rule. Several female-fronted "alternative" bands, such as the Cardigans, the Sundays, and Madder Rose, do not appear to challenge the patriarchal order, instead presenting women in a nonthreatening way.

At the same time, alternative rock has provided women with a place where they are freer to write songs, play instruments, form bands, and produce records than has traditionally been the case. This has certainly broadened the available range of powerful images of women in popular music. These images are conveyed in live performance, in print and television interviews and articles, and, most prominently, in music videos.

In the 1980s, the music videos aired on MTV and other video outlets were notable for the degree to which they objectified women. The popularity of heavy metal videos that presented women solely as sex objects, like Van Halen's "Hot for Teacher," Def Leppard's "Photograph," Motley Crue's "Girls, Girls, Girls," and many others, came under fire for their sexism (and in some cases, apparent misogyny). Even new wave bands like Duran Duran and more traditional rock/pop artists like Rod Stewart were criticized for the images of women presented in their videos. MTV became a magnet for feminist ire, and the female artists (such as Cindy Lauper, Tina Turner, and, more controversially, Madonna) who were able to put forth more complex and powerful images of women in pop/rock music were praised and viewed as exceptional.

In the early 1990s, however, changes in MTV programming made this sort of critique less relevant. Nirvana's 1991 album *Nevermind* demonstrated to record companies that alternative rock and pop could break through to the mainstream, and, as Nirvana's "Smells Like Teen Spirit" single demonstrated, it could do it with the help of music videos. Major labels and MTV became more supportive than ever of bands with nontraditional line-ups, images, sounds, and/or subject matter. Women in alternative music videos tended not to be objectified in the manner of many videos of the 1980s. In fact, bands with not particularly image-conscious female musicians like the Breeders, Veruca Salt, and Belly found their videos in heavy rotation on MTV.

Alternative rock and pop videos tend to emphasize bands in performance rather than elaborate concepts, as was common in the 1980s. Performance footage tends to code videos, and hence bands, as more "authentic," more "true-to-life" than videos with storylines, like Pat Benatar's "Love Is a Battlefield" or Duran Duran's "Hungry Like the Wolf." It is therefore telling that alternative videos featuring all-male bands in performance tend to have very few or no women in them. Because rock and pop – even alternative rock and pop – remain dominated by men, videos on MTV on the whole reiterate and reinscribe the reality that rock 'n' roll is still a man's world. Moreover, the increase in rap video programming on MTV in the late 1980s and early 1990s created a space for videos which, as a genre, often exploit women's bodies as objects of male sexual pleasure more than any other genre currently on the channel.

GENDER IN MUSICAL TEXTS: POSSIBLE DANGERS

I have argued that any thorough textual analysis of popular music and its relationship to issues of gender must take into account song lyrics, musical structures/sounds, and image. Some scholars have done excellent jobs of combining all three levels of analysis. Unfortunately, as feminist popular music studies turned toward video analysis, there was, and there continues to be, a predominant tendency to concentrate solely on video texts, while ignoring the music itself. Moreover, discussions of video imagery frequently assert that videos mean very specific things to hypothetical audiences. These assertions tend to weaken otherwise cogent analyses of music and music videos. The problem with such readings is twofold: first, they place the writer in the privileged position of passing judgment on what videos and artists mean; second, they focus on image to the virtual exclusion of all other elements. Because this kind of approach is the primary one applied in feminist readings of video texts and stars, it serves to reinforce the notion that female creativity in popular music can mainly be found in the realm of style manipulation rather than musical and lyrical composition and/or interpretation. I am arguing, by contrast, that it is not unreasonable to assume that the enduring success of female pop and rock music artists such as Madonna, Melissa Etheridge, and Janet Jackson has something to do with their music, not just with their video images.

A full appreciation of the complex relationship between gender and popular music requires an integrated textual analysis of lyrics, music, and image. Is this, however, enough? I would argue that two crucial elements have been painfully lacking from most feminist critiques of popular music: analyses of popular music institutions and economics, and analyses of practice. Popular music is part of a multibillion dollar, multinational media industry. While economics may not solely determine what sorts of lyrics, sounds, and images are made available, musical expression is formed and marketed in an environment shaped by the music industry. Its influence cannot be ignored.

The mass production of popular music around the globe has historically been dominated by men: with very few exceptions, men have been the label heads, the artists and repertoire people, the producers, the engineers, and the musicians who have shaped the sound and image of popular music. While the rise of independent labels in the 1980s helped to shift the balance a bit, even at relatively recently founded independent labels specializing in rock and pop music, men more often than not can be found in the key decision-making roles. Furthermore, the headway gained by the women at independent labels who do sign bands to contracts and perform other central functions has not as yet been replicated by the major record companies that control the vast majority of popular music released worldwide.

An equally important facet of the relationship between women and popular music is situated musical and social practices. The practices and lived experiences of women in popular music must be studied; tensions in gender relations that are evident at the level of signification in popular music are even more salient when the experiences and practices of women in popular music are examined. Women are still a relative rarity in rock bands, and studies of women's experiences with pop and rock music have indicated that girls are socialized into pop and rock music differently from boys: boys and young men *tend* to learn songs by ear and to talk about popular music's technical aspects, while girls and young women *tend* to focus on lyrics rather than on equipment and instrumentation, and to resist learning songs by ear. Miki Berenyi's experience testifies to the truthfulness of these findings:

> Girls don't have the patience to spend six years learning someone else's music. Me and Emma [Anderson] can't jam because we only know how to play our own songs. Jamming's more of a boy's thing. . . . I think that women play more imaginatively because they learn to play while they're writing songs, instead of waiting to be technically good first. (Quoted in Evans, 1994, p. 44)

These differences can make it difficult for female musicians to enter male-dominated music cultures.

However, it is not only female musicians who face barriers imposed by patriarchal practices. Women who work at record labels – both major labels and independents – often find themselves "ghettoized" into particular, traditionally "female" areas like publicity, while having little chance of snagging much more prestigious and powerful artists and repertoire positions. Female employees of independent record labels often note that, in this regard, there is not much of a difference between the gender politics of major labels and indies. Women are also employed in the music industry as booking agents for live music venues. In some cities in the

USA, in fact, the majority of booking agents at alternative clubs are women. Yet, despite the growing presence of women, problems still exist. Female booking agents claim that they are paid less and taken less seriously than their male counterparts, and that they are kept out of the male network of promoters, managers, agents, and club owners.

Similar problems exist for women who work at radio stations, even college radio stations, which have been sites from which music by female *rock* musicians has been disseminated to a much greater degree than mainstream commercial radio stations. Indeed, college radio stations, as they are popularly constructed – student-run stations that serve reasonably large campus communities and whose playlists tend to emphasize alternative rock and pop – have been somewhat hospitable places for female staffers, but inequities between males and females still exist. While at college stations there tend to be more male than female participants, women do become program directors and music directors as well as on-air personalities. However, while college radio may give women relatively open access to the airwaves, they tend to find their post-college radio industry prospects less promising than their male counterparts.

Audience practice is a final area that warrants further investigation. Fans are as crucial to the production of popular music as musicians and record companies. Listening to popular music should not be thought of as mere consumption. Interactions between cultural texts and audience members produce new and often unexpected meanings, and therefore audience members are quite actively involved in text construction. For this reason, as discussed earlier, seemingly sexist lyrics may in fact be read as emancipatory by female subjects. Yet once the step of acknowledging the polysemic nature of texts and the active role of audiences in producing them has been taken, the next step is to examine how actual audience members articulate musical texts to their own experiences and practices.

In all these cases, the gendered nature of practices within popular music, and women's experiences of these practices, demonstrate the need to understand the degree to which these practices and institutions reproduce, subvert, or attempt to escape patriarchal relations.

CASE STUDY: THROWING MUSES' "TELLER"

The complex interrelationship of all the factors described is illustrated when one attempts to bring them to bear in an analysis of a particular artist and song – for example, the song "Teller," written and sung by

95

Kristin Hersh, from *University*, the 1995 album by Hersh's band, the Boston-based Throwing Muses. Lyrically, "Teller" is a complex song with shifting subjects and subjectivities, yet it is less ambiguous than many other songs by Hersh. Still, several elements of the song invite multiple readings, beginning with the title. Who, or what, is "teller"? Is this a reference to a fortune teller? A bank teller? Or perhaps even nuclear physicist Edward Teller? Hersh answers this question in the first verse of the song when she sings, "I said to the teller / 'If this is the future / I don't wanna know'."

"Teller" seems to be a song about the narrator's reluctance to face life after, and the loss of self-esteem that goes with, the end of a relationship. Early in the song "the guy behind the bar" comments, "You cut a nice figure of a family," to which the narrator responds, "I don't know, I don't know." Indeed, confusion and mixed feelings are the dominant theme in the song; in the first verse Hersh sings, "I leave in the morning / I don't wanna go." She later adds, "I have a fear of flying / I think I have a fear of him," and she then discloses "I'm afraid of meaning nothing again." Her fear and feeling of helplessness come to the fore in the final verse, in which Hersh appears to be addressing the listeners (not, say, the teller or the guy behind the bar), and which begins with the line "Can I be stupid for a minute?" and ends with the lines "You don't have to listen to this / Tell me what to say."

It is important, however, to note how the music itself allows for more complex readings of the song. In many ways, the tensions in the lyrics are reflected in the music. "Teller" begins with a strong, steady drumbeat that drives the song forward. After each verse the drumbeat is interrupted briefly as Hersh sings "I don't know, I don't know," a momentary change in tempo that mirrors musically the hesitation expressed in the lyrics. Moreover, in the lyrically confused and conflicted final verse, the music builds: the guitar becomes louder in the mix, and layered female vocals, which are heard briefly earlier in the song, become a constant presence.

Hersh has a very distinctive vocal style. She sings in a rather nasal yet very strong alto, and her lyrics are clearly articulated, although this by no means makes it any easier to ascribe concrete meanings to what she sings. While analyzing lyrics and music are useful parts of the process of making sense of "Teller," meanings are not created by lyrics and music alone; all musical texts are intertextual, drawing meaning from and contributing meaning to other cultural artifacts. In this particular instance, it must be acknowledged that no Throwing Muses song (or Kristin Hersh solo work) can be considered in isolation. Throwing Muses gained national prominence at a time in the mid-1980s when rock and pop music released on independent record labels and played on college radio became a notable trend, independent bands that featured female musicians were increasingly more common, and music scenes in cities like Boston, outside of the entertainment industry centers of Los Angeles and New York, were gaining considerable notice from the mainstream press. For many listeners, some or all of these factors may contribute to what the music of Throwing Muses means to them. However, perhaps the most salient extra-textual factor to take into account when considering questions of meaning is Kristin Hersh's public image.

Figure 7.1 Perhaps the most salient extra-textual factor to take into account when considering questions of meaning is Kristin Hersh's public image. (Photograph by John Patrick Salisbury, used with permission of Throwing Music.)

Hersh's battle with mental illness (first diagnosed as schizophrenia, later rediagnosed as bipolar disorder) has been well publicized and has thus become central in the construction of the artist Kristin Hersh in popular discourse, connecting her intertextually to a panoply of noted artists who struggled with mental illness: Sylvia Plath, Vincent Van Gogh, Daniel Johnston, Wolfgang Amadeus Mozart, William Styron, and so on. All are part of a cultural understanding that links madness with genius, and placing Hersh in such company adds weight to her own body of work. Moreover, knowledge of Hersh's history of struggle with mental illness certainly adds another layer of meaning to her music and another prism through which her music could be read. Are her sometimes seemingly non-linear, even chaotic, lyrics and shifting tempos within songs reflections of the lack of order in her own mind? Or are they, as Hersh would prefer people to think, products of an essentially female songwriting process?

The other widely circulated understanding of Hersh *is* as an essentially "female" songwriter and performer. Hersh has contributed to this understanding. In discussing her music, she notes that she experiences her songs physically and thus uses "gut words, not brain words," in writing songs. She explains, "Maybe the fact that I'm more responsive to songs in a physical way is because I'm female. Female physicality is a much more cyclical energy" (quoted in Evans, 1994, p. 215). Such comments by Hersh about her own music make it unsurprising that many critics see her music as gendered. To give just one example, in their book *The Sex Revolts*, Simon Reynolds and Joy Press (1995, pp. 369–71) remark that the music of Throwing Muses, while adhering to many of the basic tenets of the traditional "male" rock form, tends to change tempo in mid-song and thus, "rocks . . . [to] a new female rhythm."

Of course, there is a long history, especially in literary works like "The Yellow Wallpaper" and *Jane Eyre*, of exploring the boundaries (or lack thereof) between the feminine and madness. In her partly socially constructed, partly self-constructed public image, Kristin Hersh provides a contemporary site at which discourses of femaleness and madness can and do intersect. It is therefore important to recognize that extra-textual factors such as these are as significant in understanding the ways in which listeners make sense of a song like "Teller" as the lyrics and music of the song.

Finally, any analysis of the music of Kristin Hersh/Throwing Muses requires some examination of the lived experiences of those involved in the overlapping processes of production, dissemination, and consumption. Obviously, some of Hersh's key experiences have already been touched upon, because they are also part of her image as an indie rock icon.

98

However, an analysis that foregrounds gender would also need to include something of Hersh's experience as a woman in the still-male-dominated business of popular music: how she formed Throwing Muses with her step-sister Tanya Donelly as a teenager in their home (a central site of musical practices for girls) in Newport, Rhode Island; how the band signed a major label recording contract after releasing an EP on a small independent label, a cassette on their own, and two albums on the British independent label 4AD; and how Hersh and Donelly dealt with the way that the mainstream music industry attempted to market them specifically as women in rock. On the last point, it is quite telling to note that Hersh especially has tried to resist such attempts to define and market her, noting that in the eyes of the industry she has largely "disappeared . . . because for years I gave the press really ugly pictures of myself which would make me cringe. . . . And I didn't exist! . . . They can't market you, so you don't appear to the public, so you don't have a voice" (quoted in Evans, 1994, p. 217).

It is precisely because of this that in cases of artists like Hersh it is critical to also examine the practices of audiences. Audiences create and circulate knowledge and meanings at a number of sites – with friends, in record stores and clubs, in their roles as gatekeepers at college and community radio stations, at parties, in Internet discussion forums and on Web sites, through making and sharing tapes – that may both augment and circumvent the practices of the mainstream music industry. In the case of Hersh, one can find, for instance, Throwing Muses websites that include fan commentary on releases and quote Hersh on subjects like the effect that being a mother had on the writing of particular songs or the primal femaleness of particular albums. Such disclosures are not likely to be found in standard record company press kits, yet they are clearly highly meaningful to fans.

CONCLUSIONS

A final cautionary note: for the most part, scholarly works on women and popular music have tended to posit "women" as a unitary category. In fact, gender identification is cross-cut by identifications of race, ethnicity, social class, generation, dis/ability, and so on. Gender identity, therefore, is not a stable, coherent entity but is instead a site of contestation. Furthermore, if we think of gender as something that is constructed through our interactions with systems of signification and through our experiences

99

of the social world, it must be thought of, like all aspects of subjectivity, as always in process. With that in mind, it seems important to question the usefulness of establishing firm gender lines in popular music studies.

I began this essay by discussing whether popular music, particularly rock music, is gendered as male. As female-dominated bands like Hole, Babes in Toyland, the Breeders, and the bands associated with the Riot Grrrl movement gained prominence in the early 1990s, references to "female rock" proliferated in the media. What do people who endorse gender classifications like this have to say about women who find gangster rap empowering and men who like, or even identify with, the music of Riot Grrrl bands? The important questions to ask now are not merely about whether rock/pop songs are sexist or what characterizes male rock/pop versus female rock/pop. Instead, we need to ask how, in very specific ways, popular music helps to construct gendered identities and gendered understandings through both its systems of signification and situated practices; but we also need to ask how other forms of identification cross-cut, work against, and/or reinforce gendered identities and meanings.

Resources

Bayton, Mavis (1991) How women become musicians. In Simon Frith and Andrew Goodwin (eds), *On Record: Rock, Pop, and the Written Word*. New York: Pantheon, pp. 238–57.

Evans, Liz (1994) (ed.) *Women, Sex and Rock 'n' Roll: In Their Own Words*. London: Pandora.

GoGirls "homepage for women who rock": http://www.gogirlsmusic.com/gogirls/

Karlen, Neil (1994) *Babes in Toyland: the Making and Selling of a Rock and Roll Band*. New York: Times.

McClary, Susan (1991) *Feminine Endings: Music, Gender, and Sexuality*. Minneapolis: University of Minnesota Press.

Matthew Kirkcaldie's Throwing Muses/Kristin Hersh discography: http://www.dns.net/andras/music/eyesore/html/interview/ThrowingMuses.discograpy.html

Reynolds, Simon and Press, Joy (1995) *The Sex Revolts: Gender, Rebellion, and Rock 'n' Roll*. Cambridge, MA: Harvard University Press.

Steward, Sue and Garratt, Sheryl (1984) *Signed, Sealed, and Delivered: True Life Stories of Women in Pop*. Boston: South End.

Throwing Music website: http://www.throwingmusic.com/

8
Youth

Deena Weinstein

Rock would not be possible, would be unimaginable, without youth.

Rock and Youth were born Siamese twins in the middle of that buttoned-down decade, the 1950s, joined at the hip, or perhaps at the pelvis. Rock was known as Rock 'n'Roll, a name given by its godfather, Alan Freed. But its Scout leader, Dick Clark, modified its moniker to read "Rock and Roll." Its twin, Youth, also had a variety of childhood names; until the family moved from the wrong side of the tracks, it was called JD (short for Juvenile Delinquent), Greaser, and Hood. But it was mainly called Teenager.

The twins were full of vitality and frightened many adults. Some saw the pair as evil. Reaching maturity in the late sixties, the twins were hell bent on changing the world or at least serious about not becoming like their parents. They were strong and confident, even full of themselves. They celebrated their coming of age at a big blowout party for tens of thousands held at a dairy farm in the Catskill Mountains.

Youth and Rock had a blast – Woodstock was as much about one of them as the other. But during the next decade, as they tried to find their way in society, they were not as fortunate. At least Youth wasn't. Rock went into business, became a suit of sorts, and prospered mightily. Youth, in contrast, did not thrive. It became somewhat schizophrenic – wearing its hair in a green mohawk one day, long and unstyled (the better to headbang) another. And those were only two of Youth's modes. As Rock got bigger, Youth seemed to shrivel. In the first part of the eighties, Youth sort of disappeared. Oh, its body was still there, firmly attached to Rock, but its spirit was gone. Rock would pretend that its twin was all there, but then Rock wasn't all there either.

Youth's spirit was no longer within its body, yet it did not disappear. It floated free, allowing other bodies to grasp hold of it; older, way older, bodies, and very young child bodies, too. Virtually anybody could possess Youth's spirit. For a price. In the early nineties, Rock even commissioned a song to help its twin: "Smells Like Teen Spirit." Youth was, for a time, not exactly its old self, but almost so. Its resuscitation was short-lived, and soon Rock found itself dragging around its lifeless twin's body. It had surgeons slice off Youth and went hi-tech, replacing its twin with its image in a life-like hologram. In the dead of night, Youth's body was dumped into a grave and abandoned. Lying there, six feet under, Youth began to feel its life return. It recognized that it would now only be fully alive in the underground.

For millennia humanity has used fables, but they are no substitute for analysis. Besides, the socio-historical analysis of the relationship between youth and rock is quite fabulous in its own way. Essentially rock would not be possible, would be unimaginable, without youth. From its beginnings, in the fifties, rock music was the result of a confluence of many factors, converging, like a pile-up at a demolition derby, on youth. Youth: the ground-zero of the music. "Sh-Boom" by the Chords, "(We're Gonna) Rock Around the Clock" by Bill Haley and the Comets, Chuck Berry's "Maybellene," "Why Do Fools Fall in Love" by the Teenagers featuring Frankie Lymon, Carl Perkins's and Elvis Presley's "Blue Suede Shoes," and Little Richard's (but not Pat Boone's) "Tutti Frutti": these and literally thousands of other songs made up the rock 'n' roll canon of the mid-fifties. Its musical features – particularly the beat and lyrics – the demographics of many performers, its media formats, even the criticisms leveled against it can be traced to the particular situation of adolescents in that decade.

"It's got a good beat and you can dance to it," was the teenager's critical praise of a rock 'n' roll song. The music's two major flavors were fast and slow. Fast songs like Jerry Lee Lewis's "Whole Lot of Shakin' Going On" and Berry's "Maybellene" allowed the display and discharge of abundant physical energy. Slow songs like "Eddie My Love" and "In the Still of the Nite" encouraged sexual expression (when not discouraged by ruler-bearing teacher-chaperones insisting that there be so many inches of daylight between the two dancers), as suggested by the names given to the dances – the "fish" and the "bump and grind."

But adolescents have always had a surplus of physical energy and hormonally charged sexuality. Prior generations had slow and fast dancing. These ever-same factors are insufficient to explain much more than rock 'n' roll's beat. Despite such monikers as "the Big Beat," rock 'n' roll was far more than its rhythm. The situation of adolescents in the fifties was unique – for the first time massive numbers of people in their teenage years were segregated. The increasingly affluent middle-class American family no longer needed its children to enter the workforce in their early teens to help support it. With labor-saving devices in their new suburban homes, and with fewer children in their families than in previous generations, adolescents were not needed to help, apart from some lawn mowing or a night of baby-sitting. Now teenagers, as they began to be called, were paid by their families for household chores or were merely given an allowance, money to be spent for their own pleasure.

"Industrial society has made of high school a social system of adolescents . . . set apart, in an institution of their own," wrote sociologist James Coleman (1961, p. 337). Isolated in schools, not needed by their families, and preyed upon by the market, teenagers became a phenomenon of concern for adult society. Neither children nor adults, teenagers were anomalies, and, as Mary Douglas argues, societies have always seen danger (and sometimes deliverance) in anomalies (Douglas, 1966). Teenagers reveled in their anomalous status. No longer dependent little kids nor yet adults burdened with responsibilities, teenagers had freedom.

The presence of a youth subculture could itself account for the appearance of some distinctive musical style. The millions of dollars of their disposable income was enough of a lure for businesses to create a youth market to "serve" this demographic. That rock 'n' roll was the most efficient tool yet invented to separate youth from its money is an often repeated truth. However, parental influence ceded to peer influence not only because of schools and affluence but also because it was functional for teenagers to break away from their families. By the mid-twentieth century the pace of economic, technological, and other cultural changes made too close an identification between parents and teenagers detrimental to the life-chances of the younger generation. Parents' advice and occupational skills were not as helpful as in the past.

Youth subculture developed features that were not merely different, not merely youth's own, but were oppositional to middle-class adult culture. "Youth culture," as understood by sociologist Talcott Parsons, who coined the term, "develops inverse values to the adult world of productive work and conformity to routine and responsibility" (Brake, 1985, pp. 39–40). "What are you rebelling against?" Marlon Brando's character was asked in the 1953 movie *The Wild Ones*. Tapping out a beat on the top of the jukebox, he gave his surly reply: "What've you got?"

At the beginning of the fifties, before rock 'n' roll existed, television was rapidly finding its way into most homes. If TV did not kill radio, it surely brought it to its knees. Radio's stars and programs jumped ship to TV and, of course, the audience followed. As night follows day, advertisers took their money to TV in hot pursuit of the audience, leaving radio in a state of penury. As TV prospered, radio resorted to the least expensive programming, playing popular music records that appealed to a general audience. When TV exerted its greatest attraction, after dinner, radio's audience became smaller, less general and more homogeneous. Teenagers were listening to the radio during prime time not because they were less attracted to TV than other age groups, but because the household TV (and there was usually only one to a house) had a major flaw at that time of day: parents were seated in front of it. Teenagers retreated to their bedrooms or cars, spaces furnished with radios.

A few clever DJs began playing music to suit the taste of this audience. Musicians and record labels eventually caught on and began to produce records that would be played for and bought by teenagers. The most influential of these innovative DJs, Alan Freed, coined a term for the music enjoyed by his increasingly adolescent audience: rock 'n' roll. When a major New York City radio station, WINS, lured Freed away from Cleveland in mid-1954, I began junior high school with the music he played spinning in my head. In my bedroom in the evening I did my homework, read books, and practiced my teenage sulking to the sounds of his radio show.

Rock 'n' roll music was not invented out of thin air; it was cobbled together from existing styles, specifically "race" music (known by the term "rhythm and blues" or "R&B" by 1950) and rural white music (country or country and western). Both styles contrasted with the dominant culture's taste for pop. The demographics of those associated with R&B and country music were, to put it mildly, not favored by white middle-class adults. The 1954 Supreme Court school desegregation order and the post-Second World War black migration to northern cities increased white middle-class unease. The massive migration to the suburbs in the fifties was as much white flight as it was the desire for larger, inexpensive housing. The hint of sexual relations between white and black youth was shocking, and white teenagers' embrace of black performers like Chuck Berry and Little Richard outraged their parents. Rural whites, seen as "white trash," were not deemed fitting role models either. This extra-musical symbolic rebellion was a great part of rock 'n' roll's allure to fifties-era teenagers.

Two of rock 'n' roll's major initiators – Chuck Berry, a black "Brown-eyed Handsome Man" from Missouri, and the white Pennsylvania-based Bill Haley – did their cross-breeding of R&B and country music from opposite directions. Haley and his combo, the Comets, played country swing but merged it with R&B, accenting its rhythm and producing in 1953 songs like "Shake, Rattle and Roll" and "Rock Around the Clock." From the other direction, Berry modified his R&B with up-tempo country music to create songs like his 1955 singles "Maybellene" and "You Can't Catch Me." Neither Berry nor Haley was a youngster when their new styles led to hit songs and a new genre of popular music. Yet their songs spoke to and for their teenage fans. Chuck Berry's songs, like "School Days" and "Almost Grown," were written from the point of view of someone half his age. In "School Days," a high school student can't wait for the clock to strike three to end his burdensome day and release him to the pursuit of fun. Bill Haley's "(We're Gonna) Rock Around the Clock" was a celebration of round-the-clock fun. The song took on expanded meaning and became far more widely known to teenagers as the opening track to the movie *Blackboard Jungle*, a story of high school hoods triumphing over adult (school) authority. The 1955 movie was the first of a long line of teen flicks that emphasized rock music. During the 1950s, adults seemed to prefer to stay at home to watch TV, so Hollywood made movies mainly for teenagers.

Being out of control, or at least seeming to be so, was also an affront to the bourgeois values. Little Richard and Jerry Lee Lewis, the former black, the latter white, burst on to the rock 'n' roll scene in 1956. Even though the artists were adults, their piano-pounding antics, ecstatic vocalizing, long wild hair, and song lyrics largely focused on sexuality (e.g. "Tutti Frutti" and "Great Balls of Fire") epitomized the desires of the emerging rebellious teenage subculture.

Probably no one was more responsible for the spread of rock 'n' roll to teenagers, especially those outside major cities, than Elvis Presley. Elvis embodied contradictions, some of them essential to rock 'n' roll, packaged in a good-looking, ambitious and talented guy who was in the right place at the right time. His first label, the Memphis-based indie Sun, was looking for him, and less than two years later his major label-to-be, RCA, was looking for him too. They were not after the same performer. Sun's Sam Phillips said he was looking for a white boy who could sing like a black. "'Over and over,' says Marion Keisker, Phillips' secretary, 'I remember Sam saying, 'If I could find a white man who had the Negro sound and the Negro feel, I could make a billion dollars'" (Guralnick, 1981, p. 172). Presley's five Sun singles released in 1954 and 1955 had an

R&B song on one side and a country song on the other. RCA, after waiting with other major labels for the end of the fad called rock 'n' roll, which it had been sure would quickly go the way of flagpole sitting, was trying to muscle its way into the teenage music business.

Presley mixed more than race. His demeanor was both polite and dangerous. He cultivated an androgynous sexuality in his looks, moves, and lyrics that has since been mined by a host of artists, from the sanitized Dick Clark creation, Fabian, to the far longer-running Mick Jagger and Michael Jackson. Presley saw music as a way to reach his career goal of being a movie star, and, beginning with "Love Me Tender" in 1956 and in thirty subsequent star vehicles, his image in films helped to spread the music.

By the mid-sixties, the term "teenagers" was replaced by "youth," a reflection of a change in the structural position of the age group between childhood and adulthood in American and, more generally, Western society. The period between childhood dependence and adult responsibility significantly lengthened. Children of the ever-enlarging middle class required a college education to maintain or improve upon their parents' status. College students became politically interested and active, spurred by the nascent civil rights movement and the clash between the idealism fed to them by the mass media and high school, on the one hand, and the reality that their college professors showed them, on the other. Folk music, which had been appropriated during the Depression by the political left, became popular with college students. Blues, not the R&B of the late forties and early fifties but Southern (Delta, Texas) blues and the plugged-in electrified variants of it, especially as played and recorded in Chicago, gained favor. Brits like the Rolling Stones and Eric Clapton took blues and melded it with rock 'n' roll. In the USA, Bob Dylan reinvented folk in the Woodie Guthrie tradition, and then plugged in his guitar. These new strains of older styles of music were worked into the existing framework of rock 'n' roll by bands like The Beatles, The Who, The Byrds, and countless others. The music, maintaining a flavor of progressive politics from its folk and blues incorporations, was now called rock.

Student protest activities at universities intensified with the US escalation of the Vietnam War and the draft of young men into the military, the continuing civil rights movement and the drive for increased autonomy for college students. Taking themselves seriously, the press noted, young people "began to regard themselves as a class separate from mainstream society by virtue of their youth and the sensibility that youth produced" (Greenfield, 1975). This self-consciousness of youth as a group could be seen not only in the idealistic youth movements, but also in the beginning of rock criticism. The mass media took them seriously too: *Time Magazine* in 1967 named Youth its "man of the year."

Rock, youth's politics and pleasure, meshed with the other pleasure/ politics of the era: mind-altering drugs. "Everybody must get stoned" was the marching order given by Bob Dylan in 1966. Drugs, mainly marijuana and LSD, were used to get "Eight Miles High" and to help see things more clearly, including yourself ("Journey to the Center of Your Mind"). Psychedelic music, also known as acid rock (from LSD), began in the mid-sixties in San Francisco as an attempt to sonically recreate, imitate, or enhance the mind-expanding drug experience.

Woodstock, a celebration of youth and their music in 1969, featured a diversity of rock styles appreciated in common, which demonstrated youth's cohesiveness as a social group defined by age. Jimi Hendrix, Canned Heat, The Who, Grateful Dead, Sha-Na-Na, Santana, Sly and the Family Stone, Mountain, and Arlo Guthrie were some of the performers at Woodstock, representing many different styles of music. They loudly sang with The Who, "I hope I die before I get old," and warned one another not to trust anyone over thirty. As Robert Duncan (1984, p. 29) has observed, media coverage of the weekend helped make Woodstock "the myth of the sixties, the latest myth of eternal youth."

Although the music released for the next several years assumed this countercultural age-based solidarity, it had begun to disintegrate by the summer of 1968, when the Haight-Ashbury neighborhood in San Francisco was overrun by people too needy or greedy to sustain the anarchistic community there that had celebrated 1967's "Summer of Love." A long and somewhat ugly list of blows against idealistic youth-supported causes followed swiftly, including the police riot at the 1968 Chicago Democratic National Convention and the killing of students at Kent State by the Ohio National Guard in 1970. There were two final fatal blows in the early seventies: the military draft ended and the OPEC oil embargo brought about a stagnant inflationary economy, which meant that youth could no longer expect to land a job in the cushy middle class.

No longer united by a common enemy, and lacking the assurance of a stable financial future, by the mid-seventies the counterculture or a general youth subculture no longer existed. As a result of this collapse, youth became fragmented: some young people entered a variety of subcultures, each with its own form of rock music. The Deadheads were a tableau-vivant of the sixties counterculture, following the Grateful Dead's tours around the country for decades. Metalheads kept parts of the youth

107

counterculture – like the long hair on men, marijuana, jeans and T- shirts, and music that privileges blues-based guitar virtuosity. But following Black Sabbath's lead, they replaced the key countercultural term "love" ("love is all you need") with a discourse on evil, sucking out the sunny sixties rainbow colors and leaving a somber black. Other fragments of counterculture rock included art rock, singer songwriter, and arena rock styles.

Significantly, affiliations other than those based on age began to gain social priority, especially ethnic and gender identities. Both the feminist and gay rights movements began in the late sixties, in part as extensions of the ideals of equality central to the Civil Rights movement. After the passage of civil rights legislation and especially after the murder of Martin Luther King in 1968, black pride celebrated the history and culture of African-Americans. The TV mini-series "Roots" stimulated the general public to take a prideful interest in its own ethnic ancestries. Italians, Irish, Jews, Native Americans, Scandinavians, and dozens of other ethnic groups no longer attempted to be "100 percent American" by forgetting "the old country." Instead, they began practicing the cooking, dancing, and other cultural features of their forebears. Since both the gender and ethnic movements were not age-segregated, they absorbed some of those who might have centered their interests and activities in a youth subculture.

The disintegration of a solidary youth group and culture was accompanied by the commercialization of the youth counterculture. This process included the development of the AOR radio format, the corporate rationalization of the late-sixties free-form FM format that played rock music with political or drug lyrics, or merely songs that were longer than three minutes and that the Top-40 stations avoided. Other factors in commercialization were the rise of the arena concert business, which packaged rock acts with corporate decision and precision, and the professionalization of rock criticism, as rock magazines became profitable corporate businesses. More generally, the trappings of the youth culture became fully detached from a particular age group and were sold not only to the young but to anyone who wished to buy into the image of youth. The once young baby-boom generation, having defined themselves against adults in the fifties and sixties, were loath to become adults. The culture of youth began to float free of biological moorings.

Technological and economic changes during the eighties further intensified the separation of actual young people from a culture of youth. Record companies reaped high profits from reissuing recordings of older acts on the new medium, CDs. MTV domesticated rock for the whole family, making sounds and images once confined to live concerts or record collections easily accessible on the living room TV. The cable channel's "something for everyone" programming helped make the term "rock" synonymous with popular music. Acts were developed for the sub-youth market, such as the kiddie-rock of New Kids on the Block and, more recently, the Spice Girls, Hanson, and Backstreet Boys. Radio developed a commercially successful format, "classic rock," which focused on "dinosaur bands" rather than recent releases. "Turn down that NOISE!" That was the universal sign, bellowed by parents, that the music belonged to youth. But it is rarely heard in the nineties, as parents and their children of all ages, and even their grandchildren, listen increasingly to the same music.

There have been a number of attempts by segments of youth to reclaim their own music. Punk (and hardcore) and heavy metal (especially thrash metal and death metal) had features that were both too tough for little kids and too rough for mass commercialization. For the older middle-class end of the youth demographic, there was the too-quirky-for-major-distribution indie rock/college rock scene. Alternative music, a style that borrowed from these sources, became popular with young people in the early nineties, especially its grunge variant. With Nirvana and then Pearl Jam, youth, dubbed Generation X, felt they had "their music," whose visuals (thrift-store living-on-the-street look), lyrics (pain), and sound (emotionally hurt vocals fronting an alternately loud and soft, feel strong then feel weak, instrumental arrangement) reflected their sense of their situation. But it was not long before the major labels and ambitious musicians started cloning and eviscerating alternative until it became another current in the commercial mainstream.

"Rock 'n' roll is a weapon," claims shock rock originator Alice Cooper. The composer of songs like "School's Out for Summer" and "I'm Eighteen" continues: "It's the only language and communication that the youth have against authority" (*RIP*, 1990). Expressions of youth subcultures, especially rock, are resistances to the "disciplinization" of the increasingly global hegemonic authority: the consumer culture. When rock 'n' roll emerged in the 1950s, the authorities to be resisted were parents and the schools, which were disciplining teenagers to be good middle-class adults. In the 1960s, the focus shifted to military and governmental authorities and the universities. After the 1960s, a focus for resistance was lost due to a complex of factors centering on the hegemony of consumer culture and the consequent detachment of "youthfulness" from chronological youth.

Consumer culture constantly attempts to co-opt youth-based rock and usually succeeds at this task. But as with rhizomatically propagated weeds, pulling up one shoot doesn't kill the plant – its roots are firmly established under the ground, and new shoots will attempt to emerge elsewhere. *Given the right environment, Youth still Rocks.*

Resources

Anon. (1990) Alice Cooper: nice guy with a guillotine. *RIP*, September, p. 57.

Brake, Michael (1985) *Comparative Youth Culture: the Sociology of Youth Cultures and Youth Subcultures in America, Britain and Canada.* London: Routledge.

Coleman, James (1961) *The Adolescent Society.* New York: Free Press.

Douglas, Mary (1966) *Purity and Danger.* Baltimore: Penguin.

Duncan, Robert (1984) *The Noise: Notes from a Rock 'n' Roll Era.* New York: Ticknor.

Gaines, Donna (1991) *Teenage Wasteland: Suburbia's Dead End Kids.* New York: Pantheon.

Gillis, John (1993) Vanishing youth: the uncertain place of the young in a global age. *Young: Nordic Journal of Youth Research*, 1(1), 3–17.

Greenfield, Jeff (1975) They changed rock, which changed the culture, which changed us. *New York Times Magazine*, 16 February, p. 49.

Guralnick, Peter (1981) *Feel Like Going Home: Portraits in Blues and Rock 'n' Roll.* London: Vintage Random House (originally published 1971).

Hebdige, Dick (1979) *Subculture: the Meaning of Style.* New York: Methuen.

McDonald, J. R. (1988) Politics revisited: metatextual implications of rock and roll criticism. *Youth and Society*, 19, 485–504.

Ross, Andrew and Rose, Tricia (eds) (1994) *Microphone Fiends: Youth Music and Youth Culture.* New York: Routledge.

Weinstein, Deena (1983) Rock: youth and its music. *Popular Music and Society*, 9, 2–15.

Weinstein, Deena (1995) Alternative youth: the ironies of recapturing youth culture. *Young: Nordic Journal of Youth Research*, 3(1), 61–71.

Weinstein, Deena (1996) Knockin' the rock: popular music defined as a social problem. In Craig Calhoun and George Ritzer (eds), *Perspectives on Sociology.* New York: McGraw-Hill, pp. 23–34.

Part II
Locating Culture in
Popular Music

9

Popular

Anahid Kassabian

I do not get points for assigning a three-week long unit on elevator music.

The term "popular" has a long, strange, and highly charged history. It modifies a stunning array of nouns, from uprising to hairstyle, from candidate to culture. In that last usage, popular culture, it has circulated in two related sets of debates that have significantly influenced popular music studies. First, it has figured in a theoretical dispute, described in this chapter, as a response to the term "mass culture." Second, it continues to be a focal point for a set of institutional struggles, characterized by journalists as "the culture wars," aimed at securing opportunities for scholars to study mass-mediated culture within universities. Those struggles have now made it possible to teach and study the popular – popular television, popular literature, popular film, and, central to the subject of this volume, popular music. But what do we mean when we use the word "popular"?

This chapter examines how the term popular has been mobilized, by whom, and to what ends in popular music studies. I will argue that, in the literature on pop music, the term has taken a "populist" turn, ignoring what I call ubiquitous musics – music in films, in stores, on the phone, in the office, on television, in audio books, and so on. These are the kinds of music that no one chooses for herself or himself but that nevertheless wash our everyday lives with sound. While this is the music that we hear the most of per capita, it is not routinely included in popular music studies. I want to suggest that its absence has a lot to do with the way we define popular.

In his influential book *Keywords: a Vocabulary of Culture and Society*, British culture theorist Raymond Williams devotes two full pages to the term popular. There, he traces the term from its earliest uses in English in the fifteenth century in law and politics. During the first few centuries of its existence, popular was understood as a negative term, meaning "low," "base," "vulgar," "of the common people." By the late eighteenth century, Williams tells us, it began to mean "widespread," and, late in the nineteenth century, the more familiar positive meanings we associate with "popular" began to accrue. This history is important because the meaning of the term shifts from embracing the perspective of an elite class that looked down its collective nose at the common people, to celebrating – and remaking – what those common people valued. Thus, over the course of its lifetime, the class allegiance of popular has shifted dramatically.

Yet despite this turnaround, when I was an undergraduate we did not read popular late nineteenth- or early twentieth-century stories of detectives like Sherlock Holmes or Lord Peter Wimsey, much less Kinsey Milhone and her contemporary ilk. In none of my music classes did we study jazz or The Beatles, much less punk or reggae. Over the past fifteen years or so, however, that has begun to change. Students at the university where I teach can now study, for example, gothic novels, science fiction film, and popular music. Let me briefly survey the theoretical engagements with culture that can account, in part, for this shift.

To oversimplify, since the Enlightenment, great works of culture have been understood as vessels of universal Truth and Beauty. In other words, from this perspective, truth and beauty do not change over time, do not vary from culture to culture, and are contained within the masterpieces of culture. These masterpieces are understood as the products of inspired genius – the lonely, often misunderstood artist whose unique, individual vision creates such Truth and Beauty. Think of the romantic image of Beethoven, for example.

But mechanical reproduction – photography and sound recording – challenged that understanding. Photographs, and, later, films and sound recordings created fissures in the notion of a sole artist, in the relationship between document or non-fiction and art, and in the value of a work of art. Walter Benjamin, in one of the most influential essays on culture of the twentieth century, argued that mechanical reproduction had forever broken what he called the "aura" of the great work of art. No longer could we stand in awe in front of the original, because there was no such meaningful object as an "original."

Not only the aura is broken in the age of mechanical reproduction. According to Frankfurt School theorists such as Theodor Adorno, mechanical reproduction also creates a set of economic relations in the production of culture that these writers called the "culture industry." In this Marxist model, those who produce culture are the owners of the means of production. They are profit-seeking members of an elite class who use the culture they produce to foster in audiences a "false consciousness," a misunderstanding of the audiences' own best interests.

In many ways this model is hard to dismiss. It is certainly true that culture in the twentieth century has largely been created by profit-seeking corporations, and access to the means of producing culture is not democratized. (Just imagine trying to convince a major network to let you write the news for a night, or getting it to cover a story you think is in the national interest but it doesn't.) It is also clear that some kinds of culture are permitted within this organization, while others are not. Few films are made without individual heroes, for example; similarly, popular music styles that do not adhere to the three- to five-minute song format do not easily get produced or played on the radio.

The Frankfurt School's emphasis on false consciousness also contributed to an important focus on what has come to be called "ideological critique." In this tradition of studying culture, emphasized in the collection you are reading, individual texts – novels, photographs, songs – are analyzed for traces of whose interests they serve. Much of Adorno's own work on music, in his *Introduction to the Sociology of Music* and elsewhere, paved the way for important fields of inquiry in music and other disciplines. But for some theorists, as Fenster and Swiss discuss in chapter 17 of this volume, Adorno's ideas about the culture industry were too monolithic. From the 1960s to the 1980s, British cultural studies opened an inquiry into consumption and local cultural practices that still resonates today. From the perspectives of theorists in the British cultural studies tradition, popular culture is a lived experience, irreducible to either a set of texts or a series of economic interactions. For example, in *Subculture: the Meaning of Style*, Dick Hebdige studied punk subculture not from the perspective of record labels, as a Frankfurt School approach might suggest, but from the perspective of teens who defined themselves as punks. He analyzed not individual punk songs or recordings but punk style, attempting to explain, for example, how safety pins and swastikas produced meanings within the punk subculture. British cultural studies theorists argued that audiences were not victims of false consciousness, but active participants in consumption, understood as a process of making meaning from, and contributing meaning to, popular culture. Through their work and its influences, alongside other traditions from, especially, literary studies, it became possible to argue that there is much to study and to learn from popular culture.

The place of popular culture studies varies, of course, from discipline to discipline and institution to institution. While many music departments are notoriously staid in their course offerings, some offer courses such as Caribbean music or rock history. Mass-mediated cultures form one of the major axes of communication and media studies scholarship, though popular music is not an established field in the discipline of communication. In other words, not every department in every university is comfortable with or committed to every kind of popular culture scholarship. Nonetheless, studying the popular seems now a well established part of the academic landscape.

Given such a landscape, perhaps it is time to consider again what we mean by "popular." In most of its contemporary incarnations, the term "popular" is still opposed to some idea of an elite. But these incarnations differ significantly in how they define what that elite is. In one meaning, "popular" connotes "of the folk." When invoked in this way, popular often means home-made, unmediated, and possibly – though not always – unpolished, the art and culture of "the people." From this perspective, popular music includes "Happy Birthday" and "Auld Lang Syne," garage bands, and church singing.

At other times, however, popular is opposed to both folk and "art" music, where "popular" is used to mean mass-mediated or quantitatively large, and sometimes, by implication, expensive to produce. In these uses, "folk" refers to historical practices of small (often, by implication, rural) communities, such as folk music (e.g. shape-note singing) or quilting and other forms of folk art, and "art" refers to the culture of a social elite, as in "classical" music. Popular, by contrast, means contemporary, mass-produced and consumed culture; here, popular music would include most of the musics many people purchase and listen to, from Top 40 to alternative to hip-hop to world beat music, on radio and television as well as on vinyl, cassette, or CD.

Popular can also have a more politicized meaning, in uses where it verges close in sense to populist. For example, much scholarship on punk, especially in Britain, conceived "punk" as a cultural response to an oppressive contemporaneous political reality. Young working-class Britons, who came to expect nothing better for themselves than to stand in dole lines, developed an oppositional style of music and dress that was intentionally offensive and was understood as a critique of the political economy and policies of the late 1970s. Popular culture as counterculture has, in this way, a different edge than popular-as-folk or popular-as-mass.

Particular genres or songs often – or perhaps almost always – blur these categories. One of the central dilemmas popular music studies confronted, for example, is how rock can be both commodified (popular as mass) and liberatory (popular as populist). Folk singers of the 1960s and 1970s were deeply involved in commodity relations – paid gigs and recordings, at the very least – but were also important figures in the more folk-like practices of guitar-playing and singing across the country. In this case, as in other examples, a mass-culture popular music style encouraged not only consumption of its commodities but also a folk-culture production of its style by individuals and groups.

In recent debates, all these different senses of "popular" have given rise to important scholarly enterprises. For example, the notion of popular-as-folk has led scholars to anthropological and ethnomusicological research into the music-making practices of local cultures, from Polish-American polka to Dominican bachata. The sense of popular-as-mass grounds much work in popular music, including debates about commodification (music as a terrain of economic relations) and MTV and music videos in the globalization of culture. And an entire generation of popular music scholarship is indebted to popular-as-populist models, as Robin Balliger notes in chapter 5 in this volume. This scholarship focuses on how people express social and political positions at least in part through music consumption and production; how they express themselves, as themselves, through music. In other words, from rock to reggae to punk to hip-hop, one legacy of British cultural studies in popular music scholarship is a commitment to countercultural musics and music as countercultural.

All these models share certain assumptions. They take for granted that popular culture has something to teach us about social and political life. They generally avoid the negative evaluations of Frankfurt School terms such as "mass culture." And they all assume that we consciously engage with our popular culture. From Simon Frith's *Sound Effects* (1981) to such important contemporary works as David Brackett's *Interpreting Popular Music* (1995), David Schwarz's *Listening Subjects* (1997), and Keith Negus's *Popular Music in Theory* (1997), the music under consideration is music that people choose to hear.

What about other kinds of music? There is no good name for all the musics we don't choose, but these are the musics I am most interested in. "Background music" comes close, even though it is sometimes in the foreground. "Business music" suggests its economic role, while "environmental music" points to its role in forming contexts. "Programmed music" indicates its production and distribution, but not its consumption. Most recently, I have been calling them "ubiquitous musics" – the musics that are always there, beyond our control, slipping under our thresholds of consciousness.

None of these musics and musical consumption practices is a dominant focus of popular music studies. In the entire history of the journal *Popular Music*, with over forty issues of three to five essays each, there has been one article on film music, one article on music in commercials, and one on popular film song in India. In the bibliography of his groundbreaking article in the journal *Ethnomusicology* on music in the mall of America, Jonathan Sterne notes the following published research on ubiquitous musics: four academic articles, one essay in *Smithsonian* magazine, Joseph Lanza's 1994 book *Elevator Music*, and several of Muzak's own publications. This is the extent of research, almost none of it in popular music studies, on the musics that we – at least in the USA – hear most. How can we explain this glaring absence? Can our ideas about the term "popular" explain why the acoustic wallpaper of our lives continues to go largely unexamined?

Some of the key questions that popular music studies has asked itself – How can a countercultural form exist within the economy it rebels against? How does the musical expression articulate this rebellion? How do rebels form identity through music? – cannot be asked of ubiquitous musics. They are not countercultural, and they are not consciously consumed by individuals. This, I am arguing, is the main reason why popular music studies ignores most of popular music.

Placing ubiquitous music in relation to other music deemed popular, and so how we define the meaning of popular music, has become more complicated over the past decade, as the boundaries between ubiquitous musics and consciously consumed musics erode. For example, what was the relationship between box office and soundtrack sales for the film *Clerks*? The question is not simply a business one – though it is important to note that films make significant income from soundtrack sales – but also a problem of another kind. As listeners, do we hear the same song the same way on the radio and in a film? Are we drawn to the film because of radio airplay? Does hearing a song evoke again the feelings of the film, or can we make our own separate meanings with the song? The relationship between our listening practices and the circulation of songs across the networks of multinational media conglomerates needs further study.

Now that business environment music is being sold separately, similar questions arise there. When I hear a band such as the Gipsy Kings in Starbucks, is that the same as hearing them on the radio or on a CD? If I buy the CD that I am hearing in the coffee shop, is the experience the same when I listen to it at home? Or do I listen differently? Does that then change the way I hear the Gipsy Kings – consciously or unconsciously – in other, subsequent experiences? The fact that we will hear the same music both as conscious consumers, when we choose to hear it, and as consumers of ubiquitous music, when we do not, suggests that the study of ubiquitous musics is becoming all the more urgent as these boundaries become less and less distinct.

There is still another obstacle to serious engagement with ubiquitous musics: their cultural status. As I suggested earlier in this chapter, many books have been written on "high" versus "low" and "elite" versus "popular" culture. One of the terrains of those debates is the question of value – how do we assign value to works of culture, and whose values do those works express? In the process of revaluing the popular, it is necessary to find a ground for its newly elevated value.

It is relatively easy to assign cultural value to rock and other sub- and countercultural musics – hip-hop, techno, reggae, grunge, dance hall, and so on – because their value derives directly from the degree of their opposition to high culture. A resistant cultural practice has a certain cachet, what Sarah Thornton has termed "subcultural capital." Subcultural capital is insider knowledge, a kind of proof of membership in a counter culture. For example, when I talk about counterculture music practices in my classes, I display my subcultural capital and get that cachet transferred onto me. That is, my students think I'm "cool." And this subcultural capital operates over time as well. At the age of thirty-eight, I derive my subcultural capital not only from knowing about techno and hardcore, but also from owning all of Pink Floyd and much of the Velvet Underground in first edition, on vinyl. I can also speak with some authority about, for instance, how South Asians in the UK took hip-hop and mixed it up with classical Indian and Hindi-pop vocal practices to make bhangra. I can introduce students to Lillian Allen's uses of reggae musical materials in her politically fierce dub poetry. By displaying all this subcultural capital, I accrue cool points.

I do not get points for assigning a three-week long unit on elevator music. There is no cultural cachet – and thus seemingly no value. It's not art and it's not hip; my students assume the work will be stupid, and everyone assumes it is bad music. That unit is the first thing they complain about when they look at the syllabus for my popular music course. Part of the unit includes going to a store, listening to the music on several separate occasions, finding out who makes the music choices, calling the corporate headquarters of AEI or Muzak to ask about music choices and fee structures, and generally collecting as much information about the music as they can. We discuss how the music creates the space it is played in and determines who will come into the store. We discuss the sales of CDs by chains such as Victoria's Secret and Pier One Imports and the cross-marketing of, for example, lounge music and martini glasses.

One of our most interesting conversations is always about value. My students are enormously disturbed if they like the music they hear, because they assume ahead of time that it must be bad music to be background music. Or another version of the same problem: a composer once told me he found the Starbucks coffee chain's CDs disturbing because he liked some of them but couldn't imagine having one on his shelf at home for his friends to see. Audio Environments, the company that handles Starbucks' music, also does the CDs for Olive Garden, a national chain of Italian restaurants. I really like the range of musics they put together for Olive Garden – Italian folk, Italian-American standards, and opera. Does this mean I have bad taste? What about when I'm listening to Starbucks' compilation of Blue Note recordings?

Perhaps we need to rethink our assumptions about the value of musics that we don't choose for ourselves. Even as they serve the purposes of Olive Garden, Starbucks, and Warner Brothers, some of these musics are enjoyable, pleasurable to listen to. Perhaps there is room to study ubiquitous musics not only from the perspective of how the programmed music industry functions or how we, as a culture, assign value to music, but also how listening and listening pleasure work. In "Adequate modes of listening," Ola Stockfelt analyzes his response to a piece of Mozart in an airplane. At first, he enjoyed the piece, but when he sat down to concentrate as he would have to the "original," he found this background music arrangement frustrating and bad. But, he later decides,

> Different listening situations give different norms of quality, both for the piece of music and for the activity of the listener. As long as I listened with dispersed interest, I was charmed by the sound. . . . I adopted an adequate mode of listening, and the music could therefore play a meaningful role in relation to the world.
>
> When I began to listen concentratedly, however, I applied an inadequate mode of listening – not because the music couldn't or shouldn't be adequate to listen to in a concentrated way, but because I measured it according to norms appropriate to other listening situations and other music. . . . As an "idle listener," I possessed the competence that was necessary for an adequate dedication to the music, but as a concentrated listener I was excluded by the exclusiveness of the music. (Stockfelt, 1997, p. 142)

What Stockfelt suggests here is that valuations of music will depend, at least in part, on how its judges listen to it. Lucy Green and David Brackett make a similar point in their contributions to this volume when they argue that what gets called music depends on prior, historically and ideologically grounded assumptions and values. If one assumes a conscious, analytical listening position in relation to ubiquitous musics, one will necessarily come away judging them as bad because the listening mode was not adequate to the music. The two reasons I suggested above for the absence of ubiquitous musics in popular music studies – the assumption of a conscious consumer and the assignment of little or no value – come together in Stockfelt's careful analysis of listening.

The range of existing music scholarship generated by what Stockfelt calls bourgeois concert-hall listening is impressive and important. The study of canonical music, Western art music, concert-hall music continues to pose questions and challenges that all students of music can learn from. And the study of popular musics never ceases to produce new arguments and debates that challenge thinking about all kinds of musics. Each has found a place in academic life.

To add to that range of scholarship, I want to campaign for work on the bulk of popular music – the musics heard most by the most people every day. There are ample lines of inquiry to pursue, for students at every level. For example, why do the people who are playing it want us to hear it? I think that question merits research. What are we doing with it? This suggests a complicated ethnographic project that might also connect with theorizations of listening subjectivity. Why do we like it or not? Why do we notice it or not? These questions might lead us to Pierre Bourdieu's analyses of taste. Interrogating the economic structure of this industry might begin with bottom-line financial analyses of the major programmed music companies. What the industry itself thinks it is doing and what its clients believe they are buying are again questions that might be approached ethnographically or through discourse analyses of the companies' memos and publicity materials. One might do more studies like a recent one which found that more of a store's customers bought German wine when the store played German music. Or more complicated versions, testing what clothing styles sell to what contemporary genres of music. An analysis of demographic information on who buys Starbucks' or other corporations' CDs might tell us something about the participation of corporate labels in identity formations. And we might understand Thornton's notion of subcultural capital in richer ways if we had some idea of what the buyers do with such CDs. Wear them as jewelry? Dub them and pretend the result is their own mix? Prove their subcultural capital by being cool enough to get away with it? Not "know enough" to worry about any of this?

In other words, I want to know the place ubiquitous musics have in the overall schema of music in contemporary life. But, even more, I want music students and scholars to begin to develop modes of listening adequate to the task of understanding ubiquitous musics. How can we learn to "dishearken," as Stockfelt calls what we regularly do with ubiquitous musics, and be analytical at the same time? Without such a mode of listening, inquiries into the listening positions offered to us by ubiquitous musics cannot proceed.

As I have noted, "popular" can mean – and has meant – many things to many people. I have argued here that the populist sense of the term has been at the center of popular music studies, and that the questions and answers raised by popular music studies are governed by its populist focus. Any attempt – even the most cursory – to study ubiquitous musics calls the populist focus into question. And such study is crucial to understanding the musical terrain on which we live.

To hear a new world of music requires new tools and new questions. In order to engage ubiquitous musics, students and scholars will need to develop new modes of listening. We will need to interrogate how we assign value to musics. We will have to let go of our desire to display subcultural capital. And perhaps as the very first step, we need to expand the meanings of "popular" in popular music studies.

Resources

Adorno, Theodor (1988) *Introduction to the Sociology of Music*. New York: Continuum.
Aronowitz, Stanley (1993) *Roll Over Beethoven: the Return of Cultural Strife*. Hanover, NH: Wesleyan University Press.
Benjamin, Walter (1969) The work of art in the age of mechanical reproduction. In *Illuminations*, trans. Harry Zohn. New York: Schocken, pp. 217–51.
Brackett, David (1995) *Interpreting Popular Music*. Cambridge: Cambridge University Press.
Davies, Ioan (1995) *Cultural Studies and Beyond*. London and New York: Routledge.
Frith, Simon (1981) *Sound Effects: Youth, Leisure, and the Politics of Rock 'n' Roll*. New York: Pantheon.
Hebdige, Dick (1979) *Subculture: the Meaning of Style*. London: Methuen.

122

Lanza, Joseph (1994) *Elevator Music: a Surreal History of Muzak, Easy-listening, and Other Moodsong.* New York: St Martin's Press.

Negus, Keith (1997) *Popular Music in Theory: an Introduction.* Hanover, NH: Wesleyan University Press.

Schwarz, David (1997) *Listening Subjects: Music, Psychoanalysis, Culture.* Durham, NC: Duke University Press.

Sterne, Jonathan (1997) Sounds like the mall of America: programmed music and the architectonics of commercial space. *Ethnomusicology,* 41(1), 22–50.

Stockfelt, Ola (1997) Adequate modes of listening. In David Schwarz, Anahid Kassabian, and Lawrence Siegel (eds), *Keeping Score: Music, Disciplinarity, Culture.* Charlottesville: University Press of Virginia.

Thornton, Sarah (1996) *Club Cultures: Music, Media and Subcultural Capital.* Hanover, NH: Wesleyan University Press.

Williams, Raymond (1976) *Keywords: a Vocabulary of Culture and Society.* Oxford and New York: Oxford University Press.

10
Music

David Brackett

Put another nickel in, in the nickelodeon
All I want is lovin' you and music, music, music
From "Music, Music, Music" (words and music by
Stephen Weiss and Bernie Baum)

I

Where does one begin in defining "music"? "Music" seems at once self-evident and yet so ephemeral as to be outside of language, to exist in a sort of raw, pre-linguistic ether. The 1950 hit "Music, Music, Music," as recorded by Teresa Brewer, both alludes to this belief in evanescence and implies at the same time that music is a necessity and that "music," whatever it might be, could, along with love, enable the song's persona (the person or "voice" that seems to speak from within the song) to subsist. At the same time, while "music" in this context is understood as an essence that fulfills a basic need on a par with love and companionship, the sounds of the recording project a certain sense of what music is (as opposed to what it is not), of ways in which it might be heard, of particular functions it might serve.

Despite the innocent portrayal of the idea of music in "Music, Music, Music," the music in the song is not innocent: in a sonic world such as this one, filled with barroom pianos and "dixieland" bands, juke boxes ("nickelodeons") are necessary to reproduce songs mechanically while they link songs materially to a commercial network. This paradoxical conception of music implies that what qualifies as "music" in one context may be "noise" in another, for other songs may conjure up other sonic worlds, and may function more poorly as commercial products at particular historical moments. This sense of inclusion and exclusion resonates with Jacques Attali's formulation in *Noise: the Political Economy of Music*, in which he argues that power promotes recognized forms of music-making while at the same time banning "subversive noise because it betokens demands for cultural autonomy, [and] support for differences or marginality" (Attali, 1985, p. 7). In this way, power – as it is manifested in linkages between institutions, discourses, and the resultant effects of "truth" – determines which types of organized sound may be defined as "music," and directly affects the way in which popular music is represented in two important discursive fields: the academic discipline of musicology, which was established to study music as a relatively autonomous art; and the mass media, which purport to convey the opinions of music producers, critics, and audiences about music.

For example, in the first of these fields, the disjunction between expectations of unsuspecting students who are not music majors (and who probably think of "popular music" when they think of "music") and what they are likely to find in the typical "music appreciation" class (a condensed history of Western art music) results from the content of most music courses having been shaped by the way in which "music" is defined in the academy. This definition is a very specific one, shaped by determinant historical forces, and one which increasingly differs from the idea of music brought to class by the contemporary student. How did this gap emerge between scholarly usages of "music" and everyday understandings of the term? While even attempting to answer this question is far beyond the scope of this chapter, a thumbnail sketch of the conditions in which the discipline of musicology emerged in Central Europe in the late nineteenth century will aid an understanding of contemporary musicological usages of "music."

Musicology emerged as a distinct discipline comparable to other humanistic and scientific disciplines in the late nineteenth century in Germany and Austria. Although a small number of musicologists at the time were concerned with music of the "folk," the vast majority focused on the historical study and analysis of European concert music. Due to the specific historical and geographical circumstances of its emergence, musicology developed in tandem with a whole panoply of beliefs about what the musical experience should provide, and about the relationship between performers, audiences, and composers. Audiences and scholars developed an aesthetic of distanced appreciation and a belief in the autonomous art work.

The effect of these beliefs on the discipline of musicology has been to focus attention on a small body of works (the "canon"), to encourage a positivistic approach to musical research, and to develop an analytical metalanguage uniquely suited to that canon. These factors tend to denigrate, both implicitly and explicitly, types of music that do not belong to the canon; and perhaps no body of music has fared worse in this respect than popular music since the emergence of rock 'n' roll. This is at least partially because popular music is so clearly tied to its social function(s), and so overtly connected to commercial enterprise, that it makes claims for its autonomy seem ludicrous to those attached to the idea of a canon of masterpieces that transcend commerce.

Another reason for the dismissal of popular music by musicologists lies in the way in which its aesthetic basis differs from that of European art music. Rooted largely in African-American and Euro-American vernacular musical practices, most recent popular music in North America and the British Isles generates its musical interest through subtle inflections of rhythm, pitch, and tone color within a repetitive formal framework, musical elements to which the techniques of music analysis developed for art music are almost entirely inapplicable. Thus musicology defines music, both historically and formally, according to criteria developed from European art music created between the eighteenth and early twentieth centuries (the period of the "canon"), criteria that do not facilitate or encourage the study of popular music.

An additional factor in the low esteem accorded popular music by musicologists is the way in which musicology defines the musical "work." The musical work is understood to consist of a musical score, a notated template for musical performance, which can be attributed to a historical figure known as the "composer." The emphasis on the score reinforces the concept of "autonomy" noted above. Meaning is understood to reside within the score, as being immanent in the "notes themselves." Textual analysis in much academic writing about art music focuses on those musical elements conveyed with relative precision in the score – such as discrete pitches ("notes") and mathematically proportionate rhythms (which are important in coordinating different vocal and instrumental parts). Thus, analysis and technical description focus on this printed score rather than on any particular performance, and emphasize aspects of the piece such as its melody, harmony, the interrelationship of melody and harmony, the overall form or structure of the piece, and, in vocal music, some notion of the relationship of the lyrics to these other elements. However, as the reader may have already noticed, the elements emphasized by notation and score study exclude precisely those elements mentioned in the preceding paragraph that have figured so importantly in much recent popular music.

The conjunction of the historical figure of the composer with the musical score to form a notion of the musical "work" also creates a model

126

of authorship at odds with the author-function of most popular music texts. Historical work in musicology often takes the form of the "life and works" of the historical composer, whose creative intentions are understood to underlie much of a work's meaning or are understood as background to the creation of musical works, which are understood (again) as occurring in an autonomous realm. While the "life and works" biography is definitely not dead in popular music, the genres which are most highly documented in biographies tend to be ones in which authorship can be made to function more like the Romantic model. Compare, for example, the number of biographies about Bob Dylan (many) with those about James Brown (few), even though they are arguably two of the most important figures of the 1960s in terms of their influence on subsequent musicians. Dylan, in creating the prototype of the "singer-songwriter," invites fans and biographers to hear his songs as directly related to his life, whereas Brown, in his creation of hyperkinetic dance music with minimal and impressionistic lyrics, encourages other forms of engagement. (It is important to note that this way of explaining the differential treatment of the two musicians ignores the role of race: one could theorize that predominantly white critics may unreflectively tend to see Dylan as somehow more "intellectual," and hence, more worthy of analysis and of deifying through biography than Brown.)

Authorship in popular music, however, in many cases does not lend itself easily to a simple one-to-one relationship between composer and text. The author function of the popular music text is often shared by many individuals: the singer, instrumentalists, songwriter, arranger, recording engineer, promotional photographer, video clip director, and possibly others. Listeners tend to identify the lead singer of a recording as the source of the song's emotional content, but this doesn't hold equally true in all genres or historical moments. Sometimes a producer's or songwriter's style may be strong enough to be recognized by listeners as responsible for the song's emotional impact. Dance genres such as house, disco, techno, or drum 'n' bass often are purely instrumental, or subordinate the singer to the songwriter/producer/DJ.

The idea of the autonomous musical art work also creates a strict division between text and context. One of the most interesting facets of recent popular music is the way it reinforces the idea that "there is nothing outside the text." Critics and fans read performers' lives into their recordings and videos, and then read recordings and videos back into the performers' lives; recording companies use the anti-commercial, "autonomous" status of artists and songs as a way of selling their latest products; fans use their sense of connection to stars that they have never met as a way of forging a distinctive identity that allows them to feel a bond with millions of people whom they have also never met. Clearly, the processes through which popular music produces meaning are laced with contradiction, although "contradiction" is a feeble term to describe the play of image, fantasy, everyday life, and agency and domination that constitutes part of the signifying processes made obvious by/for popular music.

So far, then, I have discussed several ways in which the discipline of musicology is indisposed toward understanding "popular music" as "music," ways which are deeply rooted in ideas emerging from a cluster of interrelated historically situated discourses, which include: (a) the idea of the autonomous art work; (b) a specific idea of the musical work; (c) a specific notion of authorship; and (d) a belief in the separability of text and context. These discourses implicitly discourage the study of music that does not fit the model, disqualifying it for being musically uninteresting, for being a standardized commercial product, or for not having sufficiently heroic figures to warrant study. Despite the ways in which the discipline of musicology may seem to thwart the study of it, the sense of difference embodied by popular music, and the challenges posed by the study of it, have spurred many people to work on popular music and to develop interdisciplinary approaches at a time when quite a few musicologists engaged with the study of Western art music have also begun to question the epistemological premises of that discipline.

The second, much larger forum of the mass media poses definitions of music that affect the way popular music is perceived. From at least the time of the creation of separate categories for different types of popular music in the 1920s, to the emergence of rock 'n' roll in the mid-fifties, to psychedelic rock, heavy metal, disco, punk, and (especially) rap, new, subversive genres have been decried and defined as "noise," specifically in opposition to other, more respectable styles of "music." The complaints against many of these genres assume a particular definition of music which the new genres do not fit. They are criticized for "having no melody," for using unusual instruments or tone colors, accused of screaming (or speaking) instead of singing, and of being too loud. These musical criticisms frequently mingle with a sense of a threat to the social order, for these genres have often brought together new social and cultural alliances, or have focused attention on the dispossessed and marginalized.

What is interesting is that mass media definitions of "noise" and "music" often rest on the same, unstated assumptions as do musicological definitions. Both privilege Romantic, European-based notions about what music should be; and both tend to undervalue styles and genres originating in social locations outside those of bourgeois, European or Euro-American society, be they working-class African-American, Latino, or rural, white Southern. I will now look at two instances of mass media reactions that depicted new developments in popular music as "noise" for ways in which definitions of "music" were invoked to repress change, and to look at what was at stake in these particular acts of defining. The first of these is that spectacularly famous instance of disruption of the popular music status quo in the mid-1950s.

II

That "Music, Music, Music" proved to be a big hit in 1950 should have come as no surprise, if only because the popular music industry lingered in a state of uncertainty at that point about what "popular music" should be. After the big band/swing era subsided following the war, the late forties were dominated by solo singers such as Frank Sinatra, Perry Como, Peggy Lee, and Dinah Shore, who were accompanied by studio orchestras. This worked to the advantage of the major record companies and publishers, as it allowed them even more control than they had had during the big band era. An interlocking system of songwriters at major publishing houses (allied with the publishing rights organization, the American Society of Composers and Publishers, or ASCAP), radio networks, movie companies, recording companies, record distributors, and studio musicians and arrangers produced recordings of songs with clear links back to the popular songs from early in the twentieth century. This system had been profitable for those who had advantageous connections to it, and it had been very effective in maintaining stylistic consistency and absorbing new influences (such as those found in swing music during the big band era). It was also very effective in keeping out musicians who produced different types of music, primarily those associated with "race" (performed by, and presumably for, African-Americans) and "hillbilly" (performed by, and presumably for, rural Southern whites) musics.

The institutional idea of "music" preferred by the popular music industry had much in common with musicological notions of "music" discussed earlier: a version of a song abstracted from any one performance and embodied in notation ("sheet music") was assumed to be more important than any individual recording, as many recordings of a song were popular at a given time, the large radio networks frequently featured versions of popular hits played by anonymous studio orchestras, and sheet music sales still figured prominently in the discourse of industry publications such as *Billboard* and *Variety*. Stylistically, popular music of the pre-rock 'n' roll era resembled nineteenth-century art music in its use of complex harmony, arching melodic designs, relatively "pure" vocal timbres, and frequent use of orchestral instruments. Authorship was more complex than in the art music model, as performers more frequently became stars, but songwriters (who were not primarily performers) were also well known to the public, and included figures such as George Gershwin, Cole Porter, and Irving Berlin.

However, cracks in the almost total control of the popular music industry by a few major companies began to appear as early as 1939. In that year, Broadcast Music Incorporated (BMI), an alternative publishing rights organization to ASCAP, was formed, enabling songwriters in hillbilly and race musics to receive royalties for their songs, and facilitating greater exposure via radio for these styles. By the late forties, the major record companies and publishers faced a more serious problem in the form of declining sales. One strategy that these companies and their associates in other media employed to maintain control was to diversify the "mainstream" of popular music, with the hope of reviving sales, resulting in a profusion of novelty songs, most notably ersatz folk and "country and western" songs (a more polite name for hillbilly music used after 1949), and cover versions of country hits.

Thus, the 1950 year-end polls for *Billboard*, the leading magazine of the entertainment industry, showed first place held by "Goodnight Irene" (a "folk" tune written by Huddie Ledbetter, aka Leadbelly), as sung by the Weavers (a "folk-singing" group descended from the late thirties Popular Front alliance between New York leftists and American vernacular music), accompanied by the Gordon Jenkins orchestra. In the top ten with "Music, Music, Music" were slick country tunes like Red Foley's "Chattanoogie Shoe Shine Boy," two versions of the vaguely Greek-sounding "Third Man Theme," old-style ballads ("Mona Lisa" by Nat "King" Cole), and another pseudo-Dixieland song, "Sing a Simple Melody," by the father–son duo of Bing and Gary Crosby. What is striking about pop music at this moment is the almost complete disappearance of swing-based dance music that had been prominent until the end of the war. Ballads in the early fifties had a beat so discreet it was almost nonexistent; uptempo numbers tended to be "novelty" numbers (featuring gimmicky sound effects or evoking idealized versions of earlier styles), versions of country or folk tunes, or some type of "ethnic" music. Many songs were still tied to musicals and films (or sounded as if they should be), and as the fifties moved along, television themes were added to the list of the most popular songs.

This was the immediate musical context for the appearance of "Music, Music, Music," a song which was entirely typical for the time. The lyrics and music of the song clearly celebrated two concepts: first, the increasingly diffuse concept of "music" held by the music industry and listeners who felt comfortable in the subject-listening position of the "mainstream" audience (assumed to be white, middle-class, Northern, urban); and, second, the idea of the song as a commodity that presents itself through a particular technological form – the jukebox or "nickelodeon" – responsible at the moment of the song's dissemination for approximately 25–33 percent of all record sales in the USA. The song celebrates an experience which it hopes that its performance will inspire, and functions as an advertisement for a service that it hopes to fulfill itself. And what is the "music" toward which the song gestures? It is music, that – in its mélange of "Dixieland" (itself a euphemism for New Orleans-style jazz), twenties' "Charleston"-type dance tune, and barroom (or is it "player"?) piano – rather strongly resembles the 1925 hit "Five Foot Two, Eyes of Blue" (written by Lewis, Young, and Henderson, and interpolated in the film *Has Anybody Seen My Gal?* in 1952), while it evokes a mythical, homogeneous past filled with innocent high spirits and hijinks.

During this period from the late forties to the early fifties, many articles in the trade magazines, and in newspapers and magazines such as the *New York Times* and *Newsweek*, derided country-based styles of music as well as the people who made and listened to them. Such publications seemed amazed that anyone other than a "hillbilly" might enjoy such "corny" music. However, "country and western" still had a major entrée lacked by "rhythm and blues" (a more polite name used for "race" music after 1949): its practitioners were almost all white, whereas rhythm and blues musicians were almost all African-American. Thus, country music had attracted the interest of major record companies and developed an infrastructure in Nashville resembling that of the popular music industry in New York and Los Angeles. The feeling of proximity of country to pop was facilitated by the involvement of the major companies in each. The unstated, yet clear, condition of this involvement was the skin color of the principal participants. Rhythm and blues never developed such a centralized infrastructure, relying from the forties through the seventies on smaller, independent companies located around the country in urban areas with large African-

American populations. Hence, the derision that greeted the acceptance of country songs into the mainstream was nothing compared to the outrage and fear that greeted the growing popularity in the early fifties of R&B, which, when it began to become popular with white teenagers, threatened to disrupt the *de facto* segregation that seemed an incontestable aspect of the social fabric of the United States.

Yet this discomfort did not result solely from entrenched racial attitudes: the sound of the music offended taken-for-granted mainstream sensibilities. In other words, R&B challenged music industry definitions of "music": rather than long, arching melodies sung in a smooth, "crooning" vocal tone, uptempo R&B songs featured short melodic phrases (or "riffs") sung in a raspy, shouting timbre; complex chord changes were replaced by simple three- or four-chord patterns; honking saxophones and electric guitars supplanted orchestral instruments; and rather than the all-conquering power of spiritualized, romantic love, R&B lyrics were filled with double entendres and frank references to sex. Eventually R&B (and "rock 'n' roll," the term for bi-racial, teen-oriented music derived largely from R&B) was to overturn received notions of authorship as well, when performer-songwriters such as Chuck Berry and Little Richard combined the two roles that previous mainstream pop had kept separate. In addition to this, R&B/rock 'n' roll contradicted Eurocentric notions of originality: many of the songs were based on the 12-bar blues form (such as Joe Turner's "Shake, Rattle, and Roll") or the so-called "doo-wop" chord progression (such as the Penguin's "Earth Angel"), and therefore relied on creative reuse of pre-existing chord changes and melodic phrases, thus foregrounding repetition rather than privileging the invention of new forms, chord progressions, and goal-oriented melodies. This emphasis on creative reuse rather than on formal invention, defined in narrow terms, is a hallmark of other African-American expressive cultural practices as well, such as oral poetry and storytelling.

In addition to questioning previously held beliefs about musical style, R&B threw comfortable ideas about the nature of the popular music text into doubt, as specific performances overshadowed the abstract template of the song embodied in sheet music, a phenomenon that accounts for why cover versions very soon failed (by 1956) to outsell the original performances. As a consequence, sheet music sales further declined, shattering the pre-eminence of ASCAP, whose critical gatekeepers believed in the priority of those musical parameters that could be easily notated over those that could not.

Even though actual recordings by R&B artists were a faint presence in

132

the pop charts in early 1955, in February 1955 a flurry of articles in the trade magazine *Variety* displayed vividly what was at stake in defining "music." These articles addressed the breakdown in the belief in the separability of the pop music text and its context: fears of miscegenation and lost profits, and incomprehension of the radically different *aesthetic* presented by R&B, congeal into an issue of morality. For example, one article correctly observes that "R&B is strictly a *sound* phenom that pushes disk sales" but then observes dolefully that this quality "pushes disk sales but doesn't move sheets [i.e. sheet music] – and that's where big publishing profits come from" (emphasis added). There are many references to the obscene and inane character of the lyrics, the "throbbing, pounding" beat, the general lowering of sexual mores, the connection to juvenile delinquency (although no one seems sure about whether the music incites it or reflects it). Furthermore, it is clear to all concerned that this is a fad, just like the "hillbilly craze" of the early fifties, that will fade by the time summer is over. R&B and rock 'n' roll (the terms used interchangeably at this point by the trade magazines, which never specify which records they are talking about) are being promoted either by people who are out for a fast buck, or by disk jockeys who are being paid off to play the records "way out of proportion to their popularity."

These anxieties came to a head with an editorial published in *Variety* on February 23, 1955, titled "A warning to the music business." The anonymous editorialist summarizes his fears of social and musical miscegenation when he writes, "In the past such material was common enough but restricted to special places and out-and-out barrelhouses. Today 'leer-ics' are offered as standard popular music for general consumption, including consumption by teenagers." When the author admits that some songs in the past contained suggestive lyrics, he (the author would almost certainly have been male) qualifies this by writing, "Only difference is that this sort of lyric then was off in a corner by itself. It was the music underworld – not the main stream."

The following week in *Variety* (March 2, 1955), several "trade execs" wrote letters that formed a rousing chorus of support for the *Variety* editorialist from the previous week. That the sole writer to disagree with the editorial remained anonymous (the letter has the heading "Defends indie labels for open door policy"), and was the only writer to do so, raises the specter of McCarthyism, which undoubtedly continued to cast a long shadow over the entertainment industry and served to suppress dissent. Eloquently elaborating on the previous week's editorial, Bill Randle, star "hit making" disk jockey of the day, explained how qualities of R&B such as its "beat," the resultant enthusiasm for "dancing," as well as its unsavory "crudity" and "primitiveness," with their "unhealthy social implications," are only "transitory" and will be absorbed back into the "continuing output of pop music," which forms the "main streams of the commercial music business." The implication? Pop music that endures is wholesome, unchanging, made by and for white people, and profitable for the established organizations of the music industry (ASCAP, the major record companies, the networks).

These fears about the popularity of rhythm and blues overwhelming that of good, wholesome pop music, along with the charge that disk jockeys were playing songs "way out of proportion to their popularity" (with the implied or overt charges of payola), were contradicted by *Variety's* own popularity charts. If we are to believe the charts, the reverse was true: for instance, on February 9, the only direct crossover (that is, an R&B song recorded by an R&B artist) on the "*Variety* Disk Jockey Poll" was the Penguin's "Earth Angel," listed at number 17 out of 45 positions. It actually ranked higher in the "Retail Disk Best Sellers" (number 9). If these hysterical charges had any basis in the material world at all, the anxiety would seem to stem from cover versions of R&B songs (that is, R&B songs recorded by pop artists) dominating the top spots, at numbers 1, 3, and 5. Two weeks later, the same kind of pattern is obvious in the *Billboard* polls, in which R&B songs actually fare *worse* in the "Most Played by Jockeys" chart than they do in the "Best Sellers in Stores." Again, one would expect the situation to be reversed if disk jockeys were actually playing songs "way out of proportion to their popularity."

The crisis did not die easily: articles in trade magazines and the popular press throughout the remainder of the fifties attest to the continued portrayal of R&B and rock 'n' roll as crude, primitive, animalistic, and linked with sex, violence, and juvenile delinquency. When confronted with rock 'n' roll's non-disappearance, ASCAP and the major companies did not go gently into that good night; they persisted in complaining, eventually managing to instigate legal proceedings in two infamous Congressional hearings of the late fifties – the BMI–ASCAP hearings of 1958, and the payola hearings of 1960 – which targeted some of the early entrepreneurs of rock and roll, most famously, Alan Freed and Dick Clark. Freed, along with several others, was convicted, fined, and imprisoned, actions which helped to re-establish the dominance of the major companies.

However, the myopia on the part of the "majors" that led to the emergence of rock 'n' roll was not a one-time event. Perhaps the most powerful reminder that these companies were fallible when it came to spotting trends was the explosion of the popularity of rap in the mid to late eighties.

III

Bass! How low can you go? . . .
Turn it up! Bring the Noise!
> From Public Enemy's "Bring the Noise"

Bring da muthafuckin' ruckus
bring da muthafuckin' ruckus
> From Wu-Tang Clan's "Bring da Ruckus"

By the 1980s, ideas about what constituted the North American "mainstream" audience had changed very little since the 1950s, and even though most of the public had thoroughly accepted fifties-era rock 'n' roll, public approbation about what was, or was not, "music" had changed very little. Not surprisingly, the music that formed the target for the wrath of critics, musicians, and a sector of the audience was a far cry from fifties rock 'n' roll. While songs like Chuck Berry's "Roll Over Beethoven" (1956) and "Rock and Roll Music" (1957) had opposed rock 'n' roll to other types of music (classical, jazz, Latin), they still celebrated rock 'n' roll as a form of music. By way of contrast, the songs by Public Enemy and the Wu-Tang Clan quoted above seem to be celebrating the idea that what they are producing – be it "noise" or "ruckus" – is *not* music in any conventional sense at all; or if it is music, it is its very "noisy-ness" that is celebrated, possibly both displaying a self-consciousness on the part of the musicians involved about how their music sounds to the mainstream, and assenting to Attali's claim that "noise . . . betokens demands for cultural autonomy, [and] support for differences or marginality."

"Rap" or "hip-hop" (a term used synonymously with "rap," but also including practices such as breakdancing, graffiti writing, and fashion) had been around for years in African-American neighborhoods in the New York City area before the first hit recording appeared in 1979, with "Rapper's Delight" by the Sugarhill Gang. However, rap, like rhythm and blues in the fifties, did not initially elicit much public disapproval, as it was "restricted to special places" or "was off in a corner by itself . . . [as part of] the music

135

underworld – not the main stream." At first, the major record companies surmised that rap was a fad (more historical echoes), would die quickly, and wasn't worth their trouble. By the late 1980s the errors of this judgement were becoming plain: in 1986, Run-DMC, in collaboration with the rock band Aerosmith, scored a crossover hit with "Walk This Way." Amid the continued increase of rap's popularity, Tone Loc's "Wild Thing" became a huge hit early in 1989 and worked its way into heavy rotation on MTV at a time when few rap videos were played. This song, in conjunction with the surging popularity of other rap recordings, led to MTV programming "Yo! MTV Raps," which quickly became the cable channel's most popular show. The fact that MTV was widely watched in the suburban hinterlands, previously thought to be hostile to rap, combined with an angrier, more militant style spearheaded by Public Enemy and N.W.A. (Niggaz with Attitude) to contribute to a rising sense of panic in the mass media.

Compared to the commentary that accompanied the emergence of rock 'n' roll, the mass media debate around rap was even more explicit about its un-musical qualities. Early in 1990, an article appeared in the *New York Times* Art and Leisure section: "How rap moves to television's beat," authored by Jon Pareles (January 14, 1990). Pareles links rap's aesthetic to that found in commercial television and video games, while at the same time reporting that rappers "insist on the durability and richness of a black street culture that's still invisible on most television." This attempt to discuss rap seriously as music apparently did not rest well with several readers of the *New York Times* (nor, by implication, with editors at the paper who decided which letters to print and which ones to ignore), whose letters to the editor were published two weeks later. Not engaging with Pareles's argument in the slightest, the letters inveigh against "such non-musical hype," "a poor excuse for music," the low quality of which "says much about a generation brought up on the empty values of television." The following letter makes clear that the definitions of music held by these letter writers are closely related to traditional musicological definitions: "I always thought that music was a combination of rhythm, melody and harmony, but after relistening to a performance of Grandmaster Flash, I found it difficult to locate either a melody or harmony, leaving only rhythm, which most definitely was present. Perhaps the definition of music has changed."

The furor over rap only increased late in 1991 when N.W.A.'s *Efil4zaggin* ("Niggaz 4 Life" spelled backwards) surprisingly shot to number one on *Billboard*'s album charts after the method for compiling the charts was revised, indicating that far more white people were listening to "gangsta rap" (at the time, the relatively new label for rap with the most violent and sexual lyrics) than had previously been assumed. Another article by Pareles in the *New York Times* (February 2, 1992) again drew the ire of readers who objected to taking rap seriously as music in much the same terms as had been used two years earlier. That same month, *Musician* magazine published an article by J. D. Considine ("Fear of a rap planet") that quoted, amidst a general defense of rap, non-rap musicians Al Di Meola, Lita Ford, and Ozzy Osbourne on why "Rap isn't music." Again, the usual reasons were cited: those who produce rap can't play instruments or sing, there is no melody, "it sounds like gang music to me" – statements that begin to arouse suspicions that the popularity of the musicians who were quoted may possibly be threatened by the growing acceptance of rap.

Some of the differences between "music" as manifested in hip-hop and in mainstream understandings resemble differences between rhythm and blues and fifties mainstream pop. As in the earlier case, the aesthetic revulsion masks social discomfort: many white listeners (and undoubtedly many black listeners as well) feel intimidated by the sound of young black males, who sound angry and exaggerate stereotypes that they may already fear. The use of profanity, racial epithets, and explicit violent and sexual imagery added to the fear (and guilt – many listeners probably believed, without being able to admit it, that African-Americans had a reason to be angry) experienced by many listeners.

However, the admission of strong social and political reasons for the dismissal of rap should not mask the very real aesthetic challenge mounted by rap to other popular music of the 1980s. Most immediately, many listeners were (and are) threatened by the playback of the music in public spaces, with its loud volume and strong emphasis on bass frequencies. The sounds of rap recordings challenge preconceptions on their own: in rap, voices do not sing or produce melody in any conventional sense, but they do not merely speak words either. Instead they produce "rhythmicized speech" (to use Greg Tate's term), in which variations of tone and relative pitch create a melody in much the same way that a non-pitched percussion instrument might. Rappers' musicality is expressed in phrasing, articulation, rhythm, and tone rather than in the manipulation of discrete pitches. The instrumental aspect of recordings also breaks with much of the other popular music of the time (especially rock), in that it sounds deliberately artificial and emphasizes that the sounds heard on the recording are produced electronically rather than with conventional instruments. In Public Enemy's "Bring the Noise," for example, amidst a dense texture of drums, bass, horns, and percussion instruments lie other sounds not so easily identified, which are probably generated electronically (or are acoustic sounds modified beyond recognition), and which include the percussive sound of a turntable needle being scratched rapidly back and forth on a record during the chorus. Compared to "Bring the Noise," "Bring da Ruckus" presents a much sparser aural soundscape, but one in which disembodied, unfamiliar sounds echo like desiccated ghosts from a sonic garbage heap, rapidly starting and stopping, with only the beat providing continuity (and even that drops out briefly toward the end).

The way in which this radically different soundscape is constructed also plays a major role in the dismissal of rap as music, as many of these sounds are taken from previous recordings. Early DJs used the technique of "scratching" to replay continuously one part of a record to provide the groove for a new rap: using two turntables playing the same record, DJs would expertly move the needle back to the beginning of a desired section on one turntable while the record on the other turntable was playing. (A compelling argument that scratching may now have found mainstream acceptance is the presence of the sound on Hanson's 1997 teenybop smash, "MMM-bop.") In the mid-eighties, sampling technology that permitted musicians to store, reproduce, and manipulate any recorded sounds became widely available. This practice of manipulating pre-existing recordings, rather than producing newly invented sounds on conventional instruments, affronted many people's ideas about authorship, originality, and musicianship; but as already pointed out in the discussion of rhythm and blues, creative *reuse* of materials has long been a hallmark of a diverse array of African-American cultural practices. In rap, many of the sonic sources are modified beyond recognition and are valued for their obscurity; however, if recognizable, the sources may create myriad connotative levels through a wide range of pop culture references, or act as a homage to a particularly esteemed musician or cultural hero. When neither scratching nor sampling can account for the sounds on a recording, often synthesizers and drum machines can. As these also aren't "real" instruments, their use provides further fuel for those who insist that rap is not really music. Lest this description of the musical construction of hip-hop seem monolithic, it is important to note that many artists do use "real" musicians, playing "real" instruments, most famously in the case of the Philadelphia-based group The Roots.

In addition to displaying changing attitudes toward the desirability of "noise," "Bring the Noise" and "Bring da Ruckus" form bookends to the period of hip-hop history under discussion. Amidst its boasts and its exhortations to militancy, "Bring the Noise" even includes a musical discussion of rap and its lack of acceptance *vis-à-vis* rock. First, the line "Run-DMC first said a deejay could be a band" raises issues of instrumental competency, authorship, creativity, and originality; and the line "Roll with the rock stars, still never get accepted as" points to differences in reception between rap and rock. Indeed, by the time rap became a major player in the national music scene, few were still questioning whether rock was music; the sounds that were so unmusical a mere three decades previously had attained a kind of legitimacy. The "noisy" threat posed by rap music had extreme consequences for many artists, including N.W.A. (harassed by the FBI and boycotted) and 2 Live Crew (arrested) among others.

The two historical case studies presented here illustrate how social fears can be disguised as aesthetic criticisms and how, at the same time, the sounds of the "music underworld," because they generate fear among those unaccustomed to them, are actually inseparable from the social fears which are displaced onto them as aesthetic criticism. And while both rock 'n' roll and hip-hop certainly do sound different from one another, both were held up to the same, unvarying, transhistorical standard of what is and isn't music, and found wanting. The dominant beliefs of the early fifties that excluded rhythm and blues from consideration as "Music, Music, Music" and the point of view that dismissed rap as non-music (even as rappers celebrated its noisiness) may be fading, but covert assumptions about what music is and is not continue to play a crucial role in how social groups associated with particular types of music are portrayed in the mass media.

Similarly, dominant definitions of "music" continue to affect access to popular music in academic study, but that does not mean either that popular music has not been studied in the academy or that scholars have confined their work to styles deemed "safe" in the mass media. Indeed, new ways of theorizing the relationship between musical texts and cultural contexts have been developed in response to the unique challenges posed by popular music. And it is important that those with specialized training in music continue responding to these challenges, since the "music" part of "popular music" refers to a medium with its own specific properties, practices, limitations, and possibilities, which musicologists are in a unique position to understand.

Resources

Attali, Jacques (1985) *Noise: the Political Economy of Music*, trans. Brian Massumi. Minneapolis: University of Minnesota Press.
Brackett, David (1995) *Interpreting Popular Music*. Cambridge: Cambridge

University Press.

Brewer, Teresa (1989) *The Best of Teresa Brewer*. BMG Music, CAK-2711.

Ennis, Philip (1992) *The Seventh Stream: the Emergence of Rocknroll in American Popular Music*. Hanover, NH: University Press of New England.

Garofalo, Reebee (1997) *Rockin' Out: Popular Music in the USA*. Boston: Allyn.

Hamm, Charles (1979) Rock around the clock. In *Yesterdays*. New York: Norton, pp. 391–424.

Hill, Trent (1991) The enemy within: censorship in rock music in the 1950s. *South Atlantic Quarterly*, 90, 675–708.

Kelley, Robin D. G. (1994) Kickin' reality, kickin' ballistics: 'gangsta rap' and postindustrial Los Angeles. In *Race Rebels: Culture, Politics, and the Black Working Class*. New York: Free Press, pp. 183–227.

McClary, Susan and Walser, Robert (1990) Start making sense! Musicology wrestles with rock. In Simon Frith and Andrew Goodwin (eds), *On Record: Rock, Pop and the Written Word*. New York: Pantheon, pp. 277–92.

Middleton, Richard (1990) "Change gonna come"? Popular music and musicology. In *Studying Popular Music*. Milton Keynes and Philadelphia: Open University Press, pp. 103–26.

Public Enemy (1988) *It Takes a Nation of Millions to Hold Us Back*. Def Jam, 314 527 358-2.

Rose, Tricia (1994) *Black Noise: Rap Music and Black Culture in Contemporary America*. Hanover, NH: University Press of New England.

Shepherd, John (1991) *Music as Social Text*. Cambridge: Polity Press.

Tate, Greg (1992) *Flyboy in the Buttermilk: Essays on Contemporary America*. New York: Simon and Schuster.

Toop, David (1991) *Rap Attack No. 2: African Rap to Global Hip Hop*. London: Serpent's Tail.

Walser, Robert (1995) Rhythm, rhyme, and rhetoric in the music of Public Enemy. *Ethnomusicology*, 39, 193–217.

Wu-Tang Clan (1993) *Enter the Wu-Tang (36 Chambers)*. RCA, 07863-66336-4.

11
Form

Richard Middleton

"Form" has always come into being in a dialogue between particular "instances" and the larger body of work, or "tradition."

Form and content: the two poles around which, traditionally, discussions of works of art revolve. *Form* is supposed to cover the shape or structure of the work; *content* its substance, meaning, ideas, or expressive effects. When the nineteenth-century music critic Eduard Hanslick declared, in an influential phrase, that music is "forms put into motion through sounds," he was suggesting that music's real content lies in its form. This doctrine of "formalism" has dominated both music aesthetics and music analysis ever since. It led T. W. Adorno to argue that popular music is deficient because its forms are predictable and schematic, whereas in "serious" music, by contrast, the form of a piece is individual – worked out afresh in each case so that all the details interrelate and cohere. (It is worth noting that a good deal of textbook analysis of "serious" pieces reduces them to little more than formal schemas as well, which Adorno also criticized.)

Adorno's theory of "standardization" links popular music's reliance on simple formal molds to commercial pressures and to the music's ideological function as he understood it. Predictable schemata, he thought, help the music industry reach undifferentiated masses of musically uneducated listeners, while at the same time the music's formulaic quality molds their consciousness into passivity. Appealing to the specific content of a given song is no help, for the details are merely a facade of "pseudo-individualization" designed to provide just enough novelty to disguise the formula. Whether one agrees with Adorno or not is perhaps less important than locating his argument in historical context. In terms of musical form, the issue really concerned the relative merits of a classicist or a modernist perspective. Adorno thought that, in twentieth-century mass societies, only a modernist approach that used new, one-off structures which disrupted listeners' expectations could offer the necessary quality of *critique*. But in any case, whichever of these views of form is taken, most popular music tends to fail the test: for classicists, its schemata (verse—chorus, twelve-bar blues, etc.) are just too basic, while for modernists, the very use of structural formulae is enough to condemn the music as reactionary.

One way of escaping this trap is to forget "form" and focus on "content" – on the music's meaning, its expressive power, its effects (on our emotions, on the body, on social behavior). And, to be sure, fans are rarely heard talking about musical form (at least in ways that musical scholars would recognize), preferring to focus on affective or visceral qualities of songs, or perhaps the appeal or particular personae of performers. For scholars, an approach not dissimilar (and probably linked) to this places the center of attention on social contexts rather than sounds: what sort of people listen to the music in question, where, why, and with what results? The danger here is that the specifically musical processes – the ways in which sounds are combined in this particular song – are ignored. This then tends to confirm the view of popular music's aesthetic poverty.

A different way to escape the formalist trap is to redefine the issue. Instead of ignoring "form," one reconceptualizes it in terms of *process*. The emphasis here is on the "internal" qualities of the musical flow, in all their detail, rather than on the "external" mold into which they may have been poured. In employing this kind of approach, Andrew Chester, Charles Keil, and some other writers have made a distinction between musical categories, a distinction with both cultural and historical dimensions (see Middleton, 1990, pp. 115–16). On one side, it is suggested, is music which is produced by starting with small components – rhythmic or melodic motifs, perhaps – and then "developing" these through techniques of modification and combination to end up with a unique, extended, sectionally articulated or through-composed structure. On the other side is music which starts with a framework – a chord sequence, a melodic outline, a rhythmic pattern – and then extends itself by repeating the framework with perpetually varied inflections to the details filling it in. On the one hand (using terms from Chester and Keil), we have music that is syntactic, embodied, extensional; on the other, music that is processual, engendered, intensional. The paradigmatic case of the first is the large-scale instrumental music of the European classical tradition (Beethoven symphonies, for instance); that of the second, open-ended African and Afro-diasporic variation forms (jazz improvisations on a pre-existing tune or chord sequence, the lengthy percussion pieces of many West African cultures). Historically, popular music in the USA and Europe seems to move (though with many variants and diversions) from an approach nearer to the first category to one closer to the second. Probably no popular music has ever been completely structurally individualistic in the Beethovenian sense; nevertheless, a comparison between, say, a Sousa march or a Strauss waltz, on the one hand, and a James Brown funk record or a drum 'n' bass performance, on the other, makes the point.

African-American literary theorists have developed the concept of "signifyin(g)" in an attempt to catch the way in which black culture as a whole favors a mode of composition organized around a "changing same" – that is, the constant variation of collectively owned, repeated materials. Applications of this concept to Afro-diasporic music reveals how a liking for varied repetition within familiar frameworks is grounded in an attitude to life – "what goes around, comes around" – that is radically at odds with the goal-directed trajectories familiar in hegemonic European modes of thought and cultural forms alike. The important role in this repertory of *riffs* – short rhythmic, melodic, or harmonic figures repeated to form a structural framework – and of *call-and-response* – repeating antiphonal relationships between voices and/or instruments – confirms the sense that form is felt here as "circular" rather than linear. Similarly, the concept of *groove* – a term now theorized by analysts but long familiar in musicians' own usage – marks an understanding of rhythmic patterning that underlines its role in producing the characteristic rhythmic "feel" of a piece, a feel created by a repeating framework within which variation can then take place.

To the extent that African-American techniques have become dominant in twentieth-century popular music, the role of these approaches to musical form is clearly important. Yet it would be foolish to disregard the fact that popular music in this period is hybrid. Thus, for example, in most songs the flow of time is shaped by periodic divisions associated with the ends and beginnings of phrases and sections; these moments, which usually coincide with divisions between lines and verses in the lyrics, articulate the temporal process hierarchically, so that, say, a shift from verse to chorus or the reprise of a previous section takes on a particular structural significance, allowing subordinate sets of relationships to work themselves out at lower levels between these "structural downbeats." Similarly, when a "hook" comes round again, or when a recollected riff returns, something in excess of mere continuity, mere groove, is inscribed in the listener's consciousness. Even in the context of the most repetitive techno or rave music, "breaks" inserted between sections of apparently endless dance beats are clearly recognized and marked in dance floor gesture. At the opposite extreme, lengthy, multi-sectional progressive rock pieces demonstrate that popular music can have

143

an extensional dimension (just as, it should be noted, good performers of classical music are aware of the significance of the intensional dimension of small rhythmic and pitch inflections).

Analysts of classical music have developed theories which try to model and account for structural hierarchy – the sense that listeners can, as it were, pull back from the level of small-scale events to take in (consciously or unconsciously) the significance of progressively higher-level moments and markers. The most influential of such theories is Schenkerian theory (so called after its progenitor, Heinrich Schenker), which sees the surface events of the musical "foreground" as a "composing out" of deeper-lying sets of "background" relationships between pitches and chords. But in suggesting a comparison between the Schenkerian approach and a need in popular music analysis to think at a variety of structural levels, I do not intend to assimilate the one to the other. Schenker had a particular conception of the way that musical language works and wanted to apply this universally. As we have already seen, however, different musical categories differ in respect of the number, location and mode of operation of their formal levels. Allan Forte's *The American Popular Ballad of the Golden Era 1924–1950*, the most thoroughgoing attempt to apply Schenkerian theory to a popular music repertory – the songs of Gershwin, Kern, Porter, and similar composers – convincingly demonstrates how in these songs the surface shapes of the tunes and their supporting harmonic progressions take much of their strength from a deeper level of coherence linking structural pitches. But Forte can do this only because the conception of musical language characteristic of this repertory is perhaps the closest twentieth-century popular song comes to that of classical music. At the same time, Forte misses the significance of a good deal of quasi-inflectional detail – rhythmic syncopations, blue notes, little repeating figures – which the composers had learned from contemporary African-American technique. Further, he ignores the fact that the written notes here are only a guide – these songs can vary immensely in different performances. In other words, he places the songs in the wrong category – or partly so.

The most persuasive approaches to popular music form have been those which emphasize the role of *conventions*. Pieces and performances can always be considered in relation to genre. (Usually they fall into a particular genre – rock, rap, ballad, or whatever – though quite often they hybridize between two or more; in any case, genre characteristics and boundaries are always pertinent.) Genres are defined, in part, by conventions governing the musical processes: what can be, what cannot be, what is usually, done; of course, this includes conventions relating to form. A genre can be thought of as analogous to a discursive formation, in the sense that in such a formation there is regulation of vocabulary, types of syntactic unit, formal organization, characteristic themes, modes of address (who speaks to whom and after what fashion), and structures of feeling. We know a Presidential State of the Union address when we hear one, without it needing to be identified as such, and we can also place generically a "rock ballad" when we hear one, without a didactic program note. In the broadest sense, approaches of this kind assume that music (like language, and other communication systems) makes sense not through the operations of intuition or any genetically inbuilt mental capacity but through acquired cultural knowledge. We "read" a song's form because we already know it (in a more profound sense than standardization theories posit). The question might then become whether such approaches – built as they are on a conception of culture as a set of systematized conventions – can avoid reifying its objects (see chapter 2, this volume). But just as (objectified) works of art can be thought of, also, as products of active *work*, so musical forms can perhaps be considered in relation to processes of active *forming*, paying due regard to the performative dimensions of cultural production and the specificities of its context.

Having cleared some ground, we can now as it were stand back and look in a more considered way at the "force field" governing the production of form in popular music. It has often been observed that *repetition* plays a particularly important role in music – in virtually any sort of music one can think of, actually. Of course, music is not unique in this. Other cultural practices often shape themselves through repetition. Language, for instance, depends upon it, for unless particular linguistic units – sound plus meaning – were repeated, their place in the language system would not be codified and collectively understood. Even life itself – the structure of consciousness, our sense of time, the production and reproduction of generations and species – is molded by repetition. But music, perhaps because of its temporal quality, perhaps because its meanings are so vague, so dependent on the *ordering* process, seems to offer a particularly strong example of the impulse to repeat. Putting it another way, we could say that music's effects are peculiarly linked to the play of repetition and difference, and difference, we could add, can be thought of in terms of the distance moved from a repeat (just as repetition can be thought of as difference squeezed to its smallest). Difference, then, can be assessed quantitatively (how far it moves from a position of identity) and qualitively (on what level it operates, on what scale, in what type of units).

In most popular music, repetition processes are especially strong. Is this to make it accessible, easily memorable, open to the largest possible audience, to energize the body (since the body can itself be seen as a bundle of interacting repetition mechanisms)? Whatever the explanation, it can be said that, in their different (and selective) ways, both the Adorno perspective and the theorists of signifyin(g) were engaging with the nub of the matter.

To emphasize the role of repetition is only to begin the analysis, however. The precise way in which the play of repetition and difference operates is culturally and historically specific. Even in a lengthy Beethoven symphonic movement, even in Schönberg's atonal works (for Adorno, the epitome of modernist critique in music), there is repetition; but it tends to be absorbed into an irregularly shaped, prose-like discourse. In most popular music, by contrast, the repetition of figures, rhythms, melodies is foregrounded. Within popular music itself, repetition works in a variety of ways. At the same time several different analytic frameworks can be used to understand it. For example, in previous writings I have stressed a distinction between repetition at the level of the short figure, often used to generate an entire structural framework, and repetition at the level of the phrase or section, which generally functions as part of a larger-scale "argument." The first type I call "musematic" (for music semiologists, a museme is a minimal unit of meaning, by analogy with the "morpheme" in language), the second type "discursive." The paradigmatic case of the first is the riff, that of the second a phrase, usually carrying a line of lyric and ending with a punctuation (a cadence, in musical terminology). For an example of the first, think of the celebrated fuzz guitar part in the Rolling Stones' recording "Satisfaction." For an example of the second, think of the first two phrases of the refrain in Henry Clay Work's nineteenth-century ballad "Come Home, Father": the two phrases are identical except for the final two notes, which make the first ("Father, dear father, come home with me now! / The clock in the steeple strikes one") "open" (that is, incomplete), the second ("You promised, dear father, that you would come home / As soon as your day's work was done.") "closed." (This song can be found in Turner (1972, pp. 246–51). The first two phrases are quoted in Middleton (1990, p. 271).)

Discursive repetition is often "nested" – especially in nineteenth-century and early twentieth-century repertories. That is to say, repetition of phrases (and even musemes, on occasion) is enclosed within higher-degree repetitions, at the level of longer phrases or sections. At the same time, in these repertories, the repetition is often sequential – in other words, the *shape* of the unit is kept but it is repeated at a different pitch. In George and Ira Gershwin's "Embraceable You" (1930), for example, the second phrase repeats the first exactly but at a higher pitch; the first is harmonically "open," the second "closed," so the effect is of complementarity. Similarly, the fourth phrase sets off repeating the third phrase one note lower, then continues in a new way (though with the same rhythm). This is the halfway point of the tune. The second half begins by repeating the whole of phrases 1 plus 2 exactly. They are followed by mostly new music in phrases 7 and 8. Phrase 7 descends, balancing the predominantly ascending shapes of most preceding phrases, while phrase 8 comprises a shortened, varied version of phrase 2, pushed one note higher so that its climactic note becomes the highest pitch in the tune (it is also one note higher than the climactic pitch at the equivalent point in phrase 4, which closed the first half of the tune); these two factors taken together point up the overall shape of the balancing two-part formal scheme. At the same time, on the lowest level of repetition, the three-note museme that opens the tune (a rising scale figure, to "Embrace me") pervades the entire song, in varied forms, at various pitch-levels; it acts like a developmental motif. Altogether, a tune like this is as close as twentieth-century popular music comes to the formal processes of classical music (see figure 11.1). The emphasis on a certain sort of *linearity* (a journey, though not too far: home, then away, then back home), on *rational control* (balance, complementarity), and on *self-sufficiency* (closure, coherence) has often been linked by scholars to a mode of subjectivity favored in traditional bourgeois culture.

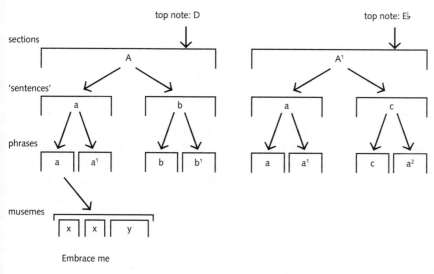

Figure 11.1   Repetition structure in "Embraceable You."

Musematic repetition works very differently. Think of James Brown's "Superbad" (1970), which has been given an exemplary analysis in David Brackett's book *Interpreting Popular Music*. There are two sections (a sort of "verse" and what Brown himself calls a "bridge"; let us call them A and B). These alternate – but the length of each section varies in an apparently unpredictable way, and the number of alternations could easily have been different: the recording fades out, and there is a sense of neither closure nor structural climax. In fact, the shifts from one section to the other seem to be arbitrary, engineered through what has been termed a "cut." It is as if, once started, the music (of either A or B) almost runs itself, for as long as seems desirable, then jumps to its alternate, and then back (and so on, for a stretch of time that is in principle infinite). The music is able to "run" itself because, at the level of the museme, it is made up of a network of riffs. Drum and bass figures, chordal interjections from the horns, and chords or melodic figures on guitar (all one bar long, for the most part) together make up a polyrhythmic matrix. On top of that, Brown's vocal is constructed in a similar way, from permutations of short, repeating figures (some little more than shouts). Two features are particularly significant. First, all the figures are formulaic; they are related to, derived from, remind us of, melodic and harmonic materials used many, many times before across a range of African-American genres. Second, all of them are continuously subject to variation. The melodic or rhythmic shape might be altered in obvious ways, but as often as not, a small-scale nuancing is achieved: slight mutations in accenting, articulation, timbre, pitch process (glides, swoops, vibrato, etc.). Brackett's analysis lays out typical band textures and Brown's core materials in tabular form, displaying both their formulaic and variative aspects. "Superbad" epitomizes the aesthetic of signifyin(g). There certainly are "structural downbeats" (at the "cuts"). Beneath this level, however, it is hard to discern more than one level of structure, since, although repetition/difference relations operate across a range of quantities, from single note to bar-long figures, these operations do not form any consistent hierarchy. The emphasis on a certain sort of formal *circularity*, on *synchronic relations* (between textural components), and on *open-ness* (to existing repertory, to tradition, to performance design) might be linked with a mode of subjectivity favoring self-construction through processes of collective participation.

It would be a mistake, though, to regard the approaches exemplified by "Embraceable You" and "Superbad" as rigidly distinct, still more to map them onto essentialized conceptions of "white" and "black" music cultures. A somewhat different angle of approach to the question of form from that constituted by the discursive/musematic distinction would be one which stressed a contrast between, on the one hand, *sectionalism*, and, on the other, *additiveness*. Clearly there is considerable overlap between the two schemata. Sectional forms – where a musical unit is divided up into clearly distinguished parts, usually organized so as to articulate an overall emotional or dramatic shape – commonly make use of discursive repetition. But the category of additive forms includes not only what one might think of as processually generated structures (such as "Superbad") but also stanzaic pieces, where a whole section (a verse) is repeated as often as necessary, each time carrying different words. The narrative ballad genre typically exemplifies this latter tendency, and its influence has fed into folk-rock and singer-songwriter repertories. An additively repeating verse can of course be formed internally out of musematically or discursively repetitive processes, or both; but, equally, so too can a sectional form, such as the 32-bar AABA structure typical of the "classic" Tin Pan Alley ballad. Similarly, in performance, such sectional structures can be iteratively accumulated – and, indeed, historically their origins are to be found in the repeating verse-and-chorus forms of nineteenth-century song. Sometimes, in an additive piece, there is such reliance on musematic repetition that a sense of groove is created which seems to overrun and pull against any sectional divisions; an example is Bob Dylan's "Subterranean Homesick Blues." In other cases, the sections in a sectional form repeat each other with such a sense of cumulation that they too point toward a potential for open-ended process. In Gershwin's "I Got Rhythm," for instance, the A phrases in the AABA form are all identical (and all harmonically closed), and when chorus follows chorus (especially at quick tempos) the effect is in a way similar to that of "Superbad" – a succession of "verses" interrupted by the occasional "bridge." The term "chorus form" is often used to denote a type of performance – typically in jazz or rhythm 'n' blues, but also sometimes in country music and rock 'n' roll – where a given structural unit is repeated an indefinite number of times. The unit itself may be sectionally elaborate, as in the case of most Tin Pan Alley ballads. It may be a twelve-bar blues, or something similar, as in the case of many R&B and rock 'n' roll numbers; here, a three-line AAB lyric, set to a three-phrase melody, is underpinned by a single gestural sweep in the harmony (see figure 11.2). Occasionally – as in some funk, dub reggae, and hip-hop, for example – it may approach the status of open-ended process.

The hybridity and range indicated here is perhaps at its clearest in rock music. Even in the 1950s burst of rock 'n' roll, when twelve-bar blues

149

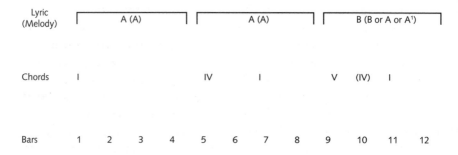

Figure 11.2 Standard twelve-bar blues. Chords are designated by their function: I is tonic, IV is subdominant, V is dominant (in C major, chords on C, F and G respectively).

form and close derivatives were predominant, some performers also included ballads in their repertories – think, for instance, of Elvis Presley's "Love Me Tender" (1956). By the 1960s, a broader range of influences, and a more flexible approach to song-writing, resulted in a variety of models. It becomes difficult to generalize, except to observe that songs were now generally constructed out of a sequence of sections of variable length, which, depending on their function and interrelationships, may be thought of as "verses," "choruses," or "bridges," and, second, that continuities are often constructed across sectional divisions through the use of riffs, similarities of figuration, rhythm or texture, or harmonically open chord progressions. In The Beatles' "She Said She Said" (1966), for instance, the sectionality (verse–verse–bridge–verse–bridge–verse–coda) is cloaked by the irregular lengths of sections and phrases, the changes of meter, and the similarities of melodic and harmonic material across sections. In the Rolling Stones' "Satisfaction," already referred to, articulation points are even more obscure: it is the prominent guitar riff which identifies some parts as having a "chorus" function and its absence which suggests "verses." Otherwise, the music (especially the pervasive two-chord alternation) seems to flow continuously.

The use of a short, repeating chord progression (a harmonic riff) to create a structural framework is especially common in rock. The Kinks' "You Really Got Me" (1964), which also alternates two chords, is often described as the first riff song, but the technique can be traced back through "Twist and Shout" (1962) and its model, "La Bamba" (1959), to "Louie Louie" (1957), and, even earlier, to doo-wop and gospel music. The subtlety with which this technique can be used is well illustrated by R.E.M.'s "Losing My Religion" (1991; see figure 11.3). The main verse (A), an irregular ten bars long, is built over a two-chord riff. A six-bar second verse (B), which keeps returning like a refrain but which, harmonically, has a transitional rather than a typical chorus feel, starts as if it will continue the riff but then extends the harmony in a different direction which can equally easily lead back to A or on to bridge 1. Bridge 1 is built on a two-chord riff that is a close relative of that in A (one of the two chords is the same, the other different), and also, from another point of view, a close relative of that in B (it follows a similar transitional trajectory). It is as if the original A riff throws out offspring which circle round the parental home. The result is that a sectionally elaborate song acquires a wonderful continuity – a quality sealed by the role of the melodic riff, played on mandolin, which runs almost continuously through the performance.

What becomes apparent is that the divergent formal principles I have discussed – musematic/discursive repetition, sectional/additive processes – are all the time mediated by the specificities of genre and style. One way of conceptualizing the range that results might refer (if yet another analytic

Intro (Br 1)	A	B	A	B	Br1	A	B	A
Bars (Inst) 8	10	6	10	6	8	10	6	10
Chordal riffs F-(G)-a-(G)	a-e	e-d-G			F-a			

B	Br 1	Br 2	A	B	Br 1	Br 1	Playout
6	8	8	10	6	8	8	(inst)
		(4 inst + 4 vocal)					

lyric transfer ↑

Figure 11.3 Form of "Losing My Religion." Chords are designated, conventionally, by their roots. Capitals indicate major chords, lower case minor.

151

map may be proposed) to a "triangulation" of impulses (and their hybrids): first, a "narrative" drive, which pulls the listener towards a goal, usually through processes of melodic and harmonic tension and release; second, an "epic" circularity, which affirms the rituals of the changing same; and, third, a "lyrical" shapeliness, which absorbs both into relations of balance, flight, and symmetry. The first privileges difference (but also resolves it in closure); the second reads difference and identity as mutually conditioning each other; the third grasps difference in terms of varying relations of equivalence (degrees of contrast, open/closed parallels, balances of pitch space, up and down, and so on). The "narrative" impulse points tenden- tially toward verse-type functions, the "lyrical" toward chorus-type func- tions, the "epic" toward choreographies of gesture. While in practice they are always mixed together, and in varying proportions, it seems clear that on the largest historical scale the twentieth century has seen a significant shift in the weighting, from a preponderance of narrative–lyric mixtures – a tendency inherited from the nineteenth century – to a focus on lyric–epic hybrids, a focus which has predominated since rock 'n' roll.

The mediation of formal impulses by the demands of genre and style runs through several different channels. For example, lyrics almost always play an important role. The effects of musical repetition are different when accompanying words are also repeated and when they are not; continuous repetition of a key word or phrase intensifies (and is perhaps generated by) musematic repetition. Similarly, hooks often have a verbal as well as a musical aspect, and act as key structural markers. Rhyme schemes may mirror musical phrase structures (though at other times they may not). Lyrics are sometimes "talismanic" rather than overtly meaningful (think of Little Richard's "Awopbopaloobop Alopbamboom"), and this seems to exert a pull towards the gestural, towards "epic" impulses. At the other extreme, story-telling ballad lyrics can push the music toward a more "narrative" mode (think of Bob Dylan's "With God on Our Side") – though this does not always follow (think of the remorseless repetitions to which Dylan's "Oxford Town" narrative is set). As this last example suggests, lyric and musical structures may work against each other – or at least intertwine in complex rather than simply supportive ways. It is just this sort of intertwining that Dai Griffiths (1988) has revealed in his analysis of Bruce Springsteen's "The River," where rhyme scheme, verbal content, melodic shape, and harmonic rhythm often follow divergent temporal patterns.

Specific choices of sound and texture also play an important role in mediating formal impulses – and these choices often relate as well to differences in generic function. For instance, the anthemic refrains so typical of "stadium rock" mark themselves out through the announcement of a characteristic sound world (loud, enveloping, uplifting; soaring guitar lines; whacking drum backbeat). By contrast, the distorted, feedback-heavy sound of classic punk rock, with its unyielding continuity designed, it would seem, to obliterate conscious awareness of "form," serves as part of a larger assault on generic norms. Compare the "expressive" cloudy textures common in "indie" music, often coupled with carefully organized dynamic shifts and textural changes at key structural moments, with the clear, spacy, percussive textures organized around open-ended repetitive rhythmic patterns typical of funk. The first demands close attention to the evolution of an expressive drama; the second invites us to dance.

A further channel of mediation, closely linked to the specificities of sound, is defined by the technologies of music production and dissemination. Top-40 radio probably encouraged the production of songs that would fit easily both into a heavily formularized generic framework and (by making them structurally amenable to fades) into programme flow. The LP record facilitated the creation of more expansive forms – for example, the relatively "extensional" processes and multi-part structures favored in some "progressive rock," or the neo-modernistic compositions of Frank Zappa – as well as the "concept album," with its tendency toward cyclic and suite-like relationships between individual tracks. At the same time, multi-track mixing opened the door to collage procedures, as, for instance, in The Beatles' "Revolution" pieces. More recently, the twelve-inch single made possible extended remixes, aimed at the dance floor and usually creating their extensions through repetition of sections or prolonged "looping" of open-ended repetitive patterns.

The prevalence in late twentieth-century pop (especially that aimed at dance clubs) of remixing, of collage textures, and of sampling as a means of generating material is of course rooted in the development and spread of digitized production technologies. At one and the same time, this tendency refocuses the formal procedures employed in popular music and orients the bundle of already existing impulses in ways that place emphasis on some techniques rather than others. Grandmaster Flash's hip-hop classic "The Adventures of Grandmaster Flash on the Wheels of Steel" (1981) has a form – a certain sort of complex, freely formed collage drawing heavily on material from other records – that is new, but its dependence on musematically repeated riffs and its "signifyin(g)" procedures place it in an old tradition.

Above all, perhaps, a record like "Adventures" raises a question about the relationship of individual pieces to the larger repertory, which certainly acquires a new intensity in the era of sampling technology but which has long been endemic to popular music practice. In this chapter I have assumed that it is reasonable to count "the piece" (a record, a performance, a published song) as the primary unit of form. In practice, however, this has never been unequivocally clear. If one thinks of the role of "covers," of the way musicians often borrow tunes, rhythms, riffs, and sounds from other pieces, of the importance of formula to song design, it becomes apparent that "form" has always come into being in a *dialogue* between particular "instances" and the larger body of work, or "tradition." When pieces can change not only their sound but also their shape from performance to performance – a process aided of course by the use of repetition techniques as both structural frameworks and potentially open-ended processes – it is easy to see how the new possibilities opened up by digital technology are readily assimilated into a long established proclivity to intertextual production (see chapter 16, this volume). In one way the implication of this is to locate the question of form at the point of reception: what counts as the unit – a performance, a piece (conceived as a collection of multiple performances), an intertextual network, or, at the other extreme, an infinitely looping riff – may well vary according to the social conditions of listening. In another way the implication is to connect musical form inextricably to the larger body of practice in the music culture. In this sphere, then, "form" can hardly be said to define, still less constrain, "content." Instead, both the particularities of vernacular behavior and the large formations of the historically evolving repertory insist that form here represents embodied cultural knowledge.

Resources

Brackett, David (1995) *Interpreting Popular Music*. Cambridge: Cambridge University Press.

Forte, Allen (1995) *The American Popular Ballad of the Golden Era 1924–1950*. Princeton, NJ: Princeton University Press.

Griffiths, Dai (1988) Three tributaries of "The River," *Popular Music*, 7, 27–34 (reprinted in Middleton, 1999).

Middleton, Richard (1990) *Studying Popular Music*. Milton Keynes and Philadelphia: Open University Press.

Middleton, Richard (ed.) (1999) *Reading Pop: Approaches to the Textual Analysis of Popular Music.* Oxford: Oxford University Press.

Moore, Allan (1993) *Rock: the Primary Text. Developing a Musicology of Rock.* Buckingham and Philadelphia: Open University Press.

Turner, Michael R. (ed.) (1972) *The Parlour Song Book.* London: Pan.

12
Text

John Shepherd

If words, images, and movement as elements of popular music's texts are linked in powerful ways to popular music's sounds in a manner that we yet do not fully understand, then . . . we may conclude that, although music can be textual, it is textual in some very distinctive ways.

INTRODUCTION

What do we mean by the term "text" in relation to music, and popular music in particular? In the everyday world, the term "text" is customarily used in relation to things that are written. We think of text as the wording of anything written or printed and also, more recently, as the wording of anything that appears on our computer screens. We think of text as a term that we would usually apply to books, articles, magazines, newspapers, pamphlets, flyers, and so on. An important element of this everyday concept of text is that texts are understood to have a tangible and visible form. They occur on paper, paper substitutes such as acetate, or on screens, whether in movie theaters or lecture halls, or those of televisions and computer monitors. Further, texts are seen as a consequence of being rendered through a tangible medium. They are not heard or, for that matter, smelt or tasted. People do, of course, refer to the "text of a speech." In this sense, the spoken, in addition to the written or printed, word enters the picture. However, when people refer to the "text of a speech," they usually mean the text from which a speech is read, or the text into which it is rendered, as when television pundits examine minutely the wording of a speech by a politician.

As described in chapters 2 and 10 of this volume, the very idea of music is itself a construct (this also applies to "language," a point usually overlooked in discussions of "music" as a construct). Music, then, is not something "given" to us by the "natural world" (any more, indeed, than is language). Having said that, however, it is nonetheless clear that people in the everyday world do know the difference between music and other forms of human expression and communication, such as language, and, as a consequence, between music and text. Text is the visible and tangibly rendered form of language. Music is not visible and cannot be thought of as such unless encoded in a score or in sheet music, a point to which I will return. Music is, like spoken language, sonic, made up of sound. It is heard. And while sound, the sound of music, may "touch" us, both literally and figuratively, we cannot touch it. Further, what distinguishes the sound of music from the sound of language is that while the sounds of language – language, if you like, in its non-textual form – are, in a certain sense, "in" the sounds of music in the form of lyrics, the sounds of music extend far beyond what we would normally recognize as sounds in the service of language. That is why people in the everyday world experience little trouble in distinguishing between music and language.

Text and music, then, seem to be very different things. Text is tangible, visible, and constituted through words. Music is intangible, heard, and while music most often "has words," it is not "of words." How, then, can the term "text" be used in relation to music? There are two answers to this question. One has to do with the development of various forms of cultural theory during the twentieth century. The other has to do with the character of musical notation and the complex relations that notation has had with the non-linguistic sounds of music over the centuries.

CULTURAL THEORY, TEXT, AND MUSIC

Much literary criticism rests on close textual analysis. This is hardly surprising, since literature – apart from "oral literature" – is almost by definition textual in character. Textual analysis in literary criticism has been influenced, if not aided, by the development of various forms of linguistic and cultural theory during the course of the twentieth century. The work of the Swiss structural linguist Ferdinand de Saussure in the early part of the century made it possible, for example, to conceptually separate the "form" of text – the shapes of letters and words as inscribed through a tangible medium – from the "content" of text – the ideas, concepts, and emotions to which such visual and tangibly inscribed shapes customarily give rise. A major point made by Saussure was the essentially arbitrary relationship between "the signifiers" – both the sounds of words and the form of their visual encoding – and "the signifieds" – the mental concepts

157

with which the sounds and visual symbols of language were customarily associated. That is, Saussure argued that there is no logical or necessary connection between the characteristics of the sounds and visual symbols of language and the characteristics of the ideas or mental concepts that are, by convention, customarily associated with them. To give an example – and to put it mundanely – there is nothing inherently "bird-like" about the sound or visual shape of the word "bird." In evoking the idea or mental concept (signified) of actual, two-legged and winged animals that fly around the sky, the sound and visual shape of the word "oiseau" could work just as successfully, which, in fact, it does in the French language.

Saussure's work was important in that it put the lie to the idea that people's view of the world is neutral, objective, and unmediated by language. For, by establishing a clear disjunction between the materials of language and the conceptual world that these materials customarily invoke, Saussure's theory of linguistic signification sugested that it was not the world that gave meaning to language, but language that gave meaning to the world. According to this way of thinking, the world becomes less of an absolute and more of a construct. This does not mean that the world is a chimera or a fantasy that has no substance. Rather, it means that because people view the world through language, different languages, as well as different usages of the same language, will give rise to "different" worlds. In other words, language mediates the world for people and presents it to them in one way rather than any other.

The work of Roland Barthes, Julia Kristeva, and others like them – work which has come to be thought of as "poststructuralist" in character – furthers Saussure's theory of signification, positing that texts somehow envelop if not penetrate people's minds, that people's awareness is linguistically constituted, and that, as a consequence, people's subjectivities are immersed, lost, or "disappeared" in textual processes themselves. Not only was it the case that language lent meaning to the world, therefore. It was now the case that language lent meaning to the world by implanting such meanings as the substance of people's awareness or subjectivity. People, in other words, were constituted as subjects by language (see chapters 1 and 2 in this volume).

Although, for Barthes as for other poststructuralists, language retained a position of primary importance in the construction of meaning through subjectivity, Barthes's emphasis on textuality as the site for the constitution of subjects was important in extending these notions to include, in principle, any cultural process or artifact that could give rise to meaning. It is pertinent, however, that, before his "textual" period, Barthes hardly mentions music. This, it can be surmised, is because musical sounds, the sounds that music characteristically manifests over and above the sounds of language that might be "in" it, are, unlike many if not most other forms of human expression and communication, non-denotative. That is, they do not refer to the objects of the external world or to concrete concepts that can be captured through language. Because of this, it did not seem to Barthes that music could on its own terms be implicated in the "meanings" of the world or its ideological messages.

In matters of ideology, music therefore seemed "innocent" to Barthes, something that became extremely important to him as he became immersed in questions of textuality. Barthes's interest in textuality was motivated by a desire to critique ideology and its messages. In this sense, Barthes's critique of ideology became a critique of meaning itself, at least in its Western formulations, a critique imbued with a sense of political struggle. But music for Barthes represented the "degree zero," the perfect, pristine, and unsullied state of "Otherness" that threw the battle with ideology into sharp relief. "As soon as someone speaks about music," said Barthes, "or a specific music – as a value in itself, or on the contrary – though this is the same thing – as a value for everyone – i.e., as soon as we are told we must love all music – we feel a kind of ideological cope falling over the most precious substance of evaluation, music" (quoted in Engh, 1993, p. 74). So, although music for Barthes was textual – along with literature, painting, film, comic books, newspapers, and so on – it constituted a very special kind of text.

NOTATION, TEXT, AND MUSIC

One answer to the question of how the term "text" can be used in relation to music is that it can be so used by extending the term to include any cultural process or artifact capable of generating meaning. Yet, as the example of Barthes illustrates, the inclusion of music as text in this way can lead to a special status for music: a signifying practice that is paradoxically "innocent" and unburdened by "meaning" in its conventional sense. Music, can, however, be thought of as text in another way, and that is through its notation in the form of a score or sheet music. Here, music is rendered into a tangible and visible form that parallels the role that text plays in relation to spoken language. In considering these roles, it is tempting to think that writing, printed language, scores, and sheet music act fundamentally as *aides-mémoire* that do little more than store the sounds of spoken language and music as performed, in this way enabling their faithful reproduction. However, as I have argued in *Music as Social Text*, the relationship between spoken language and various forms of writing and printing is not so straightforward, and there came a point in the history of Western civilizations when written and printed words took on a greater authority than the spoken words on which they ultimately rely.

A similar development can be observed in the relationship between music and musical notation, a development which followed that involving spoken language, writing, and printing. At first, as Gordon Greene has argued, notation in music was purely mnemonic. There then followed a period of uneven relations in which notation was sometimes mnemonic but at other times moved toward playing an important role in defining those sounds that could and could not be admitted to musical practice, and in the placement and manipulation of those that were. Then, from approximately the eighteenth until well into the twentieth century, notation came to play a quite fundamental role in the creation of classical and "serious" music. First, notation became both basic and necessary to the development of the large architectonic or "architectural" structures that constituted classical music in all its harmonic complexities. In other words, notation provided the tools through which the sonic components, or building blocks, of one part of a piece could be conceived, manipulated, and then stored and, as it were, put on hold while attention was being paid to another part of the structure. In this way, notation in music played a role very similar to that of blueprints in the building of ships and aircraft, and of architectural plans in the construction of buildings.

However, in addition to playing a role fundamental to the composition of music, notation also contributed to the character of classical music's soundscape. As Trevor Wishart has argued, standard music notation (that is, notation as you see it in sheet music) came to act as a filter through which all conceivable sounds could be passed to provide the rather restricted palate of sounds that were used in classical music. Since some aspects of sound are more susceptible to visual mediation and therefore notational manipulation than others, they came to be foregrounded in classical music: discrete pitches that remain largely fixed or stable and are not appreciably "bent" (as they often are in popular music, the guitar playing of Jimi Hendrix or the singing of Janis Joplin providing good examples), and rhythms that occur largely on the beat, and are also not appreciably "bent" (as they often are in popular music – this is what has largely been responsible for the feeling of "swing" in jazz, together with an emphasis on the second and fourth beats of the bar which subsequently provided the "backbeat" of rock music).

Elements of sound that are inhospitable to easy visual mediation and therefore to notational manipulation were either standardized or conventionalized. Importantly, timbre in classical music – the quality of sound itself, the tone or color of a note that tells you whether it is being played, for example, by a trumpet or a flute – came to be standardized. For each instrument and voice in classical music, an ideal and pure timbre was established. The standardization of timbres in terms of an ideal meant that the basic sonic building blocks of classical music became homogeneous. This allowed for the creation of architectonically complex pieces of music in much the same manner that the uniform and standard shape of bricks allows for the construction of large and complex buildings. Moreover, the purity of timbres in classical music – the haunting beauty of the flute or the smooth urbanity of the male singing voice – also served to render timbre relatively unobtrusive, unlikely to detract attention from the foregrounded elements of harmony and melody (which depend on pitch) and, to a lesser extent, rhythm. The flute playing of Ian Alexander of Jethro Tull, for example, with its rough and "dirty" timbres and melodic and rhythmic inflections ("bent" pitches and rhythms), as well as the timbre or tone color of Louis Armstrong's singing voice, which is absolutely unmistakable in its gravel quality, would be inadmissible in classical music, since they would draw attention away from the harmonic argument which underlies most classical music and would challenge the logic of the tightly controlled harmonic-rhythmic framework which makes such argument possible.

Sounds in classical music were thus reduced as far as was possible to the visual exigencies of notation. In this way, conceptions and perceptions of "what counts as music" within the classical tradition were determined. This reduction was, therefore, very much a textual reduction, and it is this that provides the second answer to the question of how music can be thought of as text: in terms of the reduction of its sounds to the conditions of visual notation. Indeed, this is how the academic discipline of musicology, most noticeably through its subdisciplines of music theory and music analysis, has tended to think of music (by which is invariably meant classical music). The analysis of music that is carried out within these two subdisciplines has been almost synonymous with the analysis of musical notation, the musical score. This embodiment of music within a material form, that of the score, has in turn enabled musicology (as distinct from ethnomusicology) to conceive of classical music as something apart from the rest of the world, an art form somehow independent of the social, economic, political, and cultural forces that constitute that world. Consequently, to the extent that music theorists think about the question of "meaning" or "significance" in music, they think of it as contained exclusively within music's sounds.

MUSIC AS TEXT

Music can therefore be thought of as text in two ways. First – and this is music as text in a metaphorical sense – it can be thought of as an element of culture and thus susceptible to the scrutiny of various forms of cultural theory and of the linguistic theory that supports them. In this case, music tends to emerge as curiously empty and insubstantial, Barthes's "degree zero," a perfect, innocent "Other" to the world of meaning and ideology. In this sense, it is almost as if music were an empty signifier, unburdened by the worldly significance that comes through conventional association with a signified. Second – and this is music as text in a more literal sense – it can be thought of as substantial, full to the brim with complex formal properties revealed through traditional music analysis, but only to the extent that its sonic qualities and thus its "meanings" can be reduced to the visual exigencies of notation.

These two approaches to understanding music as text might seem on the surface to be curiously disconnected, even in opposition to one another. They are, however, significantly related. First, they are related in that music is thought of as being "other-worldly." Because the sounds of music function in a non-denotative fashion and do not refer to the external world, music is thought of as being devoid of worldly significance, either "empty," or replete with formal properties, but none that would speak to the material and therefore social worlds. Further, music is in both cases conceived as text in a manner influenced largely by concepts derived from language and therefore in a manner unlikely to challenge language's social power.

The assumption here is that because the sounds of music cannot articulate "meaning" in the conventional sense of the word, any meaning ascribed to music must be the result of what people say about it. In other words, the sounds of music are assumed to exist outside the world of meaning – and therefore outside society – until interpellated into such worlds through language. This way of thinking about music's sounds – a way that derives from poststructuralism and French psychoanalytic theory – becomes clear in the attitude of many popular music scholars – particularly those with a background in sociology or communication – to the role of music's sounds in popular music. For these scholars, what is said about popular music is far more important than the formal properties of its sounds in getting at its "meaning." Musicology, with its subdisciplines of music theory and music analysis, can thus be of little assistance in this task.

In response to such scholars, we need to recognize that music theory and music analysis possess a range of impressive tools for analyzing many aspects of music's sounds, primarily those of harmony, melody, and rhythm. Yet these tools are embedded in language rather than in the music to which they are applied. This is a contentious point, and one that is difficult to establish briefly. One way of thinking about it, however, is that these tools can be applied only to the sounds of music – and overwhelmingly the sounds of classical music – through the score, through music as text in a literal sense. Music notation – which is visual, tangible, two-dimensional, and static in character – can only, as it were, identify points on the surface of a sonic world that is intangible, constantly in motion, and multidimensional. The sonic world of music – even classical music – is highly complex in the ways in which its different dimensions of harmony, melody, rhythm, and timbre (not to mention amplitude, attack, envelope, and so on) interact with one another. What notation – either as a score or sheet music – represents is but a very pale imitation of this world. It is nonetheless an imitation that allows some of music's technical characteristics to be discussed within language.

It is perhaps for this reason that Barthes once drew a distinction between what music theory and music analysis have to offer – "the system of notes, scales, tones, chords, and rhythms" – and what he was attempting to get at in his own musical criticism: "the effervescence of the beats" (quoted in Engh, 1993, p. 73). However, it is "notes, scales, tones, chords, and rhythms" that constitute music for music theorists and music analysts. While music (for music theorists and music analysts) is thus full of formal properties – neither "empty" nor "innocent" – it is, as we have seen, textually if not linguistically encapsulated, embodied materially in a manner that allows for the conceit that classical music is essentially "asocial" in character. While musicologists are for the reasons already identified hesitant to use the word "meaning" in relation to music, its formal properties are for them of great consequence in beginning to understand music's "affects" – the way it is of consequence for the lives of people. These affects are, however, understood to be entirely "intra-musical," residing within the notes of music as they impact on people rather than belonging to the external, social world.

163

Popular music, by contrast, is nothing if not social. This fact has posed considerable problems for those scholars of popular music who wish to entertain seriously the possibility that, unlike the sounds of language, the sounds of popular music are in some way connected to and of consequence for the people whose subjectivities and lives popular music affects. As Paul Willis observes, this has meant that "a really adequate account of the internal parameters of . . . music and its specific ability to hold and retain particular social meanings must be more technically rigorous than [it] has been." Because musicology has offered the only analytical tools through which to "get at" the sounds of music, the temptation for such scholars has been to take up these tools. In fact, Willis (1978, p. 76) goes on to argue that "musicology is the discipline which has the formal resources for this task." But Willis's optimism has been largely unfounded.

As discussions in other chapters have observed, the analytic tools of the musicological subdisciplines of music theory and music analysis have been drawn overwhelmingly from the study of classical music, making them less readily applicable to popular music. The most important elements in many genres of popular music are the distinctive timbres of particular performers' vocal and instrumental playing. These are developed in ways far beyond what would be acceptable in the classical tradition, just as the notes are "bent," not only melodically and rhythmically, but also timbrally, again to an extent unacceptable in classical music. The harmonic complexities of classical music – which demand uniformity of timbres, stability of pitches, and the rhythmic placing of notes with strict adherence to the beat – become in popular music the complexities of timbres and inflection (the "bending" of notes), which in turn demand a more simple and straightforward harmonic language, one which acts more as a background framework or, as it were, coathanger on which the real sonic complexities and "meaningful" elements in the sounds of popular music can be "hung."

While these technical distinctions between classical and popular music are, of course, ones of degree rather than being clear-cut and absolute (see Chester, 1990, p. 316; Middleton, chapter 11, this volume), the first reason why Willis's optimism is largely unfounded is that the tools of music theory and music analysis cannot "get at" questions of timbre and inflection, two of the most expressive elements in most genres of popular music. The second reason is much more straightforward. Because the overwhelming assumption in musicology has been that classical music is essentially asocial, with its "meanings" intrinsic to its sounds, the tools of music theory and music analysis carry no provision for linking music analysis to questions of music's social meanings.

QUESTIONS OF TEXT AND CONTEXT

Those scholars of popular music who have wished to analyze its sounds in the belief that they are of consequence to popular music's meanings have been faced with two problems: how to find analytical tools relevant to the sounds important to expression in popular music, and how to relate the findings of such analysis to questions of context – to those social, economic, political, and cultural processes external to popular music's sounds but nonetheless important in influencing their form and functioning. This question of the relationship of textual processes to those of context has been particularly pressing in popular music studies. Most popular music is obviously, evidently, and undeniably social in its significance. Moreover, a significant proportion of the popular music studied by popular music scholars has not been from other times and places but from the here-and-now of the scholar. Questions to do with the relations between context and text cannot be deferred to unfold in the fullness of academic time. This has resulted in questions of text and context being more inescapably and sharply focused than they have been in musicology or, for that matter, ethnomusicology. This has also meant that the pressure has been intense to examine musical affects as experiences mediated essentially through social and cultural processes.

One response to this pressure, of course, has been to view the sounds of popular music as "innocent" until interpellated into the meanings of the social world that are assumed to be constituted fundamentally through language. It might be tempting to view this approach on the part of some popular music scholars with a background in sociology or communication as "the easy way out," since they seldom possess much of the knowledge derived from music theory and music analysis possessed by those with a background in musicology. This, however, would be unfair, not only because the relevance of this knowledge to most genres of popular music is partial, but also because it is undeniable that contextual matters, including what people say about popular music, are highly relevant to popular music's meanings. This notwithstanding, however, most popular music scholars with a background in musicology feel that popular music's sounds do play an important role in popular music's meanings, and some have attempted to understand why and how. In this, they have had to step rather carefully between Barthes's notion of music as text and the conventional musicological wisdom on music as text, which sees "good" music (which is to say, classical music) as inherently asocial, with its meanings intrinsic to its sounds.

165

THE ANALYSIS OF SOUND AS TEXT IN POPULAR MUSIC

Attempts to understand the sounds of music as socially meaningful have occurred largely within the English- rather than French-speaking world, and for this reason have been based on a rather different kind of cultural theory. This theory acknowledges the importance of Saussure's work on language but integrates it in a way that allows a far greater role for human agency than does the work of the French cultural, linguistic, and social theorists who followed in the footsteps of Saussure. Instead of arguing that language constitutes subjects through the generation of meaning, much work in English-language cultural theory – and particularly within the earlier tradition of British cultural studies – argues that people act culturally in terms of the meanings that the social world holds for them. This means that there is a degree of negotiability in the way that people act both socially and culturally. This social negotiability of cultural meaning rests in turn on a belief not only in the arbitrary character of signification through language, but in the arbitrary character of the generation of meaning through any cultural process or artifact.

Paradoxically, the first scholar to attempt a "social" analysis of popular music's sounds was Willis, a cultural critic. Willis's analyses, to be found in his book *Profane Culture*, are based on the assumption that the two kinds of rock music he analyzed, rock 'n' roll and progressive rock, were politically oppositional. In keeping with the musical and cultural atmosphere of the 1960s and 1970s, Willis believed that the political values of much rock music were in opposition to the dominant political values of industrial capitalism as a way of life. Since classical music was viewed as the music of the social and cultural elite, the implication was that an "attack" by rock music on the established conventions of classical music was the way in which the sounds of rock music could articulate not the substance, but the temporal and spatial structures, of these oppositional values. For Willis, the motorbike culture, which identified powerfully with early rock 'n' roll, "was an attempt to stop or subvert bourgeois, industrial, capitalist notions of time – the basic experiential discipline its members faced [at] work . . . the culture did not attempt to impute causality or logic to things" (Willis, 1978, p. 78). In drawing comparisons with classical music, Willis then went on to analyze early rock 'n' roll in the following way:

> The normal rules of progression, and forms of cadence, are replaced in rock 'n' roll by a kind of anarchy . . . by avoiding conventional tonality, the music

can also avoid the great emotional structures of crescendo and decrescendo which are the essential characteristics of classical . . . music . . . the disregard for tonality in rock 'n' roll further enables it to experiment with repetition and "timelessness" – in a sense to experiment with the "space," the here and now, instead of the ordered time dimension of music. (Willis, 1978, p. 77)

Willis goes on to ask: "What is the relationship of this internal structure to the culture and style of the motorbike boys?" His first answer is that rock 'n' roll is a music based on rhythm, a music for dancing. Most crucially, he says:

this music allows for the return of the body in music, and encourages the development of a culture based on movement and confidence in move- ment. The classical European tradition has steadily forced the body and dancing out of music, and made it progressively unavailable to the masses, and progressively harder to dance to. The absolute ascendancy of the beat in rock 'n' roll firmly establishes the ascendancy of the body over the mind – it reflects the motorbike boys' culture very closely. (Willis, 1978, p. 78)

By establishing structural parallels or homologies between the characteris- tics of rock 'n' roll's sounds and characteristics of the motorbike boys' culture, Willis was able to demonstrate in a seminal fashion how an analysis of popular music's sounds could be linked to popular music's social meanings and in a way that went behind the back of language. Willis, in other words, was not talking about the content or substance of meanings but about their structures, their shapes, and their textures, elements of meaning that the sounds of music are eminently suited to articulate in terms both of their timbres and of the relations they have with one another harmonically, melodically, and rhythmically.

However, while my brief summary does not do justice to Willis's analy- ses, Willis may well have overstated the case for the way in which rock 'n' roll subverted the established conventions of classical music. This is sug- gested in some of my own work, in which I attempted to lay out a basic scheme in terms of which the social meanings of classical music as well as of many genres of popular music could be understood (Shepherd, 1991). A central component of my analysis was the notion of the "harmonic– rhythmic framework" – three chords, the tonic, the dominant and the subdominant, together with either four or three beats to a measure – which, I argued, with the central, organizing role of the keynote, could be viewed as a basic sonic code for the hierarchical structure of industrial capitalism, the social environment within which most people lived their lives. This framework, I argued, was handled differently according to the location within society of the people primarily responsible for the production and consumption of different kinds of music. Thus, with classical music, the framework was consciously manipulated in an "explicit," "external" manner commensurate with the position of those with power and influence in society. The capacity to manipulate the framework in this way seemed, in other words, to be commensurate with the capacity, if not the requirement incumbent upon such people, to manipulate and administer elements of the social environment in order to ensure its continued existence.

By contrast, this framework, whether musical or social, was something that most people other than the elite "lived within." It was something that was unremarkable and taken for granted as people concentrated more through music on their individual identity. These kinds of musical and social relations, I argued, were present in terms of social class but were also inflected by issues of ethnicity. Thus, I argued, in the sounds of the Delta blues from the state of Mississippi, where there was in the early part of the twentieth century a much higher proportion of black people to white in comparison with the state of Texas, and where, as a consequence, there was a fear of black people on the part of white people, which resulted in enforced segregation, the harmonic–rhythmic framework drawn initially from classical music was less in evidence. There was much more emphasis on a heavily inflected basic driving pulse, as well as on a declamatory and again heavily inflected style of singing, in which – and again this seems to be socially relevant – the melody rises to a plateau beyond which it cannot seem to pass, and then descends again. These different sonic characteristics of Delta versus Texas blues can be heard, on the one hand, in Charley Patton's "Pony Blues" and Willie Brown's "M & O Blues," and, on the other, in Blind Lemon Jefferson's "Long Lonesome Blues."

The fact that the harmonic–rhythmic framework is in little evidence in the Delta blues does not, however, mean that it has in some way been avoided or subverted. It means that it is still there in the background – not articulated in full, but a presence, and an important presence, nonetheless. More generally, while it is true that many of the sonic elements of rock 'n' roll – not least the vocal qualities of performers such as Elvis Presley, Buddy Holly, and Eddie Cochrane – "rub up" against the basic characteristics of the harmonic–rhythmic framework and in so doing "challenge" them socially as well as musically, it has to be understood that the absence of such characteristics in the face of challenge does not necessarily translate into subversion. There are, in fact, few sonic characteristics in popular music as a whole that are incommensurable with the basic features of the harmonic–rhythmic framework (three chords, together with rhythms built on combinations and permutations of "two" and "three"). While rock music may have been successfully oppositional in terms of style and maybe culture, there is little evidence that it has been successfully oppositional in terms of politics or broader social structures.

If "the framework" speaks to the features of the social environment, then it would seem that timbral qualities and melodic, rhythmic, and timbral inflection speak to a sense of the personal, to a sense of identity that is both individual and cultural. This leads to those sonic elements of popular music where the tools of music theory and music analysis can be of little assistance, elements to which Willis points in observing that the sounds of music act on people not only cerebrally through their ears but, as importantly if not more importantly, through their bodies in a more complete corporeal sense. In claiming that early rock 'n' roll "allows the return of the body in music," Willis in fact points to the way in which the sounds of music touch us both externally and internally.

Our bodies are inevitably implicated in the movements necessary for the playing of instruments and even more so in the actions necessary for vocalizing, where various chambers of the body, such as the lungs, the sinus passages, and the mouth, become involved through processes of amplification in the finest nuances of tone production. Since these movements and actions are as much subject to processes of social and cultural constitution as are any other aspects of awareness and subjectivity, they are experienced sympathetically, empathetically, and vicariously when music is heard. Thus, it can be argued, the raspy, constricted sound of the "macho male," which can be traced in the history of popular music from the voice of Willie Brown up through Mick Jagger and Bruce Springsteen to those of many hard rock, heavy metal, punk, and thrash singers, is, quite literally, "all mouth": the sound is forced through the mouth to the exclusion of the lungs and sinus passages. It can be argued that it signals a shutting down of the body, a repression and containment of emotions symptomatic of this gender position, which, when heard, occasions a similar, vicarious response in listeners. It is for this reason that the social, cultural, and personal messages articulated through the sounds of popular music, or, indeed, any kind of music, are *felt* as well as being recognized in a more cerebral fashion. Converse arguments can be made for the stereotypic sound of the gender position of the "woman as nurturer" – a warm and earthy tone that results from the use of all the resonating chambers of the body, but in particular those of the lungs. In this case – and the vocal qualities of Anne Murray as a singer provide a good example – the body, it could be argued, is not shut down but is more open, symptomatic of a willingness to engage in sympathetic conversation (see chapter 7 in this volume).

As with timbre, little work has been carried out on inflection. One notable exception is, however, to be found in some of the work of Charles Keil. Keil (1994, p. 96) argues quite straightforwardly that "music, to be personally involving and socially valuable, must be 'out of time' and 'out of tune'." According to this argument, popular and traditional musics emerge as more valuable than classical music. As Keil writes, "it is really only in relatively recent periods of Western music that a peculiarly rationalist approach to [the rational harmonic syntax of classical music] has managed to squeeze the mysteries of musical participation to the furthest corners of our awareness" (pp. 96–7). Keil's work is helpful in elucidating how inflections in popular and traditional musics – the discrepancies from fixed, stable pitches and from rhythms played relentlessly "on the beat" that not only facilitate but invite musical participation – are central to the expressive qualities of such music. Yet his work does not suggest how an analysis of inflections can help in gaining insights into the manner in which personal and cultural meanings are thus articulated. Indeed, Keil's work has been criticized, as has my own and Willis's, for implying that a certain "fall from grace" occurred with classical music, that a somehow natural, human essence was compromised by the advent of modern cultures – of which classical music is understood to be one element – and that various forms of popular music have worked successfully against this.

Linked to this criticism is another: that the "fits" argued for between social and musical characteristics are just too tight and too convenient, symptomatic of presumed powerful organic connections between various cultures and "their" music that are not nearly as exclusive or consistent as might be imagined. The force of this criticism has become readily apparent in the so-called "postmodern" age, when the speed and efficiency with which cultural commodities, including popular music, are spread across the surface of the planet speak to a certain draining of "meaning" as well as to the reception of the same music (or at least the same musical sounds) in significant numbers by widely different cultures. While the analyses of Willis and myself certainly understand the sounds of popular music to be articulating meanings that are constituted socially, there has always been a lingering feeling that we have not completely escaped musicology's insistence on the immanence of music's meanings to music's sounds. There has been a feeling, whether justified or not, that we have believed that music's social meanings are capable of being read from the surface of music's sounds. The path between Barthes and conventional musicology, a path that, the above criticisms notwithstanding, has been trodden with care, is nonetheless a path that has been trodden uneasily.

POPULAR MUSIC TEXTS: SOUNDS, WORDS, AND IMAGES

Relatively little work has been undertaken on issues of textuality in relation to the sounds of popular music, partly because of the difficult questions raised by any attempt to analyze popular music's sounds, partly because there are relatively few scholars who have entered this field. As Roy Shuker observes in his book *Understanding Popular Music* (1994, p. 136), "there is an acknowledged absence of textual analysis of rock in terms of the music itself . . . rock critics remain essentially preoccupied with sociology rather than sound." Implicit in Shuker's observation is the idea that textuality in popular music is not a question of music's sounds alone. Popular music has always involved live performance situations. But unlike more contemporary performances of classical music, with their hushed concert halls and musicians in uniform black and white, these performances have customarily stressed the color and bustle of movement, images, and performer–audience interaction. Words, in the form of lyrics, have also been central to the practice of popular music. Classical music, by contrast, tends to be more dominantly instrumental in character. When classical music does use words, they tend to be words that are "set" to music, often having an independent, previous existence as some form of literary prose or as poetry, rather than being words that are conceived as an integral part of the creative process, as lyrics tend to be in the composition of popular songs. It is therefore more accurate to think of popular music's texts as being comprised not just of sounds but of musical sounds in conjunction with words, images, and movement.

One reason for the idea that music's texts are essentially sonic in character is the way in which classical music – predominantly instrumental – became separated from its surrounding ecology through the isolated authority of the score. Notation in popular music in the form of sheet music – popular music's first commodity form – enabled a similar separation of "the music" from the realities of performance, a separation further perpetuated by the advent of the recording as the pre-eminent commodity

171

form for the remainder of the twentieth century. However, the use of music in conjunction with films in the silent era, together with the reliance of Hollywood on film musicals during the 1930s, the advent of "soundies" in the late 1930s and 1940s, the advent of videos in the 1980s, and the increasing interplay between films, television, videos, and music of the last twenty years or so of the twentieth century have all served as a reminder that, at heart, the character of popular music's textuality lies in performance rather than in any commodity form (see chapter 14 in this volume). It is perhaps appropriate, then, that given the paucity of studies on popular music's sounds, Shuker spends more time in his book discussing lyrics and videos than he does sounds.

A prevalent trend in the analysis of popular music – one, indeed, that rests on "sociology rather than sound" – has been content analysis, in which the lyrics of popular songs are taken to unproblematically reveal prominent social trends, particularly where young people are concerned. However, as Frith (1988, p. 107) observes, "content analysts are not innocent readers and there are obvious flaws in the method . . . they treat lyrics too simply: the words of all songs are given equal value; their meaning is taken to be transparent." Further, words are treated in isolation in much the same way that popular music's sounds have been treated. "No account is given of [lyrics'] actual performance," writes Frith, "or their musical setting" (ibid.).

There is an equally disconcerting assumption on the part of content analysts that popular music fans actually listen, or listen in full, to the lyrics of popular songs. This appears to be not always the case, a point illustrated by Shuker in his discussion of Tammy Wynette's song "Stand By Your Man." The chorus of this song, writes Shuker (1994, p. 138), "was generally interpreted as a simple clarion call for women to subserviently support their male partners, reducing the woman's role essentially to a physical one, providing 'arms' and 'something warm'." This standard interpretation has elsewhere been used to point to the complexities of popular song when both music and lyrics are taken into consideration in textual analysis. Tammy Wynette's voice, it has been argued, hard and uncompromising in the singing of the chorus, seems to contradict this presumed message in support of traditional gender roles.

The lyrical interpretation becomes somewhat different, however, if close attention is paid to the lyrics of the verses. The first verse, comments Shuker (1994, p. 139), presents "the hardships women face in their relationships with men . . . while the last line is a neatly condescending assertion of women's superior gender status." The reason for "standing by your man" now emerges in terms of the necessity of supporting men as unreliable, unpredictable, and weak, rather than in terms of the maintenance and reproduction of stereotypic gender roles. With this interpretation, it is interesting to note the change in Tammy Wynette's voice from the verse – where it is softer, more open, even at times hesitant – to the chorus, where it does become harder and more uncompromising, symptomatic of the strength necessary to support weak men rather than showing weakness in the face of male superiority.

The fact that a more superficial interpretation of "Stand By Your Man" has had greater currency does seriously challenge the assumption that fans listen closely to lyrics. If they do not, however, but it remains the case that lyrics are important (witness the small number of instrumental pieces that make the charts), then the question arises as to what role words in songs do play. Frith indicates an interesting direction in answering this question, which paradoxically reasserts the importance of sounds in music. In songs, he writes:

> words are a sign of the voice. A song is always a performance and song words are always spoken out, heard in someone's accent. Songs are more like plays than poems; songs work as speech and speech acts, bearing meaning not just semantically, but also as structures of sound that are direct signs of emotion and marks of character. Singers use non-verbal as well as verbal devices to make their points – emphases, sighs, hesitations, changes of tone. (Frith, 1988, p. 120)

Thus, if fans do not always "listen" to lyrics, it may be concluded that it is because they are not always listening to the semantic content or meaning of the lyrics, but are distracted, seduced by non-verbal, even musical, elements of the lyrics to which they are in fact listening just as attentively. Frith's perceptive observations on the role of lyrics in popular song demonstrate just how thin the line between words and music is, and how integral these two textual elements are to the success of individual songs.

A similar conclusion can be reached concerning videos. Much has been made of the way in which the advent of videos signaled the arrival of postmodernism in popular music. During the last twenty years of the twentieth century, videos have been able to take advantage of the digitization of images and their computerized manipulation to create images that are "unreal" (for example, people fading magically in and out of scenes), and sequences of images that are random and unrelated. The argument has been made that this ability to suspend narrative reality signals not only a postmodern dissolution of the traditional lines between reality and unreality, but a postmodern decentering of the subject. In other words, unreal, random, and unrelated images are taken to lead to the fragmentation of subjects through the way in which they are constituted by such videos, as well as to a questioning of subjects' "normal" sense of identity. But what this textual analysis forgets, as Andrew Goodwin (1987, pp. 41—2) observes, is that

> musical rhythms and timbres . . . hold together otherwise incoherent visual texts . . . equat[ing] non-realist visual imagery with textual destabilisation . . . reproduces as an analysis of music video a notion that has often been used as an excuse to avoid rational engagement with music itself: like the pop analysts who see music as non-representational and therefore more or less impervious to verbal description, postmodernists sometimes seem to be arguing that music video is not just beyond realism, but somehow outside the world of representation altogether.

If words, images, and movement as elements of popular music's texts are linked in powerful ways to popular music's sounds in a manner that we do not yet fully understand, then, to echo arguments presented at the beginning of this chapter, we may conclude that, although music can be textual, it is textual in some very distinctive ways.

CONCLUSION

Even if we can begin to move in this direction in thinking of popular music as textual, the fact that popular music's textuality is comprised of sounds, words, images, and movement reminds us of its staggering complexity as well as the way in which various dimensions of this complexity can reach out into the world of context. To think of popular music only as text, even if linked to and influenced by the social, economic, political, and cultural processes of context, is to think of it in a very narrow, if not anemic fashion. It is, in fact, quite difficult to draw a clear distinction between popular music as text and its contexts. Popular music performances, the occasions which remind us of popular music's textual complexities, serve as an illustration of the way in which textual properties merge almost seamlessly with the contextual processes of production and consumption. This merging has been illustrated beautifully by Deena Weinstein in her book, *Heavy Metal: a Cultural Sociology* (1991), where she describes heavy metal concerts.

Weinstein uses the concept of "backstage" to describe the rational, orderly, and sequenced work characterized by a very high division of labor that leads up to the concert (not all of this work is by any means literally "backstage"). She then contrasts this with the much more emotional and subjective world of the "frontstage": the audience "getting pumped for the concert" before arriving at the venue, the audience molding itself into a community, consuming beer and drugs, wearing the appropriate apparel, saving seats for others, not blocking the view of others, and so on. These very different, almost antipathetical, worlds need each other, as Weinstein points out, and it is the job of the performers, the musicians, to connect them meaningfully while keeping them quite distinct and separate from one another.

As providers of the complex texts of popular music, musicians – through carefully monitored and different modes of behavior that have to face in two directions at once – connect the worlds of popular music production and consumption and thus the institutions in which processes of production and consumption are anchored. As well as complex texts, the performance of popular music, whether live or pseudo-live, involves ritual, the acting out of institutionalized forms of behaviors that become convention for producers, musicians, and consumers alike. It is the marrying of the complex texts of various styles of popular music in their customary forms to the customary forms of conventional behavior that provides a feel for the concept of genre in popular music studies, a concept relatively undeveloped compared to its use in the literary disciplines and other disciplines such as film studies. In subsuming matters of popular music textuality, the notion of genre at the same time provides the necessary pathway between "text" and "context."

This is not to detract from the centrality of popular music's sounds in understanding popular music's significance. As Peter Wicke has argued, the sounds of popular music offer a structured ground capable of accepting a range of meanings – but certainly not all meanings, as the sounds of language in principle can – which may then be mediated by other textual elements, such as words, images, and movements, as well as by the conventions of genre and various processes of production and consumption. If the notion of text in popular music is to remain central and of value, then it has to be agreed with Shuker that "there has been a too ready willingness to dismiss musicology as having little relevance to the study of rock." But it also has to be agreed that musicology needs to shift its

175

ground, as Shuker points out, from "[neglecting] the social context, [emphasizing] the transcription of music (the score), and [elevating] harmonic and rhythmic structure to pride of place." Although many questions have to be answered if musicology's ground is to be thus shifted, we are beginning to see indications of how this might be done.

Resources

Chester, Andrew (1990) Second thoughts on a rock aesthetic: The Band. In Simon Frith and Andrew Goodwin (eds), *On Record: Rock, Pop, and the Written Word*. New York: Pantheon, pp. 315–19 (originally published 1970).

Engh, Barbara (1993) Loving it: music and criticism in Roland Barthes. In Ruth A. Solie (ed.), *Musicology and Difference: Gender and Sexuality in Music Scholarship*. Berkeley: University of California Press, pp. 66–79.

Feld, Steven (1994) Communication, music, and speech about music. In Charles Keil and Steven Feld, *Music Grooves: Essays and Dialogues*. Chicago: University of Chicago Press, pp. 77–95 (originally published 1984).

Frith, Simon (1988) Why do songs have words? In *Music for Pleasure: Essays in the Sociology of Pop*. New York: Routledge, pp. 105–28.

Frith, Simon (1990) What is good music? *Canadian University Music Review/Revue de musique des universités canadiennes*, 10(2), 92–102.

Goodwin, Andrew (1987) Music video in the (post) modern world. *Screen*, 28(3), 36–55.

Greene, Gordon (1972) From mistress to master: the origins of polyphonic music as a visible language. *Visible Language*, 3, 229–52.

Keil, Charles (1994) Participatory discrepancies and the power of music. In Charles Keil and Steven Feld, *Music Grooves: Essays and Dialogues*. Chacago: University of Chicago Press, pp. 96–108 (originally published 1987).

Keil, Charles and Feld, Steven (1994) *Music Grooves: Essays and Dialogues*. Chicago: University of Chicago Press.

Shepherd, John (ed.) (1990) Alternative musicologies/Les musicologies alternatives. Special issue of *Canadian University Music Review/Revue de musique des universités canadiennes*, 10(2).

Shepherd, John (1991) *Music as Social Text*. Cambridge: Polity Press.

Shuker, Roy (1994) *Understanding Popular Music*. London: Routledge.

Tagg, Philip (1979) *Kojak – 50 Seconds of Television Music: towards the Analysis of Affect in Music*. Güteborg: Skrifter från Musikvetenskapliga Institutionen.

Tagg, Philip (1991) *Fernando the Flute: Analysis of Musical Meaning in an ABBA Mega-Hit*. Liverpool: Institute of Popular Music.

Weinstein, Deena (1991) *Heavy Metal: a Cultural Sociology*. New York: Lexington.

Wicke, Peter (1990) Rock music: dimensions of a mass medium – meaning production through popular music. *Canadian University Music Review/Revue de musique des universités canadiennes*, 10(2), 137–56.

Willis, Paul (1978) *Profane Culture*. London: Routledge.

Wishart, Trevor (1977) Musical writing, musical speaking. In John Shepherd, Phil Virden, Graham Vulliamy, and Trevor Wishart, *Whose Music? A Sociology of Musical Languages*. London: Latimer, pp. 125–53.

13
Images

Cynthia Fuchs

For myself, I no longer hear new music except visually; if it pleases me, I inscribe it on a staff in the brain, photograph that notation, take it home, and develop film which can be preserved indefinitely. This manner of recall is not, I think, unusual to many composers.

Ned Rorem, *Settling the Score*, p. 228

Question: Are you really scary or is it an image?
Marilyn Manson: This is the way I look, people can perceive it how they like.

Marilyn Manson, AOL Chat, April 30, 1996

Madonna. Chuck Berry. Luciano Pavarotti. Tupac Shakur. Guns 'N' Roses. Will Smith. The Spice Girls. Amadeus. Bob Marley. Garth Brooks. Miles Davis. David Bowie. Metallica. The Sorcerer's Apprentice. Patsy Cline. Missy Elliot. Marilyn Monroe. Marilyn Manson. The Beatles. The Artist Formerly Known as Prince. Elvis Presley. Whitney Houston. The Jets and the Sharks. Bessie Smith. The Partridge Family. The Wu-Tang Clan. Robert Johnson. David Lee Roth. Billie Holiday. Puffy Combs. Judy Garland. Michael Jackson.

It is hard to think about any of these musical performers or performances without images: Mickey Mouse battling floods of water, Miles Davis bent intensely over his trumpet, The Beatles walking across Abbey Road. For all the sound, rhythm, and noise that music brings into the world, it also generates and is generated by graphic elements – notes on staff lines, artists on a lighted stage, art on album covers, advertisements on the Web – that help to initiate and organize its effects. From Greek tragedies and Italian operas to Tin Pan Alley concerts, from go-go shows in Washington, DC, and Celine Dion's Christmas Special to productions by Judy Garland and Mickey Rooney in an Andy Hardy movie, music and images have been linked.

In this chapter, I examine the relationship between popular music and images, especially the cultural, political, and commercial dimensions of this relationship. I look at links among artists, consumers, and images, as well as the perpetually mutating correlations of music and images with notions of authenticity, identity, and signification. In order to examine these complex configurations of popular music and images, I consider three specific cases: Madonna, Prince, and the Wu-Tang Clan.

Popular music's connections to images are varied and flexible as much as they are fixed in and by collective awareness. Consider, for example, maximum-blonde Madonna gyrating in a Gaultier bullet-bra, Michael Jackson moonwalking at Motown 25, Judy Garland strutting in sheer stockings and cocked fedora, Prince loving his guitar, Pavarotti booming, David Lee Roth jumping, Will Smith getting jiggy with it. But think again, and in your mind these well known images morph into different shapes, colors, sizes, and attitudes. Madonna is dark-haired in S/M gear, an Afroed Michael Jackson is performing "Dancing Machine" with his brothers, a pigtailed Judy Garland is singing "Over the Rainbow" to Toto. Such second thoughts underline the fact that images are, as Donna Haraway observes, produced in part through and by processes of consumption, experiences of perception, listening and viewing subjects in specific situations. She writes:

> The topography of subjectivity is multi-dimensional; so, therefore, is vision. The knowing self is partial in all its guises, never finished, whole, simply there, and original; it is always constructed and stitched together imperfectly, and therefore able to join with one another, to see together without claiming to be another. (Haraway, 1991, p. 193)

It is this "knowing self" that shapes relations between music and images in ways both insidious and intense. Consider, for example, what you think you know about Michael Jackson, as this knowledge is arranged in and by music and images. Where is the line between knowledge and self? Which constitutes which? If at one moment you think of Michael Jackson singing "Billie Jean" on the television special Motown 25, at another you may recall him as part of the Jackson 5, performing "Dancing Machine." And then, you might conjure up still other Michaels, in a hyperbaric chamber, with his face covered in a surgery mask, kissing Lisa Marie Presley for a screaming MTV audience, posing in *Life* magazine with his son. While any one of these images constitutes something to know about Michael Jackson, something that affects your experience of his music, each also affects the others. The succession of images (whether in chronological order or not) is attached at every point to music. Even those images that seem definitively private have, eventually, everything to do with his career, his public persona, and his music (for example, he has used his seeming torment by the press as source material in "Leave Me Alone," "Black or White," and "Scream"). As representations of himself, his music and his images remain as available and as elusive as any possible concept of his emotional, spiritual, or social existence.

Michael Jackson may be the extreme example that illustrates the rule. If, on the one hand, it seems sensible to acknowledge that music and images are interdependent (especially given their marriage in marketing campaigns, films, and music videos), on the other hand such a notion can seem to show disregard for disciplinary distinctions. At one of my first presentations at an academic conference on popular music, I showed clips from MTV and BET videos during my analysis of "white boys" who explore and exploit "black styles" of music (the Beastie Boys, the Jon Spencer Blues Explosion, and others). At the end of my presentation, a member of the audience questioned the relevance of videos to popular music. I wasn't surprised at this. In fact, I anticipated that a musicologist might wonder about my appearance at the conference, considering my professional training in film and other visual media studies.

At the same time that I understood the question, however, I found it difficult even to begin to answer, because the question assumed a clarity of distinctions between genres, experiences, and sensations, not to mention performing and consuming practices, that seemed impossible to maintain. Still, I understand concerns that "popular" music becomes popular largely as a function of its availability – in particular, its visibility in glossy magazines like *Rolling Stone, The Source,* or *Vibe,* and online magazines like *Addicted to Noise.* I also understand the often expressed worry that the relationship between music and images is increasingly out of balance, the worry that a mass cultural (read: crass, commercial, "too" popular) privileging of images dilutes the so-called purity of music. John Fiske (1994) frames the problem rather aca-dramatically, saying that music television amounts to "the foregrounding of the signifier over the signified." Put another way, as does Will Straw, a contributor to this volume, music videos can seem to make " 'image' more important than the experience of the music itself" and "result in a diminishing of the interpretive liberty of the individual music listener" (Straw, 1993, p. 3). These anxieties, Straw continues, have to do with fears that "rock music," once conceived as a resistant, underground cultural force, is being absorbed and manipulated by the mass medium of television (p. 4). Straw worries that resistance is impossible in the new medium, that assimilation is the cost of representation and accessibility. Drawing from Dick Hebdige's and Iain Chambers's well known analyses of bricolage and appropriation as means for consumers to undermine dominant meanings (through recontextualization), Straw finds in "post-punk youth culture" – as filtered through music videos – a "tribalist pluralism" rather than a "genuinely subversive element" (p. 19).

This common complaint overlooks the multiplicity of consuming practices, the ways that fans use music videos as background noise, convenient forms of advertising, new narrative models, or style inspirations. But such multiplicity is, nonetheless, quite clearly marked for those who would recognize it. And there is perhaps no artist who has understood so quickly and completely the significance and variety of representations offered by MTV than Madonna, who ascended, for the first time anyway, during the 1980s, which serve as Straw's focus. Certainly, her creative combinations of music and images to effect a series of self-images are well known. Accused of lacking vocal, instrumental, and songwriting talent and exploiting her own body as a hypersexual (that is, too visible) object, Madonna has intelligently (and sometimes cynically) turned such critiques back on her wannabe detractors, reabsorbing condemnations as part of her own promotional machinery. Perhaps most famously, she turned the tabloid revelation that she had once posed nude into a "so what?" campaign, incorporating *New York Post* headlines into her stage show at the time. For most of her career, her music has been a function of her image. She has changed musical styles repeatedly, sometimes starting trends and sometimes, as with her 1998 album *Ray of Light*, following them. What remains constant with Madonna, however, is her self-assured, room-filling personality – or should I say "image" – an image represented in the 1991 documentary *Truth or Dare* (directed by Alek Keshishian) and her press materials and interviews.

It wasn't always so. Word has it that in the beginning, back in 1981 or so, when Madonna's self-titled debut single was released, her label decided to leave her picture off the album cover. As Amy Robinson (1993, p. 340) recounts, "According to . . . sources, Warner Studios had assumed that Madonna was black and attributed her popularity in the Black and Latino communities to a similar misconception." In this instance and others having to do with Madonna, Robinson points out, identification is aligned with consumption, such that Madonna's "black" sound is credited with selling her music to audiences of color. And even after her image

181

was released (i.e. she was outed as white), Madonna went on – in interviews and performances – to identify with black cultural signs, events, and characters, suggesting that she early on comprehended the importance of crossover appeals. This is not only a matter of broadening or multiplying niche markets; it is an astute business strategy. Even before the explosion of dance and hip-hop, white consumers often desired black-identified musical products.

This desire initially helped to launch Madonna's career. By the time of her video "Vogue," however, her use of black images and styles was wearing thin. In 1989, Madonna's song and video "Vogue" were enormously popular: the video features Madonna and her dancers (black, Latino, Asian, white) posing in expensive evening wear (gowns and tuxedos), their hands framing their perfectly made-up faces, their gestures precise, their expressions ravishing. These moves were lifted, with no effort to disguise the sources, from the practice of voguing then popular among black and Latino gay communities in New York City. As it happened, *Paris Is Burning* – Jennie Livingston's documentary on these communities, their houses, and balls – was released at the same time that "Vogue" was in heavy rotation, so that comparisons and accusations were easy to make. The central problem was that the moves were glamorized in old-school Hollywood fashion – filmed in soft-focus black and white, deeply and artfully shadowed, and carefully composed in close-up shots – and accompanied by lyrics extolling the dazzling visual wonders of white movie stars, including Greta Garbo, Jean Harlow, Marilyn Monroe, Rita Hayworth, even Fred Astaire. These allusions to white icons and contexts raised questions about Madonna's respect for the black and Latino artists and transgendered individuals who created voguing as a means to act out dreams of wealth, luxury, and upper-class "white" experiences. These doubts led to others, especially concerning her self-declared authentic investments in AIDS prevention and queer activism (causes she often and very publicly supports).

Such attention to Madonna's authenticity might be considered ironic, given that she has, to an extent, made her career out of conspicuous artifice, celebrations of pop faddishness, and explicit critiques of institutional Christianity, nuclear-familial structures, celebrity worship, and educational systems. You might say that Madonna-marketing practices have long since given up on notions of authenticity or, rather, that they have focused closely on it to reveal its cracks and tricks. Most often, Madonna is presented as a powerhouse of glorious fakery, a blatantly ambitious non-blonde, a whiz at self-promotion, and a cunning survivor. These qualities are managed visually such that her many incarnations, facades, and moods have become, ironically, her trademark image: she has no fixed look. Madonna's enthusiasm and talent for self-reinvention might be said to ally her with the voguers she emulates in the "Vogue" song and video in the proposition that image is as important as depth or, more precisely, that there is no difference between them. So, to those who would complain that Madonna lacks genuine musical skills (and they might make the same complaint concerning any number of currently and fabulously successful acts, including Janet Jackson and the Spice Girls), we might respond that music and images are codependent elements in constructions of popularity, authenticity, and identity.

Unlike Madonna, The Artist Formerly Known as Prince (TAFKAP) is generally recognized, by industry insiders as well as zealous fans, as a phenomenally talented artist. He plays a number of instruments, sings, dances, composes, runs his own label, and produces music for other artists. Like Madonna, however, TAFKAP has undergone many changes in image and music over the course of his career. Once sexually ambiguous, overtly promiscuous, and (occasionally) expressly bisexual, TAFKAP has recently undertaken to proclaim his spiritual reawakening, in part through his soul-melding with and marriage to Mayte Garcia, in part through his liaison with a Greater Being, and in part through his legal split from Warner Bros. His change has taken unusual forms, namely much-asserted monogamy, heterosexuality, attempts to promote his own material over the Internet, frequent appearances on the Today Show, and a generally more subdued image. He is less outrageous, less aggressively erotic, more talkative, and more fully clothed.

Even when he was Prince, TAFKAP was a master at arranging and rearranging his image, always presuming that his image and music were inextricably linked and, moreover, that they were about performance, play, and varieties of excess rather than the expression of a single or unyielding identity. Surrounding himself with talented musicians, Prince became the swirling center of profoundly energetic and prolific productions, including (eccentric but ambitious) film projects like *Purple Rain* and *Under the Cherry Moon*, the soundtrack for Spike Lee's *Girl 6*, and innovative videos, including "Kiss," "7," "Diamonds and Pearls," "Sexy MF," "Gett Off," "Cream," and "Darlin' Nikki" (one of the songs that inspired Tipper Gore to inaugurate the Parents' Music Resource Center and its attending Parental Advisory warning labels for albums).

If TAFKAP perpetually reinvents his integration of music and image, reaching back into history to recreate the ground he works from, the Wu-

Tang Clan is a bright new incursion on that ground. The Wu may be the best current example of the indivisibility of image and music. From their inception, the band had "a plan from A to Z," a plan that included signing the individual Wu members to various labels so that each would have his own career in addition to single collaborations with a range of other artists. While the group pull their predominant metaphor and image from the kung fu movies they adore, each member has a distinct personality perpetrated through images and performances: Ol Dirty Bastard is a lunatic, Method Man a charismatic leading man, Raekwon an inventive freestyler, GZA a master fighter and strategist, Ghostface Killah a graceful and creative lyricist, RZA a magnificent producer and life-designer.

The group are serious about images. They have a clothing line (Wu-Wear), a video production company, and a planned, as yet unrealized, "series of Wu-themed entertainment centers." The Wu members are equally serious about their hip-hop legacy. As most hip-hop 101 primers insist, the culture is a combination of style, affect, ideology, and philosophy. Its roots include graffiti writing and tagging, breakdancing, MC-ing, and DJ-ing. Hip-hop was a culture immediately self-conscious, concerned with recording its own history, in lyrics and images. It worked to recover moments lost to black histories (the oppressions felt by black and Latino communities, the police harassment, the social violence), documenting in oral and visual forms the moments and figures who preceded. As Tricia Rose (1996, p. 251) notes, hip-hop expresses an "inherent tension between a desire to preserve personal agency and free will (e.g., fight the power, self-destruction) and a necessary acknowledgment of structural forces that constrain agency (e.g., institutional racism, white supremacy, class oppression)." In expressing this tension – in clothing, demeanor, manners of speaking, language, metaphors, painting, movie-making, and video imaging – hip-hop has transformed the surrounding culture. The "mainstream" has absorbed baggy jeans and the booming jeeps and hummers, the jewelry, the hairstyles, and the swaggers, turned alluring by Tommy Hilfiger and any brand of SUN, Mariah Carey and Whitney Houston, FAO Schwartz and Disney.

In 1998, RZA, one member of the Wu-Tang Clan, reappeared in another guise – Bobby Digital. It is an alter ego and a dream persona, an incarnation that allows him to perform like a seventies pimp Superfly guy with access to enemy-decimating, recording, and imaging technologies that Shaft could never have imagined. Bobby Digital is a figment, all image, but he is also a declaration, the embodiment of a new music made of sampled, just-invented, and barely recognizable sounds, densely layered and luminous. He is imperfect, sometimes resorting to standard sexist images, then laying down a serious, auspicious, and respectful love song that is unusual in the realm of rap. He has taken up the challenge to hip-hop that Tricia Rose observes – its institutional and internal policing by markets and mass-media representations. Bobby Digital is a suave and cagey motherfucker. He can imagine beyond the limits of hip-hop as violent delirium or merchandising Valhalla. For Bobby Digital and the Wu-Tang Clan, hiphop is a way of seeing the future, a way of communicating to "the children" that there are options, that envisioning difference is the first step.

At the moment it is clear that popular music – the industry, the various cultures, the concept – continues to be enthralled with multi-threat performers. Artists such as Brandy, Will Smith, Madonna, Puffy Combs, Ice Cube, Jennifer Love Hewitt, Nas, Queen Latifah, DMX, LL Cool J, Usher, Janet Jackson, Tupac Shakur, Dee Snyder, RZA, and TAFKAP have assembled careers that cross generic and competence boundaries: they sing, produce, choreograph, direct, promote themselves, pitch products, write, and act in film and television. They understand that they are performers and images, creators of music and themselves. And by understanding this about themselves, they understand something more about their culture. They understand, and reflect back without judging, the constructedness of authenticity and identity, the currency of representation, and the value of consumption.

Music and images are social, commercial, and political representations. They correspond, intersect, and inform each other, impure and inviting. They depict, bear, and transform cultures and cultural values. Together, they demonstrate the pervasive interconnections between visual and music cultures, their abiding and intricate appeals to "youth" audiences, and their insistence on their own sense of urgency and immediacy. This sense of time passing suggests a more profound aspect of these intertwining representations – their understanding of and ease with the instability of identity. They do not insist on definitive declarations of self, on absolute and unchanging roots, or even on authentic backgrounds, documentable and fixed. Instead, like those consumers they might be said to represent, they embrace ambiguity and generosity, looking beyond Bennetton to coalitions and diversities. Imagine it: RZA and Zack de La Rocha are captioned "100% Aggression" on the cover of *Rolling Stone*; Lil Kim, Missy Elliot, and Foxy Brown pose in crowns and royal robes under the title "Rap Reigns" on the cover of *Vibe*; Sheryl Crow sings the theme song for the latest James Bond picture; Tricky and Method Man perform while high fashion models stalk the runway on MTV's *Fashionably Loud*; Fiona Apple's picture announces *Spin*'s "Girl Issue"; Busta Rhymes makes a guest appearance on Cosby; Mariah Carey smiles with sexy confidence on the cover of *Cosmopolitan* to demonstrate her new, post-marriage freedom; Marilyn Manson debates with G. Gordon Liddy on ABC's *Politically Incorrect*; and, of course, the Spice Girls spice up everyone's life with a world tour, multiple hit singles and videos, and *Spice World*. These are the images that portray, articulate, enhance, and help to engender popular music today.

Resources

Badsubjects. Listserv@english-server.hss.cmu.edu

Bennett, Tony, Frith, Simon, Grossberg, Lawrence, Shepherd, John, and Turner, Graeme, (eds) (1993) *Rock and Popular Music: Politics, Policies, Institutions.* London: Routledge.

Burnett, Ron (1995) *Cultures of Vision: Image, Media and the Imaginary.* Bloomington: University of Indiana Press.

Fiske, John (1994) *Power Plays, Power Works.* London: Verso.

Frank, Lisa and Smith, Paul (eds) (1993) *Madonnarama: Essays on Sex and Popular Culture.* Pittsburgh: Cleis Press.

Frith, Simon (1996) *Performing Rites: on the Value of Popular Music.* Cambridge, MA: Harvard University Press.

Frith, Simon, Goodwin, Andrew, and Grossberg, Lawrence (eds) (1993) *Sound and Vision: the Music Video Reader.* London: Routledge.

Gray, Herman (1995) *Watching Race: Television and the Struggle for "Blackness."* Minneapolis: University of Minnesota Press.

Haraway, Donna (1991) Situated knowledges. In *Simians, Cyborgs, and Women: the Reinvention of Nature.* New York: Routledge, pp. 183–201.

Hebdige, Dick (1979) *Subculture: the Meaning of Style.* London: Routledge.

Hebdige, Dick (1987) *Cut 'n' Mix: Culture, Identity, and Caribbean Music.* London: Comedia.

Lipsitz, George (1997) *Dangerous Crossroads: Popular Music, Postmodernism, and the Poetics of Place.* London: Verso.

Robinson, Amy (1993) Is she or isn't she? Madonna and the erotics of appropriation. In Lynda Hart and Peggy Phelan (eds), *Acting Out: Feminist Performances.* Ann Arbor: University of Michigan Press.

Rorem, Ned (1988) *Settling the Score.* New York: Harcourt.

Rose, Tricia (1996) Hidden politics: discursive and institutional policing of rap music. In William Eric Perkins (ed.), *Droppin' Science: Critical Essays on Rap Music and Hiphop Culture.* Philadelphia: Temple University Press.

Shuker, Roy (1994) *Understanding Popular Music*. London: Routledge.

Straw, Will (1993) Popular music and postmodernism in the 1980s. In Simon Frith, Andrew Goodwin, and Lawrence Grossberg (eds), *Sound and Vision: the Music Video Reader*. London: Routledge.

14
Performance

David R. Shumway

*Performance has remained the ideal locus of rock authenticity long after it has
ceased to be the real origin of rock music.*

Music has long been defined as a "performing art," the sort of work that is
fully realized only in a specific event, a playing or a performance. A novel
or a sculpture may be experienced differently in separate readings or
viewings, but we take these artistic works to be complete in themselves.
Before the advent of film and sound recording, music and drama had to be
performed anew each time the song or the play could be experienced as
such. On her live album *Miles of Aisles*, Joni Mitchell complains about the
special burden that performing artists face. Responding to the audience's
shouted pleas for songs that they want to hear, she observes that painters
don't have to face such demands. "No one ever said to Van Gogh, 'Paint
Starry Night again, man!'" She then offers up "The Circle Game" as what
seems a concession to the audience's demands, but she also asks the
audience to sing it with her. The result is a kind of performance different
than the one in which Mitchell would have sung by herself. The live
audience perhaps does not get quite what it wanted: the authentic "Circle
Game," the one on the record. On the other hand, a listener to *Miles of
Aisles* experiences a decidedly different version than the one recorded on
the earlier release, *Ladies of the Canyon*. This new version might be regarded as better or worse than the original, but it will have a certain value
because it is not merely a repetition of the studio recording. Mitchell's
words and the live version of her song call attention to the unusual and
complicated meaning which *performance* has within rock 'n' roll.

In ordinary discourse we typically use *performance* to mean a particular
action or course of action undertaken by an individual or group. We speak
of an individual's performance on the job, or a team's performance in a
game or over the course of a season. Used in this way, performance

strongly implies that the action so named is subject to evaluation. In this sense of the term, all forms of music offered for public consumption, whether recorded or live, are performances. Here we might distinguish performance from *practice* or *rehearsal*, where music (or a drama) is played but not for public evaluation or consumption. *Performance* thus carries the sense of being for an audience.

In the performing arts, performance has traditionally been distinguished from the text or work. The former is temporary and to a certain extent ephemeral, while the latter is permanent and is often treated as an essence. William Shakespeare wrote one *Hamlet*, but there can be an infinite number of performances of the play. It is significant that *interpretation* is often used as a synonym for *performance* in this sense. The standard songs of American popular music are often said to be given different interpretations by the various singers who perform them, just as a production or a performance of *Hamlet* can be called an interpretation of it. Notice that this distinction presumes that there is a stable object, the text of the play or song, which varies only in performance. But we all know that critical readings of the text *Hamlet* are at least as varied as performances of it. When one adds music, the problem of distinguishing between text and performance becomes even more complicated. It is safe to say that most listeners do not know Cole Porter's "Night and Day" from reading the music. The song for them is an essence that they know only through the various interpretations with which they are familiar – by Frank Sinatra, Ella Fitzgerald, U2, and so on. The fact that standards are performed by so many interpreters means that they are seldom identified with any one of them.

The different cultural practices associated with musical forms such as classical, jazz, country, and folk all treat the relation of text and performance somewhat differently. Popular standards remain identified with the songwriter, and thus with a sort of ideal text. "Night and Day" remains Cole Porter's no matter how familiar listeners may be with Frank Sinatra's treatment of it. This is not the case with every song with which Sinatra is associated. "Strangers in the Night," for example, is far more identified with the singer than the songwriter. In such an instance, the distinction between text and the recorded performance may disappear. This is at least in part a result of the prominence recording has come to have in popular music. Recording, however, has not had the same impact on classical music. In that practice, performance is strongly opposed to composition. The musical work is identified primarily with the score. Performances are understood as serving the work of the composer, a condition that restricts

189

the latitude interpreters may exercise. Differences in interpretation of classical works thus tend to be rather subtle compared to those in pop or jazz.

In jazz, relations between performance and composition are virtually the reverse of those in classical music practice. Performance is understood as at least an equal site of creativity with composition, and usually the more important one. If a classical performance is usually an interpretation of a canonical work, a jazz performance is most characteristically an improvisation on a familiar but distinctly non-canonical text, usually a popular song. The jazz musician is free to not play the music as the songwriter wrote it because the song is not regarded as having transcendent value. Its status as popular culture, or as entertainment rather than (high) "culture," makes it perfect fodder for the jazz musician's art. Rather than respecting the work, the jazz player transforms it into his or her own creation, which is the performance. The jazz ideal is for each performance to be a unique event, an improvisation that will never be exactly reproduced.

Since jazz and sound recording more or less grew up together, however, jazz improvisations have long since taken on the permanence that recording permits. Moreover, there is also a long history of jazz composition, practiced by such leading performers as Duke Ellington, in which the relations between work and performance adhere much more closely to the classical pattern. Still, the dominant tendency in jazz has been for performance to have priority over composition.

This leads us to one more distinct sense the term *performance* carries now. In this definition, a performance is not *of* a work; it *is* the work. Those works called "performance art," or sometimes just "performance," are not performances *of* something else, a text that could be performed again by someone else. Rather, they exist *sui generis* as performance. This is an odd turn in the history of *performance*, for it abolishes much of the sense of doubleness that we have noted in the term. While performance art is still performance *for* someone – and thus cannot escape the context of evaluation – it is designed to prohibit comparison to an ideal or original. Of course, once performance art became a recognizable genre, such a prohibition could not hold completely, since artists and audience cannot help but generate ideals, conceptions of what performance art should and should not be. Still, even if performance art cannot escape generic expectations, it does represent one extreme toward which *performance* may tend. We will see that rock 'n' roll performance has sometimes tilted toward this extreme.

If *composition* has been the term most strongly opposed to *performance* in jazz and classical music, it is *recording* that holds this place in rock 'n' roll. Composition of music or lyrics is only one element in producing a record, and as rock 'n' roll has developed, it has become increasingly integrated into that process. While, in the 1950s, songwriters like Leiber and Stoller continued to work on the Tin Pan Alley model, providing material for rock performers, The Beatles provided a new model that became dominant in the 1960s. Instead of going into the studio to perform a previously composed song, rock 'n' rollers increasingly "wrote" their songs in the studio as they recorded them. While the process of composition doubtless occurred there, it was no longer the creation of a song represented by notes and lyrics. Rather, it was the album track or single that was now composed, printed notes and lyrics having become a secondary phenomenon. When The Beatles appeared on the scene in the early 1960s, it was something of a scandal that songwriters John Lennon and Paul McCartney could not read music. But by the time The Beatles stopped recording as a group, they and their producer, George Martin, had transformed music production by making the recording studio the primary site of musical creation rather than that of mere reproduction.

Even before composition and record production merged, however, the meaning of *performance* in rock 'n' roll had already begun to evolve away from that of classical and jazz. From the start of sound recording in the late nineteenth century, up until after the Second World War, the music on records was the reproduction of performances. Whether the musicians were performing for a "live" audience, they were performing in real time in the same way they would have had they been on stage. Recordings thus were understood as adding another layer to the double of composition and performance, with the work or text being the essential or original, the recording being a mere derivative or copy, and the performance lying somewhere in between. Today, classical critics can still regard recording simply as a means of recalling live performance, even though most listeners to classical music doubtless hear much more recorded than live music.

There is some justification for this view of classical recording, since it has never stopped reproducing performances. But rock 'n' roll recordings, almost from the beginning, have been products of studio manipulation and not simply the electronic representation of "natural" sound. It has long been recognized that Sam Phillips's Sun Records was a success not only because Phillips had the foresight to record Elvis Presley and Carl Perkins, but also because of the distinctive sound his studio was able to produce. Even before the days of multitrack recording, the particular acoustics of different studios helped to distinguish rock 'n' roll from musically similar styles. The process of recording changed completely with the advent of multitrack technology, for it was now possible to record a song without recording a performance of it. While multitracking was first used to augment or modify the recording of a performance – for example, to add backup vocals or a string accompaniment – it is now common for a song to be built up entirely out of separately recorded tracks, some of which may not originally have been intended for use together. Rock recordings, in other words, are as often as not created of spare parts, pieces of tape that when mixed add up to a new piece of music.

It is curious, then, that the old view of recording as reproduced performance continues to exist in both rock critics' discourse and rock fans' common sense. As Theodore Gracyk (1996, p. 69) has observed, "there is a continuing temptation to regard recorded rock as a mere substitute for – a documentation of – performances we cannot attend." Gracyk blames visual representations of rock for this error: we often see still or moving pictures of musicians performing or seeming to perform, but seldom do we see images of what goes on in the studio. The importance that images continue to give to performance is for Gracyk simply a marketing ploy. While, as I will argue, this claim reflects a misunderstanding of performance in rock, even if we were to accept Gracyk's position, we would still be entitled to wonder why this ploy should work. In my view, the reason it works is that performance has remained the ideal locus of rock authenticity long after it has ceased to be the real origin of rock music. As we will see, this adds significant complexity to the relation of performance and recording.

In Gracyk's aesthetics, the recording serves rock 'n' roll in the same way that the composer's score serves classical music: it is the transcendent object of which performance can only be a mere reflection. It is safe to say that most rock listeners never thought of it this way, and not merely because most of them are not philosophers. Gracyk's view exactly reverses the traditional conception in which the recording is a mere reflection of performance – which itself was a mere instance of the composition. As far it goes, this is accurate enough. Recording has assumed priority over performance in rock. Not only is recorded music the kind people are most likely to encounter these days, but rock fans typically take recordings to be the standard by which live performances are judged. Rock 'n' rollers are expected to be able to reproduce on stage at least a credible imitation of the sound of their recordings, an often difficult demand since the recorded music wasn't performed to begin with. The last thing rock audiences seem to want is the sort of spontaneous transformation of familiar material that is expected in jazz performance. The audience at a jazz performance, at least in theory, hopes for novelty; a rock audience, by contrast, demands the repetition of what it already knows and loves.

Given the priority of the recording, why do rock fans continue to go to concerts at all? What is the point of a "live" repetition of something that can be repeated perfectly *ad infinitum* on the home stereo or portable listening device? To answer these questions, two points need to be understood. The first is that, although recordings have aural priority because they are the means by which any rock 'n' roll song is likely to be first and most often heard, live performance continues to be an aesthetic ideal by which recordings themselves are judged. This ideal is not absolute. Albums such as The Beatles' *Sgt. Pepper's Lonely Hearts Club Band* and *Abbey Road* flaunt their dependence on the studio and eschew entirely the immediacy and imperfections of performance. Yet, over the course of its history, rock 'n' roll has not been dominated by this studio aesthetic, and few successful performers have consistently devoted themselves to it. Rock 'n' roll has oscillated between movements like punk and grunge, which take live sound and performance as their ideal, and those such as techno, which reject performance and embrace the studio. In my view, the aesthetic of live performance has been on the whole the more powerful in defining rock 'n' roll as a practice.

The second point is that rock 'n' roll has never been a purely musical form. Of course, no kind of music exists purely as music. Classical music, for example, has distinctive rituals that define its concerts as much as the music itself does. But rock 'n' roll has from its emergence been especially bound up with non-musical forms of expression. Rock performances are not limited to the playing of music for live audiences. Televised performances were extraordinarily important to rock 'n' roll in the 1950s and 1960s. Movies have presented rock stars in both musical and non-musical performances, and rock videos helped to define the rock 'n' roll of the 1980s.

Moreover, rock stars cannot be considered simply as musical performers even when they are on the concert stage. In addition to the music, rock 'n' rollers have performed "themselves," or rather, the role or roles they inhabit as stars. This is perhaps most obvious in the case of rock 'n' rollers like David Bowie or Madonna, where the star has made a point of inhabiting many different characters or images. But even Mick Jagger's much more consistent persona is one that has been created and developed in collaboration with the other Rolling Stones, their management, the record

193

companies, and many others. No rock star is in performance the same man or woman who exists off stage, even if some stars' personas entail precisely that fiction.

Thus, while records are undeniably rock's most significant product, performance in its various forms is indispensable to rock 'n' roll. To illustrate this point, I will focus on performance in two senses: the performance of music for an audience, whether live or mediated by film or television; and the performance by the star of his or her persona. I will take the King himself as my example. One can understand Elvis Presley's cultural impact only by taking into account his performance in both senses. Elvis is frequently cited for the musical innovation of combining country and R&B to make rock 'n' roll. This assumes that "country" and "R&B" are, like chemical elements, themselves indivisible, when in fact both of these are made up of the same threads of musical practice that are also woven into rock. I don't mean to suggest that Elvis's recordings lacked any musical or aural innovations. I have already mentioned the distinctive sound that Sam Phillips's studio produced, but that is not all. If one compares Elvis's versions of the R&B songs he covered to the originals – for example, "Mystery Train" (Junior Parker), "Good Rockin' Tonight" (Wynonie Harris), or "Hound Dog" (Big Mama Thornton) – it is clear that Elvis makes each of these songs his own, bringing to them not only a distinctive vocal interpretation but a new instrumental arrangement.

These distinctive aspects of Elvis's records were a necessary condition of his rise to stardom, but they were not sufficient. Elvis's performances, first live and then on television, were of at least equal importance. Just as Elvis seemed to have developed the basics of his vocal style prior to his first recording sessions at Sun, he seemed already before his first club date to have taught himself the movements that would distinguish his stage act. And from the first, this act produced the screams from teenage girls that would continue until Elvis gave up the stage in 1958. There is good reason to believe that Elvis's dancing, like his singing, was an adaptation of the styles of black performers such as T-Bone Walker, Wynonie Harris, and Charlie Burse. (The last of these Elvis could have seen regularly at the Gray Mule club on Beale Street in Memphis.) Elvis's innovation was not the general style of his dancing – his wiggling, shaking, and gyrating – but the use of this style in a new context. In the beginning, this new context meant performing for an audience of whites, especially white girls. But the more significant break came with television. Elvis shocked the United States by performing on national television in a style that had previously

194

been available only in small clubs frequented mainly by African-Americans. The television camera itself focused the attention of the audience on his body and its movements.

Elvis's television performances transformed him from a pop singer to a rock star. The key performances in this transformation occurred on the *Milton Berle Show*, especially the one on Elvis's second appearance on June 4, 1956. Elvis had previously appeared six times on the Dorsey Brothers' *Stage Show*, but the *Berle Show* reached a much larger audience. Both shows were broadcast live, but the *Berle Show* performances convey the excitement that Elvis generated in the studio audience. In the June 4 performance, Elvis's dancing was more extreme than it had been on previous television appearances, and he incorporated new gestures, such as pointing at the audience, that may have intensified the exchange of energy between crowd and performer.

Unlike on the *Stage Show* telecasts, however, the audience's response could now be heard, and, more importantly, it could also be seen. The director cut between shots of Elvis and his band and shots of the audience. One adolescent girl is shown several times standing and screaming with a rapt, ecstatic expression on her face. The girl's face tells the television audience how to respond to Elvis. The excitement of the live audience is contagious; it makes the television audience feel the star's power. The images are a perfect illustration of Simon Frith's claim that, in pop concerts, "it's not just the *stars'* emotions on show. The power struggle between stars and fans is what gives concerts their sexual charge" (Frith, 1988, p. 167). Moreover, whether or not Elvis's act was planned in advance down to the last detail, it seems as though he also was feeding off the audience's energy, playing to them, with them, for *them*. It is hard to imagine that anyone who witnessed this performance of "Hound Dog" could have worried about whether it sounded like the record.

We don't need to speculate about the impact of this performance, however. In its wake, cries of outrage arose across America. While it would be a mistake to see these reactions as solely a response to the *Berle Show* performance – negative reaction to Elvis had been growing – this performance was clearly a catalyst for its expression. Berle's network, NBC, received letters of protest, and the various self-appointed guardians of public morality attacked Elvis in the press. As a result, for Elvis's next television appearance, on Steve Allen's show (also on NBC), he was forced to wear tails and sing "Hound Dog" to a live basset hound.

Why had the *Berle Show* performance been so disturbing? For one thing, it was most unusual in the 1950s for a man to display himself as a sexual object, and I have argued at length elsewhere that such display feminized Elvis. Paradoxically, however, the audience reaction seems to have stirred almost the opposite fear. Here in black and white was evidence of the damage this man could do: make our daughters lose their inhibitions. But the daughters clearly liked losing their inhibitions in a safe, imaginary relationship with a star who to them may well have seemed all the safer because he seemed a bit feminine. They went on not only to buy Elvis's records and to see his movies, but also to buy an enormous assortment of Elvis trinkets and paraphernalia. This last phenomenon strongly testifies to the fans' desire to relate to Elvis rather than merely listen to records.

If music were the only thing for which Elvis was valued, if the audience knew Elvis only through the sound of his records, then the response of his fans from 1956 to the present would be impossible to comprehend. To comprehend it, we need to consider not just Elvis in performance of his music, but also his performance of Elvis Presley, rock 'n' roll star. To begin with, it should be noted that Elvis was the first person to play the role of rock 'n' roll star. There were other recording artists emerging about the same time as he did, some of them – Chuck Berry, for instance – arguably making better records. But no rock 'n' roller before Elvis commanded the devotion of enough fans to be called a star.

Stardom is a particular kind of celebrity. A star is not revered only for his or her ability or achievements; fans imagine a personal relationship with the stars they worship. In order for such imaginary relationships to be constructed, the artist cannot appear merely to be a professional, no matter how excellent his or her work. For the star to be a star, he or she must appear as an attractive, winning personality. With the help of his manager, Colonel Tom Parker, and the star-maker machinery of the entertainment industry, Elvis was presented as such a personality.

To say that Elvis performed this personality is not to say that he faked it. Like a performance artist, Elvis was not performing a work distinct from the performance itself. In creating Elvis, he was creating the work. All of the media in which Elvis performed contributed to this work, his star persona. In this performance, the recordings are one element, together with television appearances, concert and club appearances, film acting, and representations in fan and news media. Not all of this performance can be attributed to Elvis's own effort or design, and it is properly understood as a collaboration. Elvis, however, is not only the principal author, but the only actor. His success in this performance is reflected in the enormous longevity of his personality, which continues to attract fans more than twenty years after his death. No phenomenon makes the performative character of Elvis clearer than the impersonators. These people are not known for their musical abilities. The culture's interest in them is not in how they sing or play an instrument, but in their bringing to life the character Elvis Presley first performed.

With the phenomenon of Elvis impersonators, we no longer have performance as an event staged by a professional *for* an audience. Instead, we have an instance of the mass cultural audience taking over and remaking what had been previously a commercially produced object of consumption. The impersonators are fans, members of Elvis's audience, who stage their own performances, eviscerating the distinction between star and audience, sound and dramatic role. Here the stable object performed is no longer the written score but the role of Elvis the King, now (since Presley's death) open to possession by the ambitious fan. From performance evaluated according to its relation to the song text, we have performance as an occasion for the merging of the performer with the ultimate star role of Elvis. The text being performed here is the performer himself – Elvis, or rather, "Elvis," something understood as constructed and liable to reconstruction by actual performers and fans alike, ephemeral but enduring through the fans' actions. If pop music has in the past borrowed its notions of performance from other musics, it distinguishes itself now from the practices of these other musics by its substitution of the performer for the text performed.

However interesting the phenomenon of the Elvis impersonators, we should not be misled into thinking that this is the typical way that popular music is now performed. If performance remains key to the realization of all musics, musics differ in what performance is seen as realizing. Popular music in the twentieth century has embraced a plethora of *performances*, from the presentation of an interpretation of a standard, to the replication of a recording, to the creation of a star persona, and finally to the collaboration of erstwhile performer and fans in reconstituting the performer as star. These forms of performance, available for use by artists and fans, continue to exist simultaneously, making popular music the music richest in the possibilities of performance.

Resources

Carlson, Marvin (1996) *Performance: a Critical Introduction*. London and New York: Routledge.

197

Frith, Simon (1988) *Music for Pleasure*. New York: Routledge.
Frith, Simon (1996) *Performing Rites: On the Value of Popular Music*. Cambridge, MA: Harvard University Press.
Gracyk, Theodore (1996) *Rhythm and Noise: an Aesthetics of Rock*. Durham, NC: Duke University Press.
Palmer, Richard (1977) Towards a postmodern hermeneutics of performance. In Michel Benamou and Charles Caramello (eds), *Performance in Postmodern Culture*. Madison, WI: Coda, pp. 19–32.
Shumway, David R. (1991) Rock & roll as a cultural practice. *South Atlantic Quarterly*, 90, 753–69.
Shumway, David R. (1997) Watching Elvis: the male rock star as object of the gaze. In Joel Foreman (ed.), *The Other Fifties*. Champagne: University of Illinois Press, pp. 124–43.
Taruskin, Richard (1995) *Text and Act: Essays on Music and Performance*. New York: Oxford University Press.

15

Authorship

Will Straw

Authorship is in question these days in part because so much popular music now unfolds within highly specialized cultural niches – complex clusters of influence and cross-fertilization marked by tiny moves ahead or to the side.

In the 1960s, as film critics began to advance claims about the creative autonomy and primacy of directors, they looked outside the cinema for models of authorship. Was the direction of a film like the writing of a novel, many asked: did it involve the inscription of fictional worlds and narrative events upon a blank page? Or was it, rather, like supervising a construction site, working with a blueprint, coordinating the labor of others, and producing a finished product? Might the film director most resemble the conductor of an orchestra, offering personal inflections of pacing and color to a score and performances created by others? Debates over authorship in the cinema acknowledged the multiple kinds of labor and creativity which went into the making of films, but sought to establish a hierarchy among these. Claims that the director stood atop this hierarchy found large numbers of adherents even when the precise function of directors was not always clear. Dissidents who suggested that actors, cinematographers, or producers might be equally entitled to stand there – that they were the real "auteurs" of a film – made their cases without much success.

Music, of course, is different from the cinema in many important ways, but the problem of isolating authorship within it is no more easily resolved. It might be, were we content with simply enumerating the various sorts of creative labor involved in the production of a musical artifact: the composition of a musical piece, the vocal and instrumental performances of it, the arrangement and engineering of that performance as it is recorded, and so on. If ideas of multiple authorship were satisfactory, we might well judge a musical performance in the way that we judge a meal in a restaurant: as resulting from an interplay of skills and practices for which we credit a series of different people. Typically, however, we evaluate a musical recording or concert as the output of a single individual or integrated group. The unique character of music evaluation in this respect stems from the willingness with which we grant this primacy to performers (few would do the same for film or theater). The precise input of composers, producers, engineers, and back-up musicians is, most of the time, unclear to us. In any case, we find it convenient to see such personnel in terms of how they have shaped the performance which we see them as serving (see chapter 14 in this volume).

The muddy complexity of popular music and the cinema has traditionally been invoked to set them against writing or painting, forms in which authorship has seemed less problematic. Novels and paintings seem free, usually, from the messy problems of collaboration and coordination which have haunted these other forms. Both writing and painting involve acts of creation we imagine as solitary; each begins with a blank surface upon which the hand begins to make its imprint. Music and cinema, in contrast, seem more obviously to involve selection from among pre-existing materials already present in the world. With the most minimal analytical distance, however, we can begin to cast these distinctions into doubt. The invention of the printing press helped, with time, to enshrine the name of a book's author as the distinctive form of branding which gave it an identity in the marketplace and in the circulation of creative acts. At the same time, however, the public quality of printed books served to make the circulation of knowledge and ideas a much more collective endeavor. As everyone came to read the same books (or maps, or scientific treatises), each came to respond to – and build upon – these works. The broader fields of knowledge and creativity in which books circulated developed in ways we might imagine in collective terms: each book presumed familiarity with its predecessors, incorporating this prior creative labor as one element in its own comprehensibility. Literary theorists have used the term "intertextuality" to designate this dependence of any one text on the body of texts which precede or surround it. To write is not to confront a blank page but to build upon an existing body of writing. In this respect, it is neither solitary nor the production of meaning from nothingness.

Musical performers often build upon prior performances and thus evoke similar tensions between what is pre-given in the history of a cultural form and what is novel and original in any new performance. These are aesthetic questions, but their implications, as Rosemary J. Coombe has ar-

gued, may sometimes become legal. In conceiving many of her performances, Madonna may have drawn on the music, dress, and postures of
drag subcultures, but there is no widespread sense that these things were
the legal possessions of those subcultures or that her borrowing was an act
of theft. However, when these elements become part of Madonna's own
legally protected performances, their subsequent borrowing by others
may be judged as an act of plagiarism or direct imitation.

More obviously than that of most other cultural forms, the history of
popular music is marked by movement back and forth between collective
tradition and moments of individual transformation of that tradition. We
may acknowledge this as one source of popular music's richness, while
noting the ongoing aesthetic, legal, and economic questions it cannot fail
to raise. Aesthetically, we often look to elements of tradition to supply the
historical depth or socio-cultural "thickness" of a musical performance (as
when we are drawn to the dub reggae influences in Bristol trip-hop).
Legally, we have evolved complex (if dubious) ways of distinguishing
between collectively developed standardized genres (such as Chicago blues
or house music) and instances of plagiarism. In economic terms, the
music industries have helped to develop forms of celebrity through which
collective musical traditions can become the object of protected investments (as when Celtic musicians from the Canadian Maritimes are given
national, televised variety specials.)

The problem of authorship in popular music has normally been reduced
to one of the relationship between songwriter and song. Here, again, we
may search for models elsewhere. Is the singer of a song like the performer
of a theatrical text, inhabiting (while inflecting) a persona whose broad
parameters have already been defined? Under certain circumstances, is the
singer like the spokesperson for a community, giving concrete voice to
themes and styles produced through lengthy, collective processes? If neither of these is entirely satisfactory, it is because we live in an age which
expects that singing will be more than the simple "interpretation" of a
song or embodiment of a collective spirit.

These increased expectations for popular music "authorship" are confounded by a number of qualities of popular music and of the electronically mediated forms in which we typically hear it. For example, the
invention of the electric microphone helped to heighten the experience
of the voice and of its modulations. As Simon Frith has pointed out, the
microphone has come to serve many of the functions of the film close-
up. It not only gave us a new sense of closeness to celebrity performers
but meant that we came to judge them more and more in terms of

201

personal honesty and authenticity and less according to purely technical musical skills. What is now our "normal" experience of hearing singing suggests that personality is present in music in ways which go beyond the simple expression of words created in another time or place. The difference between singing and songwriting has come to feel like an uncomfortable difference, the sign of a potential incompleteness in artistic expression.

Since the Second World War, popular music has worked to resolve this incompleteness in two principal ways. The first is to be found in the move toward performers writing their own music. Here, musical composition has come to be redefined less as the craft of producing new texts according to well established rules and criteria than as part of the building of a coherent public persona. (Much of the time, craft now stands as the ability to carve that personality into textual form.) In addition, the problem of interpretation has found partial resolution through the slow acceptance of the idea of the "career," the body of work through which this personality takes shape. In a circular process, the body of a performer's work endows that performer's personality with a unity, just as the presumption of that unity gives meaning and coherence to the body of work. The sense of a unity allows compositions by the performer to coexist (on albums and in performances) alongside cover versions of songs by others, the cover versions chosen according to affinities about which the former compositions have already taught us. For example, we are prepared for Luna's cover version of Serge Gainsbourg's "Bonnie and Clyde" because their own compositions suggest a cleverness and historical connoisseurship which this choice of cover confirms.

This unity allows, as well, for changes of style in the course of an unfolding career to appear as marks of development or the signs of a productive engagement with the rest of musical culture (rather than as simple adaptation to changing market demands). The shifting thematic concerns and stylistic allegiances of a performer's career now appear to be meaningful in ways which transcend the simple economic story of that career's rising and falling commercial fortunes. We may find David Bowie's engagements with drum 'n' bass in the late 1990s laughable, but we assume they were genuinely intended as part of Bowie's ongoing interest in the music around him, rather than cynically calculated.

In this respect, covering and borrowing have become personalized. Performing the songs or adopting the styles of others might once have been seen largely as the result of performer and songwriter working within a shared cultural "system," or as having established professional relationships. Now, these are increasingly read as gestures of affinity and allegiance meant to illuminate the performer's own creative sensibility. When No Doubt perform the Specials' song "Ghost Town," they are clearly doing more than adopting materials produced within the same professional and cultural system. They are indicating a wide range of affinities – with the tradition of ska, with the early 1980s' moment of ska's revival, with the political project of the song and of the group who first recorded it.

Ideas of authorship are bound up with the commodity status of music in a variety of ways. It is not simply that the performer becomes the hook through which musical performances are given distinctiveness and marketed (as "stars" have long served to differentiate films). Over the long term, the continuity of performer careers is seen as a way of bringing order into the musical marketplace by introducing a particular kind of predictability. The identities of performers help the music industries to plan the future, to see this future as a sequence of new releases that will build upon (and draw their intelligibility from) the activity of the past. Almost as importantly, the continuity of performer careers helps to make the musical past (the record company's back catalogue) more than merely a bunch of individual events. It becomes a complex map of unfolding careers and lines of biographical development, with each event on this map linked to others through the continuity of people's lives. The predictability associated with performer careers is often contrasted to the flimsy, risky quality of short-lived musical fads, which offer quick returns on investment but an uncertain future.

The extent to which ideas of authorship inflect our experience of music has much to do with the channels through which we hear it. Since the 1950s, most radio stations have relied on recorded music as their principal source of programming. Nevertheless, standardized ways of introducing or contextualizing songs have given widely varying levels of importance to performer identities or artist biographies. In North American radio, for example, the degree of prominence accorded to performer identities serves as one of the key criteria according to which programming formats have differed from each other. Top-40 radio embedded the playing of songs in detailed sorts of information which drew attention to a record's rise and fall on the charts. In this, it focused attention on the specific, distinctive characteristics of each record, but the Top-40's emphasis on the single and the chart as a whole detracted attention from the performer's career in which that single was an event. In contrast, the album-oriented rock (AOR) radio of the 1970s located each cut or track within the context of

203

a performer's unfolding career (both past and present). Career retrospective (of Eric Clapton or John Lennon, for example) – sets which included several songs from an album, interviews, and concert broadcasts – all worked to reassert the totality of a performer's oeuvre. Adult contemporary stations are dominated by music in which distinctive vocal styles dominate, and such stations presume a high degree of listener familiarity with a limited number of artists (such as Céline Dion or Whitney Houston).

The story of disco music in the 1970s is full of lessons about the relationship between musical form, music industry strategies, and ideas of musical authorship. From 1973, when the music industries began to invest heavily in disco music, through the perceived "collapse" of disco in 1979, the music provoked ongoing anxieties about the place of performer identities and the status of authorship within disco music. In the late 1970s, when the US music industry experienced its first decline in sales since the Second World War, much of the blame for this slump was placed on disco music. Disco, it was claimed, had lured record companies away from their proper mission: the development of long-lasting artists with distinct identities and stable careers. It had led them to seek easy money from a series of records featuring faceless, forgettable performers. Now, the trade magazines claimed, record companies were paying the price.

Before it came to designate a musical style, the term "disco" was used for any records which crossed over from discothèques to Top-40 radio and retail sales charts. The system for marketing disco music, as a business journal described it in 1977, would translate the success of records in nightclubs into initial sales of a single in record stores. These sales would, in turn, result in radio airplay of a song; eventually, that airplay would pull the record up the charts. Finally, widespread familiarity with a song and single would translate into the sale of albums, the desired endpoint of the whole process. A process which began in the fragmented and turbulent culture of nightclubs was to conclude within the familiar marketplace for full-length albums on major labels. Recognizably distinct performers were to provide the ballast which brought order to this system.

Almost immediately, the failure of this process was evident. With a few exceptions, the sales of albums by disco performers remained low relative to expectations. Initially, record companies claimed, this was a result of the genre's relative newness: once the music had been around for a few years, the argument went, disco fans would develop the sorts of loyalty toward artists that was common within the culture of rock music. When this failed to occur, it became apparent that the problem was more fundamental, rooted in formal characteristics of the music, in the ways in which it was produced, and in the role played by distinctive performers within it.

In the early years of disco, record companies pleaded with disc jockies in night clubs to speak the titles of songs and names of performers before playing a record (or, at the very least, to place a record's cover on the window of the DJ booth). This request, rarely acquiesced to, signaled one of dance music's unending problems – that of granting distinctiveness to performances and performers within an unbroken sequence of musical tracks. Between the dancers' relative uninterest in distinguishing musical selections and the disc jockies' concealment of professional knowledge, the identity of recordings and their performers often went unmentioned. The introduction of the twelve-inch dance single in 1975 intensified this problem. Increasingly, the vocal elements of disco music – those elements which allowed one to still think of disco tracks as "songs" – were subordinate to the maintenance of an extended, consistent instrumental sound. In the construction of this sound, studio producers frequently played a more significant role than did musicians or performers. Many successful disco "bands," such as the Ritchie Family, were in fact temporary groupings of studio musicians brought together by a producer for the purpose of recording, and with no collective existence as a unit outside the studio. This characteristic, in turn, limited the ability of such "groups" to undertake live performance tours and to acquire the kinds and levels of celebrity which live performances normally helped to establish.

Major record companies, accustomed to developing "careers" and selling albums, found in disco a formidable challenge to their usual ways of operating. Because the marketing of disco music involved few live tours or large-scale media events, small record companies were able to enter the markets for disco music with low levels of investment. These firms had little interest in developing long-term cumulative loyalty toward performers, and less still in building up back catalogues. The rapid stylistic change of dance music meant that albums were likely to become obsolete in the interval between the release of a successful single and the putting together of an album, unless the latter was a hastily assembled collection of tracks which copied the hit. While the album had become, for the record industry, the dominant form through which a performer's identity found expression and assumed value, the lengthy periods normally required for its production and promotion were at odds with disco's rapid turnover and development.

Major firms were increasingly confounded by the disco market, in which the sales of twelve-inch singles appeared to eat into the sales of albums, the former attracting buyers who wanted little more than an individual song and who recognized that disco albums consisted primarily of filler material. As the commercial market for twelve-inch singles expanded, small companies moved in to meet the demand. Two parallel systems came into being during this period, setting in place a broader industrial structure which persists to the present day. While major record companies began to limit themselves to those dance artists whom they felt could be marketed as distinct, recognizable celebrities, another strata of dance culture developed in the direction of an underground, almost artisanal subsystem. By the end of the 1970s, major record companies had begun to speak enthusiastically of "dance-oriented rock," relishing the emergence of a dance music whose performers (such as Blondie or The Cars) offered a model of celebrity and authorship more like that of rock music than of disco. In the dance music system which diverged from this line of development, professional roles (those of producer and remixer) assumed primacy over (or become indistinguishable from) those of performer and artist, just as the "track" displaced the song and the twelve-inch single replaced the album as primary recording format.

When music industry observers spoke of the "glut" of disco recordings put onto the market in the late 1970s, they were designating a body of works from which few high-profile cases of celebrity and authorship had emerged. Stylistic distinctiveness in disco would reside in individual producers, or in small, independent labels, or in regional scenes, more often than it would in performers, who were typically the vehicles through which the collective history of the genre found expression. These kinds of authorship, legitimate in themselves, were poor fodder for the sorts of investment in stable, long-term careers through which major record companies had hoped to find value in disco music.

Claims that the status of musical authorship has been transformed significantly in recent years are usually followed by reference to sampling, or to other practices (such as turntable-mixing) which have served to undermine notions of originality (see chapters 10 and 16 in this volume). However, these are only part of the story. Authorship is in question these days in part because so much popular music now unfolds within highly specialized cultural niches – complex clusters of influence and cross-fertilization marked by tiny moves ahead or to the side. In speaking of these niches, we might consider Brian Eno's claim that creativity now operates at the macro-level of whole genres, not at the micro-levels of individual artists. In place of "genius," Eno awkwardly suggests, we must speak of "scenius," in which it is the entire scene (of deep house music or electronica) which is the creative force, producing collective movement in particular directions and leaving individual contributions to that movement to be seen as minor and transitory. In the words of McKenzie Wark, we might profitably see acts of creation within these niches as "moves in an information landscape" rather than the full-blown creative gestures typically associated with other genres and other times.

In important ways, of course, the situation described here is no different from that of other tightly knit and formula-dominated musical communities through history, from dixieland through surf music. When a British musical celebrity like Norman Cook operates under different names in different musical fields, however – as Pizzaman when making techno-house, or as Fatboy Slim when releasing big-beat records – we are in a different regime of aesthetic and economic value. By changing names as he shifts genres, Cook (best known in the United States for his 1998 Fatboy Slim CD *You've Come a Long Way, Baby*) refuses to build the obvious points of continuity between these different practices, to let each new style add to the asset value of his name over time. In other periods, or in other styles of music, this would be commercially foolhardy, but in the field of contemporary dance music it is strategically appropriate. Within the dance music community, little value is attached to the idea of a creator retaining a consistent identity through ongoing changes of style and genre. If anything, such changes are read as signs that the individual's origins in (or commitment to) any one style are not genuine, that the individual's participation in that genre's unfolding history is merely a momentary visit. And so, Norman Cook (itself a pseudonym) will subdivide his identity, producing distinctive versions of himself to work and flourish in specialized musical genres from which particular identities seem inseparable.

Resources

Barthes, Roland (1977) The death of the author. In *Image – Music – Text*, trans. Stephen Heath. New York: Noonday, pp. 142–8.
Coombe, Rosemary J. (1998) *The Cultural Life of Intellectual Properties: Authorship, Appropriation, and the Law*. Durham, NC and London: Duke University Press.
Foucault, Michel (1977) What is an author? *Language, Counter-memory, Prac-*

tice: Selected Essays and Interviews, ed. and trans. Donald F. Bouchard. Ithaca, NY: Cornell University Press, pp. 114–38.

Frith, Simon (1986) Art versus technology: the strange case of popular music. *Media, Culture and Society,* 8, pp. 263–79.

Reynolds, Simon (1995) Rage to live: 'ardkore techno.' In Hanif Kureishi and Jon Savage (eds), *The Faber Book of Pop.* London: Faber, pp. 730–6 (originally published in 1992).

Stibal, Mary E. (1977) Disco: birth of a new marketing system. *Journal of Marketing,* October, 82–8.

Wark, McKenzie (1991) Fashioning the future: fashion, clothing, and the manufacturing of post-Fordist culture. *Cultural Studies,* 5(1), 61–76.

16
Technology

Paul Théberge

Too often, "technology" is thought of simply in terms of machines – sound recording and playback devices, synthesizers, computers, etc. – rather than in terms of "practice" – including not only the various uses of machines but also, in a more general sense, the organization of production and consumption.

Few would deny that the technologies of sound production and reproduction have become central to contemporary popular music culture. Nevertheless, "technology" remains a controversial and misunderstood term and, perhaps more surprisingly, one of the most undertheorized concepts in popular music studies. There is a persistent tendency among those who regard music as a form of essential and authentic experience to vilify technology as a corrupting force. Alternatively, among those who champion the use of technology in music-making, the tendency is to glorify it as a form of liberation for both musicians and audiences alike. At the same time, technology is regarded by the recording industry as important to the circulation of music commodities as currently organized and, also, a potential threat to that organization. The existence of such polarities marks technology as one of the essential factors and key discourses through which individuals make sense of their experience of music – on the one hand, guiding and justifying the choices they make in creating and listening to it and, on the other, a foundational element upon which the music industry is based, an inherent component of its operational strategies and its ultimate profitability. A more thorough understanding of technology – as object, medium, social phenomenon, system, discourse, and ideology – is thus critical to a better understanding of music, the recording industry, and popular culture as a whole.

TECHNOLOGY AND POPULAR DISCOURSE

One of the most common and often conservative popular critiques of technology pits sound recording and its associated practices against "live" performance as the norm toward which all music should strive (see chapter 14, this volume). This critique has its roots in early twentieth-century reactions to the recording apparatus of the day: John Philip Sousa, for example, argued that "canned music" – a metaphorical expression inspired by the shape of the early phonograph cylinder – would lead to a general deterioration of musical taste and the undoing of amateur music-making. As more complex technologies and practices of sound recording have come into use, such as those associated with the multitrack studio, this argument has been taken up and elaborated again and again (see, for example, Hunter, 1987). The simple positing of "live" music as the essential mode of musical production and reception inevitably leads to the portrayal of technology as a corrupting force, falsifying both musical performance and the experience of music. Curiously, the discourses of "high fidelity" promoted by the audio industry have reinforced the notion that the ideal sound reproduction device is one that is transparent in its operation, thereby collapsing any differences between the live and the recorded. The more critical task of addressing technology's actual mediation of "live" performance, as we know it today, has been seldom undertaken. But, as Steve Wurtzler has argued, the notion of "live" versus "recorded" music as mutually exclusive categories is socially and historically constructed and can account for neither the variety of contemporary, hybrid representational practices nor the relationship of audiences to the events posited by them.

In coming to understand "technology," it is useful to recognize, first, that virtually all music-making is based on some form of technology (an acoustic guitar is, in this regard, a "technology," even singing usually requires some level of training and practice, however informal, and people experience music more often in pre-recorded form than in "live" performance). Second, it is useful to recognize that the possibilities offered by technology are never exploited or accepted to the same extent in every sphere of music-making. This latter point is the source of much of the conflict in musical aesthetics and values that has accompanied the introduction of various technologies into pop music during the past half-century, and is clearly linked to notions of musical authenticity. Furthermore, the specific uses or the explicit rejection of various technologies are often instrumental in defining both the aesthetics and the politics of musical genres.

Such conflicts have become increasingly pronounced in recent decades with the introduction of powerful new electronic and digital technologies. Indeed, in most popular discourse, the word "technology" is not used in a general fashion (as I have used it above) but to designate a very narrow range of technologies. Hence, electric guitars and amplifiers were regarded as anathema to the folk movement of the 1960s; the multitrack recording studio, which was in large part developed to meet the needs of rock music, came to be regarded with suspicion by many rock-oriented critics of disco in the 1970s; and digital synthesizers and sequencers were often singled out, by a variety of detractors, as the devices that lent a "cold" and "inhuman" feel to much dance and electro-pop music of the early 1980s (even the label "electro-pop" speaks of its origins in terms of a particular technology).

In isolating particular technologies in this way, critics and proponents alike tend to ignore the degree to which other (favored) genres of pop music are also technologically based, thus rendering the wider field of technology transparent. I am reminded here of an interview with a noted rock guitarist that I once saw on television: as the conversation turned to issues of synthesizers and sampling in pop music, the guitarist rose from his seat, looked directly into the camera, and, pointing to his guitar, defiantly declared: "This is a *real* instrument." With that single gesture and statement, he seemed to mobilize all the ideological assumptions that have been used to support the notion that rock music is more "authentic," more genuine, than "synthetic" pop. It was as if the mere presence of vibrating strings (and the player's contact with them) cancelled out all other characteristics of the technology – from the cherry-red lacquer that covered its body, increasing its rigidity and preventing it from resonating, to the electro-magnetic pickups that captured the (rather puny) sound of the unamplified strings, to the many special effects devices (for which the guitarist was a known enthusiast) that transformed the sound, to the tubes, circuits, and massive speaker systems used to project the sound out to the audience. All this, not to mention the wide variety of other spectacular technologies used in the band's live performances, recordings, and videos, was made to disappear, neutralized in a tacit argument that pitted one form of technology, and the aesthetic bias of its users, against another.

Not all popular musicians, critics, and fans display such prejudices. But while there appears to be some public awareness of the intimate role played by technology in the production and reception of music, it is seldom articulated in any clear or systematic manner. A notable exception to this rule can be found in the writings of pop musician and producer Brian Eno. In an early pair of articles entitled "The studio as compositional tool," Eno lays out his view of the multitrack recording studio as a compositional environment. His discussion of the various choices made in the adding, layering, editing, and stripping away of sonic material in studio production reveals a constructivist approach to the medium. Furthermore, in these articles and in other writings and interviews, Eno has attempted, albeit often in a self-consciously ambiguous and elliptical manner, to place these studio practices and his emphasis on the manipulation of sounds within a broader context of pop music experience, and to argue for a redefinition of the roles of artist and consumer.

A similar, more theorized, attempt to deal with the constructive possibilities offered by sound recording technology can be found in the work of Chris Cutler. In *File Under Popular*, Cutler elaborates a theory of technology and music that divides history into three broad eras, each based on specific "modes" of production: the "folk" era/mode, based on memory and oral/aural transmission; the "art/classical" mode, based on music notation; and the "new," or popular mode, based on sound recording. Cutler understands the last to possess a "revolutionary" potential as yet unrealized because of the domination of mass media and commodity relations. Cutler's broad periodization of history, opposition of technological forms in terms of their supposed perceptual bias toward ear and eye, and opposition between communal and individual ideals come explicitly from Marshall McLuhan's ideas. One of the more significant aspects of Cutler's argument is the degree to which the tendencies that he sees in each of these modes of production are regarded as "inherent" properties of the technologies in question. In this way, Cutler articulates, in a most overt and extreme fashion, a deterministic attitude toward technology, derived from McLuhan, that usually exists just below the surface of much popular commentary.

The impact of the ideas of Marshall McLuhan on popular discourses about technology is still quite prevalent, despite the fact that his theories have been relentlessly criticized in academe (and in many more public forums as well), his logic and his particular brand of technological determinism denounced. In recent years there has been a considerable revival of his ideas, especially the notion of the "Global Village," for example, in the music industry promotion of World Music and, especially, in computer culture, where *Wired* magazine declared him its "patron saint." Moreover, in drawing on some of Cutler's work and other similarly derived theories, even pop music scholars such as Simon Frith, while

212

operating out of a different set of assumptions and oriented toward a very different set of conclusions, have elaborated various arguments about technology without always acknowledging this underlying source and its limitations. In this way, discussions about music technology are often conducted in a theoretical vacuum, ignoring the sources and contexts of technological discourse in society at large.

There is also a range of popular and institutional discourses, equally deterministic in their own way, that cast technology as, on the one hand, a source of artistic freedom and consumer choice and, on the other, a kind of *agent provocateur*, encouraging theft and market anarchy. Until the introduction of the cassette tape recorder, most consumer technologies did not allow sounds to be recorded. Disputes over technology tended to be the result of internal conflicts and competition between industry inter- ests (e.g. the so-called "battle of the speeds" between LP and 45 r.p.m. standards during the late 1940s and early 1950s). However, with the widespread adoption of audio cassette technology during the 1970s, the rise of digital sampling in music production during the 1980s, and the more recent emergence of the Internet as an alternative means of distribu- tion, conflicts over new technologies have more often pitted the record industry directly against musicians and consumers. I return to some of these issues in more detail below, but, for the moment, it is important to recognize that while these disputes often revolve around specific tech- nologies, and while the solutions to them are often posed as technologi- cal, legal, or economic sanctions and controls placed on these technologies and their use, "technology" in these instances is often little more than a focal point for the deployment of a wider set of discourses concerning issues of democracy, political economy, and social control.

TECHNOLOGY AND POPULAR MUSIC STUDIES

Perhaps due to the relative youth of the field of popular music studies, much academic writing on the subject of technology in popular music can be regarded as an elaboration of these various discourses (and others) already circulating in popular culture. Unless conducted in a critical man- ner, such strategies risk, as noted above, reproducing the assumptions and theoretical frameworks of these discourses. And while there are a number of essays in the literature that are provocative and insightful in themselves, the interdisciplinary nature of the field is such that relatively little commonality of perspective or approach exists between them, at least little

213

that would be suggestive of an emergent "theory" of technology as it relates to popular music studies.

What common ground does exist lies in the continued importance of what is often referred to as the "Adorno–Benjamin debate" of the 1930s. While it is not my intention to replay this so-called "debate" here, it is worth mentioning that much of the work in popular music studies that uses Adorno and/or Benjamin as a starting point (whether implicitly or explicitly) usually ends up emphasizing the polemical aspects of their work – Adorno's notion of the "regression" of listening, for example, versus Benjamin's characterization of film reception as "distraction," the nostalgic cultural elitism of Adorno versus the progressive politics of Benjamin – at the expense of exploring some of the substantial similarities that exist between them.

What is curious in all of this, however, is the fact that while Adorno's general theories of mass culture find expression in a number of works devoted specifically to music – hence his importance to the field as a whole – he wrote relatively little on the subject of sound recording technology *per se* (his commentaries devoted to film technology and radio are more substantial). Further, the essays on recording that do exist are actually more ambivalent toward the possibilities offered by the medium than one might expect. Even more curious, though perhaps not surprising, is the importance attached to the work of Benjamin, who wrote virtually nothing on the subject of music and whose considerable influence on a variety of discourses associated with technology (including those found in art history, film studies, and postmodern theory) often reduces to little more than a passing familiarity with what is probably his most well known essay, "The work of art in the age of mechanical reproduction." My point is not that Benjamin's ideas should not be applied to music but that various aspects of the essay are, in my opinion, ambiguous and quite contradictory in relation to much of his other work. The application of his ideas to music should therefore be undertaken with some care and with a clear understanding of the differences between the experience of film and that of popular music.

One of the problems with the influence of both these theorists on popular music discourse is a tendency for scholars to adopt a high level of generalization and theoretical abstraction, while ignoring the specificities of musical practice and experience. For example, in his essay "The sound of music in the era of its electronic reproducibility," John Mowitt outlines the theories of Adorno and Benjamin (among others) and then attempts to reunite them by arguing that electronic technologies, as the supposed antithesis of mechanical means of reproduction, have become the vehicle

for the restoration of the "aura" and the evacuation of the political potential in mechanical reproduction envisioned by Benjamin. Mowitt performs
this dialectical sleight of hand by making an analogy between Benjamin's
notion of the "fragment," embodied in the film frame, and the "bit," the
binary unit of digital technology. But while the film frame lies below the
level of perception for the cinema viewer, it still exists at a very concrete
level in the practices of film editing; the same cannot be said for the "bit,"
which exists in machine logic and has perceptual significance for neither
audiences nor music producers. Despite this imperceptibility (indeed,
because of it), Mowitt argues that bit-oriented logic conditions subjectivity in specific ways, undetected by consciousness, and limits possibilities
for community. Mowitt's arguments, with their basis in a kind of radical
formalism that seems to allow for no escape, bear the mark of Adorno's
totalizing reason. However, drawing on Attali's concept of "noise," Mowitt
is able to claim that while a music industry based on bit-oriented technologies is capable of rechanneling and profiting from the "noise" it
produces, it is still somehow unable to satisfy the very needs that it creates
among consumers, thus generating more "noise." This creates the conditions in which at least some consumers and producers are apparently able
to realize the critical potential hidden within their technologically engendered subjectivity. How this occurs, however, is not entirely clear.

Mowitt's arguments are unconvincing, in part, because they posit a
uniformity in listener response to the new technologies of reproduction
that is entirely out of keeping with the dynamics of popular music culture.
Furthermore, while he claims to go beyond the polemical divisions that
separate Adorno and Benjamin, he is ultimately dependent on the original
terms of that older "debate." Indeed, even in the turn of phrase, "At a
time when the aestheticization of theory is becoming increasingly prevalent, music has responded by sensualizing cultural politics" (Mowitt,
1987, p. 196), Mowitt offers faint echoes of Benjamin (in this instance,
his famous comment on Fascist aesthetics) in an attempt to find a moment
of liberation within the totality that he has constructed.

The enduring influence of the Adorno–Benjamin polemic in popular
music discourse on technology is significant in at least two ways. First, it
offers testimony to the complexity and depth of the ideas formulated by
these early twentieth-century thinkers and to the continued relevance of
these formulations, even though the conditions that gave rise to them
have long since passed into history. Second, and more problematically, it
may signal what is essentially a paucity of new theories dealing with the
role of technology in popular music studies.

SOME PERSONAL REFLECTIONS ON THE PROBLEM OF
TECHNOLOGY

To some degree, then, the influence of Adorno and Benjamin is inescapable in popular music studies and in cultural theory in general – and this is not necessarily a bad thing. While my ideas about the role of technology in popular music owe some debt to them, my own perspective is also the result of an attempt to bring together two broad areas of experience and study. First, my personal knowledge of music technology is derived, in part, from my own experiences as a musician and composer. My perspective is thus intimately related to a set of acquired technical, musical, and social *practices*, as well as a more formalized type of musical knowledge and training. Any individual's personal experience is, of course, limited and hence a precarious foundation upon which to develop theory – in the case of Adorno, his considerable familiarity with music as a discipline may have been as much a liability as an advantage, given the cultural biases that it seemed to carry with it. What personal experience does offer, however, if complemented with detailed observation of the practices of others and a respect for their own attempts to make sense of their experience (itself, a kind of "theoretical" activity), is an opportunity to comprehend, empathize with, and interpret a range of specialized cultural practices that might appear, to the outsider, as opaque or esoteric in nature. This is, in a sense, the basis of "participant observation" as a methodology. But beyond method, it is important to integrate practical knowledge, however acquired, with an understanding of the larger social, economic, and cultural contexts within which practice becomes meaningful.

The second source of my interest and perspectives on technology comes from my study and teaching within the fields of media studies and communications. Technology is, in many ways, a central concern of these fields – where there exists an extensive literature on technology, ranging from the early writings of Lewis Mumford, for example, to Jacques Ellul, James Carey, Innis and McLuhan, and Raymond Williams, among others. Working within them has allowed me to explore a wide range of questions concerning the role of technology in media and society. It is not my intention to survey this literature here, but to suggest the manner in which ideas derived from it can contribute to a more layered approach to the study of technology in popular music.

Too often, "technology" is thought of simply in terms of machines –

216

sound recording and playback devices, synthesizers, computers, etc. – rather than in terms of "practice" – including not only the various uses of machines but also, in a more general sense, the organization of production and consumption. Thought of in this way, the design characteristics of technologies (which are themselves subject to the possibilities and constraints of capitalist modes of production) are significant for how they structure, enable, and limit various specific musical or cultural practices, keeping in mind that the full range of possible uses to which any technology can be put are never fully understood at the design stage, that innovative uses have the potential of redefining technologies in significant ways. Furthermore, individual technologies should not be studied in isolation. The rise of digital sampling production techniques during the 1980s, for example, cannot be separated from various other technologies and practices – turntable "scratching" and multitrack studios – or from the larger contexts of consumption – dance club venues and radio airplay – of which they are only a small part. Individual technologies are thus not simply isolated objects but always part of a larger system of technologies and practices and a more general technological, economic, and cultural environment.

The development and use of technology can thus be understood as a kind of nodal point where the musical, the socio-cultural, and the economic intersect in a variety of concrete ways. By studying the accommodations in musical practice that accompany the introduction of new technologies, it is possible to reveal much about the very nature of that practice and its relationship to social and cultural practices at large. But, as mentioned above, it is important to realize that technologies are never used in the same manner in all spheres of music-making. Indeed, there is a type of inertia both at the industrial level, where investments and institutional pressures may inhibit the adoption of certain technologies, and at the cultural level, where sedimented values, dispositions, and the necessity of acquiring specialized knowledges may predispose individuals toward some technologies or uses over others. Thus, to understand technology in this way is not to argue for a vision of a structurally uniform relationship between music and society, as Adorno so often did, but to explore the various relationships and contradictions that exist between them.

Finally, and perhaps most important in the context of the present volume, technology must be understood as a kind of discourse. The various technical, theoretical, social, and aesthetic arguments that are put forward in order to explain, justify, or promote the use of technology in music-making (especially new technologies) are ideological in character

217

and related as such to a more general set of ideologies and discourses manifest in society (see chapters 1 and 2 in this volume). The larger social contexts and political economy of technology can thus be felt within the sphere of music in the ways in which discourse utilizes the concepts and rhetoric of that larger world. Equally importantly, discourses influence the manner in which musicians and consumers make use of technologies and integrate them into their everyday lives. In this regard, it is important to stress that I do not see these various aspects of technology, musical practice, society, and discourse as separate, but rather as integrated parts of a whole – different facets of a single experience.

SAMPLING: ONE TECHNOLOGY, MANY DISCOURSES

The relatively recent introduction of digital sampling technology into contemporary popular music practice – a technology that has been the object of much controversy – is, in many ways, illustrative of a number of issues described above. Digital sampling was introduced during the late 1970s and early 1980s and is thought of primarily as a studio production technology used by musicians, engineers, and producers. A full analysis of its role in music-making is not possible here. My aim is, rather, to simply highlight certain aspects of the introduction of this technology as a pop culture phenomenon and as a moment in which the intersection of various discourses was extraordinarily pronounced.

Digital sampling is a technology that allows sounds (typically only brief snatches of sound) to be recorded, manipulated, and subsequently played back from a keyboard or other musical device. It was developed by synthesizer manufacturers initially as a more convincing means of emulating conventional musical instruments – a task for which most synthesizer technology, which made use of simple electronic waveforms, was ill-suited. The technology has been used in a wide range of applications: in professional music production (both on stage and in studio), in creating music and sound effects for film and television, in playback-only forms in contemporary digital synthesizers, drum machines, organs, and pianos designed for the semi-professional and home amateur markets, in computer sound cards, and even in children's toys.

Some of the early discourses surrounding the use of samplers, especially those promulgated by musicians' unions, stressed the adverse effects of the technology on the employment of session musicians in studio production – string players, horn players, and drummers were particularly hard hit in this regard – thus reflecting a more general set of discourses relating to political economy and the introduction of technologies into the workplace. The relevance of such discourses in contemporary music production has always been somewhat questionable: the fact that sampling technology was used by other musicians as much as by "employers" (i.e. record producers) was seldom raised.

As it has come to be most commonly used in popular music discourse, however, the term "sampling" is related to a more specific and, indeed, more spectacular set of practices associated primarily with rap, hip-hop, and dance music of the 1980s. Here, the term refers to the use of pre-recorded sound and music – drum and other instrument sounds culled from decades-old rock albums, percussion breaks, James Brown's vocal pyrotechnics, bits of film and television sound tracks – in the creation of rhythm tracks for use in hip-hop and rap, in dance remixes, and in so-called "mastermixes," with the origins of the sounds being more or less recognizable depending on the intentions of the artists and the knowledge base of their audience. That such practices were never intended by the designers and manufacturers of samplers bears testimony to the possibility of culturally redefining technology through significant and innovative *uses*.

From the perspective of the record industry, the sampling of pre-recorded music was equivalent to a form of theft, and in support of such an allegation (and in actual court proceedings) it mobilized a variety of discourses, ranging from the moral and artistic (based on romantic notions of the uniqueness and integrity of artistic expression), to the legal and economic (copyright infringement). In the industry press, in specialized periodicals devoted to musicians and engineers, in the consumer-oriented music press, and even in a number of general-interest mass-circulation periodicals, articles appeared throughout the 1980s debating sampling technology and issues of ownership ("Who owns a sound?"), identity, the nature and value of musical performance and expression (a new twist on the "live" versus the "recorded" debate, sometimes read as a clash between rock aesthetics and pop), the boundaries of compositional prerogative, the role of the record industry in stifling new forms of creativity, and the challenge to (and for some, the imminent demise of) copyright law. In each of these debates, a variety of discourses drawing on notions of originality, artistic freedom, musicianship, and property rights, among others, were assembled as a means of strategic support for each author's position. In many ways, sampling became the focal point around which a wide range of pre-existing tensions and conflicts within the matrix of music, culture, and commerce could be

219

made manifest and addressed through a (partially) new set of concepts and terms.

In academic writing, a number of these debates were taken up, elaborated further and, most often, complemented with a more theoretical discourse on sampling practices as a form of "postmodern" collage, with some writers being more specific than others as to which sampling practices could, or could not, be considered "postmodern." And wherever postmodern theory was invoked, the influence of Walter Benjamin and his ideas on mechanical (now updated to include "electronic") reproduction and the destruction of the "aura" of the work of art also figured prominently. In fact, the idea of collage or pastiche as an aesthetic, sampling as a "transgressive" practice, quotation as cultural appropriation, the blurring of distinctions between traditional, popular, and avant-garde art, and other elements of postmodern discourse were taken up in a number of the more hip, popular periodicals as postmodern theory made its influence felt in popular culture as well as academe. To some extent, the application of these discourses to sampling had as much to do with the diffusion of "theory" during the 1980s as it did with sampling practices per se. Indeed, as Andrew Goodwin has argued, sampling came to be regarded as a key element in the defense of the "idea" of postmodernism – a popular form that both confirmed and legitimated the theory.

Whether they promoted or criticized the use of sampling in popular music, however, many of the industrial, popular, and academic discourses of the 1980s tended to isolate sampling technology from the larger contexts of musical production, seeing it variously as a determining force in either creating new artistic possibilities or precipitating a cultural, legal, and economic crisis. As some of the controversy around the technology subsided, the discourses were also modified or at least put aside whenever the possibilities of profit intervened. By the 1990s, even the record industry could be found contradicting much of its earlier, idealist aesthetic and legal discourse by allowing the sampling of copyrighted material, provided that artists paid for the privilege, on terms set by the industry, in advance. At the same time, a fuller understanding of sampling as it relates to earlier DJ practices, such as the isolation of break beats in turntable "scratching," and the dynamics of the dance floor as the cultural context for many of these practices, has emerged. Some recent work has offered an even more substantial challenge to a number of the earlier discourses (if only implicitly): for example, Tricia Rose's more situated analysis of sampling practices highlights the manner in which specific "cultural priorities" manifest in black culture can influence the use of not only sampling but a wide range of other technologies of music production and consumption as well. In her analysis, sampling practices can thus be understood as an expression of a unique, collective identity, as opposed to earlier, essentialist notions in which sound samples themselves were considered the embodiment of personal identity.

Finally, as evidence of the further evolution of discourses surrounding sound sampling, one might consider the appearance of the Blue Note/US 3 record project during the early 1990s (US 3, *Hand on the Torch*, Blue Note, B2 26708, 1993). In this instance, rather than prosecute US 3 for using samples of Blue Note's recorded repertoire in some of its hybrid jazz/rap productions, the record label offered US 3 virtually unlimited access to its back catalog and a contract to produce an entire CD of its "acid jazz"-like combination of sampled and improvised music. The rationale behind this benevolent attitude was that by allowing the sampling to take place, a new, younger audience might be exposed to jazz – and, not coincidentally, to Blue Note's extensive back catalog of recordings as well. Realizing that such a move might still create controversy among seasoned jazz fans, Blue Note was careful in its liner notes to construe the act of sampling as the continuation of a tradition – "all of the samples here are from Alfred's legacy" (referring to Alfred Lion, Blue Note's legendary founder and producer) – as opposed to its rupture. But perhaps more important is the liner notes' apparent reversing of that tradition as well: it is as if Lion had posthumously taken part in the project – "he produced every note sampled here." Interestingly, while Lion's role in producing the original sound recordings is credited, the role played by the various musicians in producing "every note" is not (they are credited elsewhere). For their part, the musicians might have a very different point of view on the use of "their" music in this project, but they have no legal claim of ownership in the sound recordings themselves, while Blue Note does. Thus, Alfred Lion, as record producer, takes his place, or so it would seem – "And yeah ... Alfred would have really dug this" – among a new generation of producers: the sampling artists.

CONCLUSION

Discourses are not static. Insofar as they constitute a strategic resource, they change in order to meet the demands of new situations, new challenges, and, not least of all, new technologies and practices. The significance of the various discourses outlined above lies, in part, in the ways in

221

which these discourses have defined sampling within popular culture: celebrating a very particular creative use of the technology, on the one hand, and vilifying it, on the other, all the while virtually ignoring the broader contexts of its application. In this way, "technology," as manifest in discourse, is often more limited, more circumscribed, than the actual range of social and artistic practices associated with any given technical apparatus.

While discourses may change, they are also always in short supply. And this is especially true of the repertoire of discourses that the record industry has used in its confrontation with new technologies during the past two decades. Indeed, the number of moral, artistic, legal, and economic discourses that it has actually employed in its attempt to gain greater control over the introduction and use of new technologies is extremely limited. Of necessity, they have been complemented by the considerable institutional, economic, and legal pressures that the industry is able to bring to bear on governments and the marketplace. Words, it seems, are never quite enough.

In this regard, apart from the various debates that have raged between various genres of popular music over questions of authenticity and the acceptable uses of new technology, one of the key technological issues of recent decades centers on the increasing technical ability of both musicians and consumers to record and distribute music as well as to reproduce it. There has been a pressing need for the industry to exert some degree of technical or legal control over this new ability or, at the very least, to be able to derive a significant level of profit from it. Hence, in the case of audio cassettes and home taping, the industry has concentrated its efforts on convincing governments in many industrialized countries around the world to introduce blank tape levies. The introduction of DAT (digital audio tape) technology into the consumer market in North America was stalled throughout the 1980s while the industry lobbied government to legislate the implementation of a technical fix – the Serial Copy Management System (SCMS). In the end, SCMS has probably been a less significant factor in curbing digital piracy than the simple fact that the industry lobby (which lasted several years) effectively crushed any possibility that the technology would ever gain widespread acceptance among consumers. And, as mentioned above, the potential threat to copyright that digital sampling may have originally posed was essentially contained, primarily through legal intimidation, while the industry organized its own, internally managed system of payments and fees for sampling privileges.

Finally, the most recent technological challenge faced by the industry has come from the sudden rise in popularity of the Internet and, in particular, the increasing use of Web sites for the distribution of recorded music (both legally and illegally obtained). Curiously, in addition to the Internet itself, a most unlikely "technology" has become the center of this controversy: the so-called "mp3" digital compression format. While the sole claim for mp3, from a technical point of view, is its capacity to compress digital audio files to a manageable size while maintaining audio quality, manifold discourses have accumulated around it, ranging from the most idealistic expressions of the desire to use technologies such as mp3 and the Internet as the vehicle for a new, more direct relationship between independent producers and consumers, to predictions of the eventual role they will play in the demise of the entire record industry. Such discourses can be found in abundant supply on Web sites, such as MP3.com, where the mediating role of the Web sites themselves in organizing, classifying, and making available the recorded material tends to be ignored. The record industry has responded, in typical fashion, by pursuing legal action against Web sites distributing pirated recordings and by attempting, for the most part unsuccessfully, to block every commercial venture (such as the introduction of portable mp3 players) that might extend the influence of mp3 outside the Internet and contribute to its acceptance as a standard audio format.

What is significant in each of these examples is the degree to which technology is construed by the record industry as a driving force behind the desire to violate copyright. Indeed, in most industry discourse, the simple capacity of these technologies to both record and reproduce music is taken as a direct provocation, as an "encouragement" of piracy. On the opposite side of the debate, the availability of these same technologies is taken as a virtual guarantee of artistic and individual freedoms. Surely no single technology contains, in itself, the capacity to support such disparate claims. Indeed, "technology" in these instances loses its physical profile, becoming something of an immaterial entity, a nodal point, a site for the playing out of a diverse set of artistic, social, and political tensions between industry and popular culture.

Resources

Attali, Jacques (1985) *Noise: the Political Economy of Music*, trans. Brian Massumi. Minneapolis: University of Minnesota Press.

Benjamin, Walter (1969) The work of art in the age of mechanical reproduction. In *Illuminations*, trans. Harry Zohn. New York: Schocken, pp. 217–51.

Cutler, Chris (1985) *File Under Popular*. London: November.

Eno, Brian (1983) The studio as compositional tool – parts I and II. *Down Beat*, July and August, 50–3, 56–7.

Frith, Simon (1986) Art versus technology: the strange case of popular music. *Media, Culture and Society*, 8, 263–79.

Frith, Simon (1996) Technology and authority. In *Performing Rites: On the Value of Popular Music*. Cambridge, MA: Harvard University Press, pp. 226–45.

Goodwin, Andrew (1988) Sample and hold: pop music in the digital age of reproduction. *Critical Quarterly*, 30(3), 34–49.

Harley, Ross (1993) Beat in the system. In Tony Bennett, Simon Frith, Lawrence Grossberg, John Shepherd, and Graeme Turner (eds), *Rock and Popular Music: Politics, Policies, Institutions*. London: Routledge, pp. 210–30.

Hunter, Mark (1987) The beat goes off. *Harper's*, May, 53–7.

Levin, Thomas Y. (1991) For the record: Adorno on music in the age of its technological reproducibility. *October*, 55 (Winter), 23–55.

Middleton, Richard (1990) *Studying Popular Music*. Milton Keynes: Open University Press.

Mowitt, John (1987) The sound of music in the era of its electronic reproducibility. In Richard Leppert and Susan McClary (eds), *Music and Society: The Politics of Composition, Performance, and Reception*. Cambridge: Cambridge University Press, pp. 173–97.

Porcello, Thomas (1991) The ethics of digital audio-sampling: engineers' discourse. *Popular Music*, 10(1), 69–84.

Rose, Tricia (1994) *Black Noise: Rap Music and Black Culture in Contemporary America*. Hanover, NH: Wesleyan University Press.

Wurtzler, Steve (1992) "She sang live, but the microphone was turned off": the live, the recorded and the *subject* of representation. In Rick Altman (ed.), *Sound Theory/Sound Practice*. New York: Routledge, pp. 87–103.

17

Business

Mark Fenster and Thomas Swiss

It is important to concentrate on the ongoing tension between music's role as a form of cultural expression and music's position within an economic and industrial context.

This chapter begins with an assumption common to other chapters in this book, namely that any commercial popular musical recording or performance is produced within an economic and industrial context. In order to understand contemporary popular music, it must be seen as produced and used within a specific industrial structure of production, distribution, and sales that is itself located within a capitalist economic system. In order to understand contemporary popular music, one must understand something of "The Business."

While music is a creative art form and audiences strongly identify with the music and musicians to which they listen, economic imperatives and the commodification of live and recorded music have an impact on music production and consumption. The development of fan support and consumer demand requires an enormous amount of capital. Music companies, agents, promoters, and others within the music industry must invest in new artists if the artists are to achieve national and international success. The expense of producing, distributing, and promoting recorded music creates economies of scale and competitive advantages that enable a handful of large corporations to dominate the contemporary recorded music industry, as has been true for most of the twentieth century. Although fans might think their favorite bands' CDs are "true expressions" of their creative talents and might dismiss other artists' CDs as "sell-outs," all are commercial products sold as commodities by large corporate conglomerates in the popular music marketplace.

There are several ways to understand the relationship between cultural production and the economic structures within which such production takes place. We begin by looking at three of the leading positions in this debate (also see chapters 4 and 9 in this volume). The first is often seen as a "critical" stance against the commodification of the culture industries, while the second and third emphasize the relative autonomy of audiences and artists. Each of the accounts has its shortcomings, but, taken together, they provide important insights into the current state and future of the music industry.

APPROACHES

First, some critics have argued that the market for popular music recordings, and therefore the pop music audience itself, are essentially created by the music industry. Record companies, according to this argument, generate and fill demand for standardized products with their mass-produced commodities. Articulated most famously by Theodor Adorno in the 1940s, this critical approach works from the assumption that the production of a mass cultural form like popular music is similar to the production of any mass-produced product, such as an automobile or a bar of soap. Recordings generally sound the same, with some variation due to the handicraft nature of music production, because record companies seek to maximize profits by limiting the costs of production and the risks involved in innovation. Artistic expression and cultural significance have no place within the assembly line of what Adorno and his co-author Max Horkheimer termed the "culture industries."

For most popular music artists and fans, however, this argument is unsatisfactory (although, ironically, it is a familiar trope that fans use to criticize artists and genres that they don't like: "That music sucks; it sounds like it's cloned by the industry"). While there *is* a good deal of repetition within some genres of popular music – for example, many dance tracks and country ballads feature similar rhythms, instrumentation, and lyrics – this does not necessarily mean that there is standardization. Any casual listener of a Top-40 countdown radio show will be struck by the wide variety of sounds and styles that constitute contemporary pop music. Furthermore, despite the fact that two songs within a particular genre might sound the same to listeners who don't know or don't like the style, most followers of a genre like "ska" or "folk" could quickly point out differences in instrumental sound and vocal styles that become apparent with repeated exposure to and emotional investment in a particular form of music. The repetition of elements within certain styles of music may be understood as a musical convention, but this is not equivalent to the standardization and assembly-line production of automobiles or bars of soap.

In addition, as in nearly all forms of cultural production, making a profit in popular music production is a difficult and complicated project. Most CDs released by major companies fail to recoup their costs of production, manufacture, distribution, and promotion, and few records actually make money for the company that produces them. Because pop styles change so rapidly and consumer tastes are so fickle, even products that are heavily supported and promoted by a major music company can fail miserably. Exacting and temperamental stars can be slow to deliver a finished product or can take an artistic turn in sound or style that proves unpopular and unprofitable, while the overnight success of a new artist or genre might vanish as quickly as it seemed to arise.

In short, selling popular music recordings is a highly unpredictable process due to the intense and inexplicable peaks and valleys of the business and the uncertainty of success. For example, the rapid collapse of disco in the late 1970s proved that trends can be only temporarily profitable. At least one label, Polygram, lost millions of dollars as a result of disco's demise. New trends often surprise record labels, as in the rapid development of a large market for rap records in the mid-1980s and, more recently, for "alternative" music in the early 1990s. In both cases, major labels were forced to scramble in order to remain current with popular taste. They were successful: profits from sales of rap and alternative rock proved ultimately to be worth the investment that labels made. Yet such investments in new music and promotion can be expensive, and the success they bring can be difficult to maintain. While "Candle in the Wind 1997," Elton John's wildly popular musical eulogy to Princess Diana, surprisingly boosted overall record sales by 30 percent for several weeks, steep marketing costs during the year nevertheless continued to eat away at industry profits.

Ultimately, the notion that markets and audiences are simply created by the music industry provides only a partial explanation of the history of audience participation in the production and consumption of popular music. Audiences' activities as fans, participants, and consumers of emerging musics are critical in the development of new musical sounds and artists. Although the industry attempts to manipulate, categorize, and profit from its market (the record-buying public), it cannot predict success or failure, control the output of established and emerging artists, or dictate individual and collective tastes in cultural products. There is, however, one general rule of thumb for the music industry: because the major companies make decisions as to what music they will record and distribute

227

according to the commercial demands of profit-making, they will ignore or eventually quit producing any music from which they cannot make money.

If the music industry cannot entirely control the "business" of popular music, what role do audiences and artists play? Two competing approaches privilege the roles of these groups in music production. The audience-focused approach emphasizes the resistance of individuals and groups to the ideological dominance of the culture industries and of mainstream culture in general. According to this approach, people produce their own meanings for popular texts and artifacts (including music) through ritual, recontextualization, and alternative readings. These cultural practices are active, not passive, and are a crucial site of the struggle over individual and group identity that occurs within an otherwise exploitative capitalist economy. In the past two decades, cultural theorists' emphasis on consumers of popular culture as creative readers and users has generated important empirical and theoretical work on musical subcultures and fandom.

A more traditional approach in popular music scholarship focuses on the exceptional creativity of certain popular music artists, genres, and record labels. This approach, which often appears in histories and biographies of popular music and musicians, assumes that certain artists can transcend the otherwise materialistic music industry to create moments or careers of innovative, powerful, and often politically significant music. In such biographies and histories, usually aimed at the mass market, the industry is an adversary attempting to ignore or suppress the creative intentions of the transcendent individual or movement, or is simply absent, having no effect upon the artist's creative impulses.

If the "culture industries" approach grants too much power to the furies of capitalist production, the audience- and artist-centered approaches err in the opposite direction, assuming that popular music is a form of culture that can remain untouched by or exist completely outside those forces. It is too simplistic, however, to consider popular music culture and the economics of the music industry as though the two were separate entities. The music industry is extremely powerful in its ability to control the vast proportion of music that is produced and distributed. This situation deeply affects the relationship between creative artists and their public. Although a relatively small number of stars might have the capital and power to make demands on the companies that produce and promote their records and live performances, even these artists depend on the structures of the industry for access to their audiences. Similarly, audiences depend on the music industry for access to music – access which is available predominantly through such economic transactions as purchasing records and tickets, selling advertising, and so on. Both "resistant" audiences and "transcendent" artists operate in a marketplace structured by capitalist firms and the uneven distribution of wealth.

These three approaches represent distinct poles in thinking about the relationship between the "art" and "business" of popular music. Most analysts fall somewhere in between, arguing that different artists, records, institutions, and periods in the history of popular music represent different – and very complex – combinations and relationships of power. Indeed, in contemporary popular music studies, the most common and productive way to consider "business" is to examine the relevant social forces involved in the historical development of music as a cultural commodity, and to study how forces such as economics, technology, and government have shaped and constrained musical recordings, performances, and consumption. This is generally labeled a "political economic" approach.

It is important to concentrate on the ongoing tension between music's role as a form of cultural expression and music's position within an economic and industrial context. Contemporary popular music is a mass cultural phenomenon involving the large-scale national and international distribution of millions of recordings. As such, it depends at all times on the economic structures that are able to support such a phenomenon. Of course, artists and audiences have an enormous role to play in the kinds of music produced and in music's cultural meanings, and other chapters in this book look more closely at the social issues involved in the practices of musical production and listening.

In the remainder of this chapter, we turn to a few broad examples of the "business" of popular music. We focus first on record companies, with an emphasis on the changing relationship between the "majors" and the "independents" and how this relationship structures changes in the relationship between production and consumption. Next, we take up the topics of licensing and publishing. We conclude by discussing the business of broadcasting popular music and addressing the emerging medium of the World Wide Web.

RECORD COMPANIES: "MAJORS" AND "INDEPENDENTS"

Most of the compact discs and cassettes available in stores are produced by what are known as "major" record companies or "labels." When we speak of these "majors," we mean fully integrated companies: firms which

229

oversee or control the production, manufacture, distribution, marketing, and promotion of the recordings of their own artists. In addition, majors may perform one or more of the same duties for smaller, independent record companies. The majors dominate the marketplace of popular music, and the recordings on their main and subsidiary record labels dominate mainstream commercial music radio and the shelves of most record stores, despite the fact that majors don't own a significant proportion of either radio stations or retail outlets. Currently, the largest major companies in the international music industry (known as the "Big Five") are WEA (based in the USA, owned by Time Warner), Sony (based in Japan, owned by the consumer electronics firm of the same name), Bertelsmann Music Group (BMG, a privately held German conglomerate), EMI (based in the UK), and Universal Music Group (whose Canadian corporate parent, Seagram, recently purchased what had been the sixth major, Polygram, from the Dutch electronics manufacturer Philips).

In the past fifteen years, there have been two important developments in the structure and operations of major integrated record companies. First, they have increased in size and scope by acquiring and creating smaller domestic and international music companies and music publishing firms. Second, the majors have been increasingly consolidated within and controlled by corporate conglomerates that own or control companies around the world. In addition to popular music, all these "multinationals" reap profits from other types of business. And all of them have some stake in other forms of entertainment software, such as movie and television production studios (Time Warner, for example, also produces films, television shows, magazines, and other media products), or in consumer electronic hardware, such as compact disc players and portable cassette players (Sony).

Many of these changes are part of general tendencies within the media industries and the international economy that have taken place throughout the history of the recording industry. Yet, in the past decade, the march toward consolidation of the major record companies within multinational corporate conglomerates has been particularly acute, and the degree of major label control in other areas of the industry has also greatly increased. Indeed, many critics currently argue that because the music business is but one element of a global media economy, it can no longer be examined apart from the other industries with which it is integrated.

This new corporate structure has a number of important effects that condition the ways music is produced, distributed, and heard. First, because many record companies are subsidiaries of larger corporations, the software they produce (recordings, song copyrights, and so on) is often supported by and used to support other products within the larger corporation. Time Warner, for instance, uses its record company to promote the products of its movie studio and to create commodities related to the studio's films, like soundtrack albums. It can also use its magazine division to promote and advertise its musical recordings. Similarly, a consumer hardware company like Sony may use its record company to introduce and promote new formats for recorded music, such as new digital recording media on tape and disc.

Second, record labels' large corporate parents increase the amount of capital and global corporate infrastructure available to produce, distribute, and promote musical recordings. Over the past decade, the majors have sought to expand their presence throughout Eastern Europe and Asia, as well as other areas around the world where they feel that their penetration can be profitable. In doing so, they are not only creating audiences for records produced in the USA and the UK but also attempting to record and distribute local artists, some of whom can then be marketed throughout the world to the growing audience for international and "world music" sounds. These business practices raise a set of new controversies over the imperialism of Western culture and capital, and the eradication and commodification of indigenous or local cultures. Because the "world music" and "world beat" categories were created to aid marketing, for example, many musicians are now not categorized by their music but by their race or ethnicity. That is, even if musicians make music recognizable as jazz or rock music, if they aren't North American or British, their sound is labeled and marketed as "world music." Also problematically, some Western artists, as well as major and independent record labels, increasingly appropriate non-Western sounds and styles without acknowledgment or remuneration, incorporating the "Other" as an exotic aesthetic fashion for wealthy American and European audiences.

The changing scope and roles of major record companies have also affected their relationship with what are called "independent" record companies ("indies"): commercial firms that produce recorded music and remain, to varying degrees, independent from the production, distribution, and manufacturing facilities of major record corporations. By "varying degrees," we refer to the fact that while some independent record companies are fiercely independent and attempt to produce, manufacture, distribute, and sell their records without the help or interference of majors, other indies may rely on majors to perform one or more of these tasks, such as distributing or manufacturing. "Pure" independence is a difficult status to achieve and maintain, given the expense of production and distribution of musical recordings and the ubiquity of majors and erstwhile independent companies affiliated with the majors in all sectors of the industry. Independent companies are often forced to choose between, on the one hand, settling for a meager profit level (if any at all) and limited distribution to retain their independence, or, on the other, working within the structures of the major record companies.

Of course, major record companies typically don't behave like cartoon villains seeking to destroy poor, defenseless indies by ripping them off or stealing their artists without compensation. Indeed, majors often find it easier and more profitable to establish formal and informal corporate and financial relations with independent labels. At other times, however, majors simply ignore independent labels and different musics, allowing them to operate on the margins until it makes financial sense for the majors to buy or contract with them. Independent companies are therefore central to the functioning of the music industry, especially in terms of the development of new artists, new genres, and innovative business strategies. For example, consider the role of independent labels in the rise of "alternative rock." Many of the most successful alternative bands, such as R.E.M. and Nirvana, began their careers with small independent companies that represented and "packaged" these bands to specialized audiences in ways that the majors would not and, at the time, could not. As the independent records of individual bands proved successful, these bands were signed to major labels, which in turn began to sign more artists within this genre. Ironically, majors began to buy indie alternative rock labels in whole or in part – as majors also did with labels that specialized in other genres, like rap and metal – and even started their own small, "fake" indie labels to attract artists and fans who might otherwise be turned off by a large label.

The ongoing development of the World Wide Web and other means of distributing music as digital sound files may offer indies cheap, efficient, and instantaneous ways to bypass major labels and their distributors by selling directly to their customers. Yet the necessary technological, legal, and marketing infrastructure for a potentially radical reconstruction of the operations of the music industry is still a mere future possibility. Such a solution to the indies' dilemma may in fact not constitute a new era of independence for musical innovators and entrepreneurs, but instead may turn out to be merely a new stage in the business relationship between majors and indies.

To sum up, at different moments in the rock era, the relationship between indies and majors has varied. At certain times, independents have been visible in the music industry, and their releases have been successful in the popular music marketplace. At other times, the majors have so dominated the structures of the music industry that indies have been forced to the margins of the market. At all times, however, the economic and industrial structures of the music industry have strongly influenced what music consumers hear and how they hear it.

LICENSING AND PUBLISHING

Most listeners to popular music don't concern themselves with the concept of the "intellectual property rights" that attach to such things as musical recordings, music publishing, and the band logos that appear on T-shirts, except to the extent that fans may knowingly own copies of illegal "bootleg" performances or unauthorized merchandise for which artists and record companies receive no compensation. Yet such rights are central to the profitability of the music industry as it currently operates.

Under US law and industry practice, these property rights include the ownership by artists and music publishing firms of song compositions, and record companies' ownership of sound recordings. Both sets of rights, called "bifurcated" rights in the sense that separate rights attach to the recording and the underlying song, have separate privileges and values for their respective owners. For example, if movie producers or advertisers want to use a recording or re-record a song for their audio soundtracks, they must "lease" the rights to that "property" from the copyright owner, typically through the payment of royalties to the label that owns the rights to the recording and/or the music publisher that owns the rights to the song.

With these exploitable property rights, major music companies do not simply and solely produce and distribute music to individual consumers of compact discs and cassettes. They also sell or lease material to other entertainment corporations, even within their own conglomerate, for television and film soundtracks, advertising jingles, and so on. Music is increasingly "pre-sold" before it reaches the consumer, and at times before it is even recorded: the rights are leased for soundtrack packages and optioned for other commercial purposes. A "song" thus becomes a potential commodity in a seemingly infinite number of ways prior to its material manufacture as a cassette, compact disc or record for sale. In addition, major labels fully exploit their back catalogs of recordings through repackaging (for example, "greatest hits" CDs and compilations based on themes like "surf" or "party" music).

As the domestic and international use of pop songs increases in advertisements, films, and television shows, and through the performance of hits by other artists, the value of music publishing has steadily risen, and the largest and most powerful publishing firms are purchasing smaller ones around the world. Publishing is an important and lucrative aspect of the music industry because there are few significant costs involved. Publishing is perceived as a fairly steady business, unlike recorded music, which tends to fluctuate wildly between good years and bad. Moreover, newer communication technologies like cable television, home video, and the World Wide Web represent new ways to sell and profit from music copyright ownership. Since most major music companies own music publishers as well as record labels, the consolidation within transnational conglomerates of rights over recordings and publications has enabled major record companies to more effectively exploit these rights for licensing.

Finally, the merchandising of paraphernalia associated with pop and rock stars (T-shirts, posters, and other material goods) is an increasingly profitable aspect of the music industry. Merchandising supplements artists' main streams of revenue from recording contracts and performance fees. For example, during U2's 1997 tour, the average gross sales of such merchandise at authorized sales booths were more than $12 per person, meaning that the band can generate hundreds of thousands of dollars in gross sales at a single concert. Indeed, merchandising is now seen by major labels as crucial to the success of a rock or pop act, both in the sales it is likely to achieve and in its overall potential as a source of profit. Major labels are more likely to sign and produce those acts that are seen as especially suitable for merchandising and have demonstrated an ability and commitment to merchandising themselves. This business practice, too, clearly has an effect on our consumption of popular music.

BROADCASTING AND CABLE

Radio and music video are integral to the music industry in their ability to promote popular music in general and specific recordings in particular. Radio stations and cable television channels are separate businesses from record companies, however, and their interest in using the products produced by the recorded music industry in order to be profitable can occasionally conflict with the short- and long-term interests of the record labels. All commercial broadcasters and cable channel owners depend upon the sale of advertising for revenue, and are therefore interested in musical recordings and videos in terms not only of the *size* of audiences that they draw and that can then be sold to advertisers, but also of the *kinds* of audiences that will tune in. Broadcasters and cable channels generally care little about the types of music, artists, and record labels they play; they are interested only in those forms of content that attract particular demographic groups that can be sold to advertisers at a profit. Those audiences with the greatest disposable income and propensity to spend it are generally those that are most attractive for advertisers. Those stations that best capture these "attractive" audiences can charge more for advertising time during their schedule.

This difference between drawing audiences and selling records is at the center of the sometimes conflictive relationship between record companies and broadcasters. Record companies perceive the most important part of their business to be selling new recordings and emerging artists. Many radio stations, on the other hand, play proven artists and styles of music, while ignoring emerging and even profitable forms of music (like techno and rap) that might "alienate" audiences sought by advertisers. Because radio stations are independent of record companies and have separate, different sources of revenue, their different goals – for record companies, the sale of records; for radio stations, the sale of their audiences' attention to advertisers in the form of commercial time – often coincide but occasionally do not.

Music video broadcasters like MTV and VH-1 are similar to radio: although they rely on record companies for videos (as radio stations depend on the music industry for their records), video outlets are relatively independent in their choice of which videos to play. Yet there are some important differences between radio and music video channels. For example, over the past decade, MTV has been more open than most radio stations to playing emerging forms of music and new artists (while at other times, especially in its early years, it was condemned for not playing new music by African-American artists). MTV was instrumental in the success of post-punk new wave in the early eighties, of rap for a white audience in the mid-eighties, of alternative rock bands in the early nineties, and, recently, of techno bands like The Prodigy and difficult to categorize performers such as Björk. In the late nineties, VH-1 has been critical to the emergence of "adult alternative" artists like Sarah McLaughlin and Jewel, while the local Video Jukebox outlets on cable have been important avenues for rap artists. Still, as critics have pointed out, although music video has had an extensive, far-reaching influence on the recording industry, these influences have amplified existing features of the business – especially the predominance of major record labels (which can afford to pay for and promote increasingly expensive music videos).

235

One key term for the function of broadcasting in general is "gatekeeping" – a concept that media and popular music scholars have increasingly explored in their research (see chapters 4 and 6 in this volume). Commercial radio (and to a lesser extent music video) programming is based on what are known as "formats," particular groupings of music by which radio and cable stations identify themselves to listeners and advertisers. Examples include country and all-talk radio, as well as various formats based upon contemporary hits and rock. Formats are important not only for listeners to identify the type of music a station plays. They also help radio broadcasters and advertisers to reach a specific audience segment or demographic. The radio audiences for country, contemporary hits radio, and rap stations are obviously different and will attract different advertisers. Similarly, when MTV, VH-1, and more genre-focused outlets like Country Music Television and Black Entertainment Television's video shows decide to add new videos, they base their decisions at least in part on what the audience they wish to reach will want to see. To choose a format and songs for a playlist, then, is a business decision based on which demographics a station wants to attract and which format the station believes can best attract them. In that sense, broadcasters and cablecasters do not so much give their listeners "what they want" as decide what demographics they want and decide which format and songs best correspond to those demographics.

Although major record labels and video outlets might wish broadcasters were more willing to play emerging types of music and artists, radio and video playlists are nevertheless skewed heavily in favor of major label recordings. This is particularly true in the various pop, rock, and country radio formats, which are almost completely dominated by major label recordings. Although labels might not like the specific choices stations make in their role as gatekeepers, majors are ultimately favored by the gatekeeping process. This is not because the majors release the "best" records (though clearly the best known artists record for the major labels); rather, the majors spend a good deal of money and time promoting their records and have a great deal of influence on radio stations and MTV, despite broadcasters' supposed independence.

THE MUSIC BUSINESS AND THE WEB

With the advent of the World Wide Web, "cyberspace" has increasingly become a means of promoting and distributing popular music, with ef-

236

fects on the music industry similar to those resulting earlier from the introduction of radio and television. The number of music-related sites – including retail outlets, homepages for artists and record labels, and fan pages celebrating (or trashing) particular artists – dramatically increases on a weekly basis. In the early days of the Web's development, computer-savvy artists, entrepreneurs, critics, and fans embraced the Web as a space to develop and promote an "indie" aesthetic. Indeed, one of the reasons why the Web and rock music are seemingly well suited for each other even now is the fact that they operate under similar, if often complicated or contradictory, notions of participation, independence, innovation, and community.

While discussions of the Web by those involved in popular music are sometimes characterized by a millennial utopianism, it is more useful to think of the Web as a technological entity located within fields of power where designs of corporate colonization and desires for communal creativity and individual autonomy often merge or collide. Music-related "independent" sites and fan pages designed on home computers, for example, both supplement and compete with well financed corporate sites. Even as some major labels include links on their "official" sites to fan pages and other "unofficial" sites, the Recording Industry Association of America employs a staff of full-time Web surfers who comb the Web daily, searching for copyright infringements. Gatekeeping in general has become more complicated with the arrival of Web sites with stereo sound clips, videos, downloadable CD-quality songs, and so on.

For students of popular music, this new space of cultural production and reception offers ample opportunity for considering the complex social and cultural processes at work in the business of popular music, which simultaneously enables and commodifies an expressive, creative art form and active audience participation. From the global heights of popular music – such as "We Are the World" and the phenomena of Michael Jackson or The Spice Girls – to the localized moments of a struggling local band hawking its self-produced compact disc in a small neighborhood bar, the music industry and its structures and processes are present.

Resources

Addicted to Noise. http://www.addict.com/

Banks, Jack (1996) *Monopoly Television: MTV's Quest to Control the Music*. Boulder, CO: Westview.

Billboard Online. http://www.billboard-online.com/

Burnett, Robert (1996) *The Global Jukebox: the International Music Industry.* London: Routledge.

Dannen, Frederic (1991) *Hit Men.* New York: Vintage.

Feld, Steven (1988) Notes on world beat. *Public Culture*, 1 (Fall), 31.

Frith, Simon (ed.) (1993) *Music and Copyright.* Cambridge: Cambridge University Press.

The National Entertainment State III: Who Controls the Music? *The Nation*, special issue, August 25, 1997.

Negus, Keith (1992) *Producing Pop.* London: Arnold.

Sanjek, David (1998) Popular music and the synergy of corporate culture. In Thomas Swiss, John Sloop, and Andrew Herman (eds), *Mapping the Beat: Popular Music and Contemporary Theory.* Malden, MA: Blackwell, pp. 171–86.

Taylor, Timothy D. (1997) *Global Pop.* New York: Routledge.

18
Scenes

Sara Cohen

"Scene" is a familiar term in popular music studies, but it has generally been used uncritically or interchangeably with terms like "subculture" or "community."

INTRODUCTION

The term "scene" is commonly and loosely used by musicians and music fans, music writers and researchers to refer to a group of people who have something in common, such as a shared musical activity or taste. The term is perhaps most often applied to groups of people and organizations, situations, and events involved with the production and consumption of particular music genres and styles. Indeed, it first came to be linked with popular music during the 1950s, with reference to jazz and a "jazz scene." In most cases, the term is used to describe situations in which distinctions between informal and formal music activity, and between the activities and roles of music audiences, producers, and performers, are blurred.

However, the term "scene" is also used to refer to music activity within specific geographical areas: for example, the Seattle rock scene, the South London rock scene, the New Zealand rock scene. It is this association of scene with place and the local that has recently become a focus for theoretical consideration within popular music studies. In place of using terms like "subculture" and "community," which imply music-related groups that are bounded and geographically rooted, some writers have preferred to use "scene," thereby emphasizing the dynamic, shifting, and globally interconnected nature of musical activity. In this chapter, I discuss some of this literature on popular music scenes, looking at the ways in which the term "scene" has been defined, used and reconceptualized. Further, I assess the term's usefulness by relating it to the specific case of "indie" rock music in Liverpool. (The term "indie" is used here to refer to music that is associated with independent record labels and with "alternative" as opposed to "mainstream" culture; see chapter 17 in this volume.)

MUSIC SCENES AS LOCAL CULTURE

There are various ways in which so-called indie rock music in Liverpool could be described as a "local scene." First, its production depends upon a particular group of people. Most notably, there are the five hundred or so bands, each typically comprised of four or five musicians, using drums, bass, and lead guitar, and sometimes keyboards, and generally performing their own musical compositions. Most of them are white, working-class men in their twenties and thirties. Their reasons for getting involved with music-making include the fact that it offers them: a particular lifestyle; a social network and identity outside of work, family, or home; a sense of purpose, status, and prestige; a unique means of communicating emotions and ideas; and the lure of artistic and financial success. For most, their overwhelming ambition is to "make it" – that is, sign a contract with a major record company in order to sell records and reach wider audiences. Yet this quest for success is frustrating and elusive. Within the music industry, the imbalance of earnings is striking, and audience tastes in music and thus commercial success are notoriously unpredictable. The chances of "making it" are thus slim, and being in a band involves a day-to-day struggle to raise funds in order to rent or purchase instruments, find audiences and opportunities to perform, compose commercially viable songs, and attract the attention of music journalists and record companies, all of which intensifies the preoccupation with success and failure. The music activities of these musicians are supported by local audiences and those involved with a broad and diverse range of local music businesses and organizations (many of these people are also musicians) that includes music education, training, and community arts, and local record labels, recording studios, and record shops.

The scene is created through these people and their activities and interactions. Many forge close relationships with each other and form clusters or cliques, while others are part of looser networks or alliances. Such relationships involve a regular circulation and exchange of: information, advice, and gossip; instruments, technical support, and additional services; music recordings, journals, and other products. Such relationships comprise an informal economy. Through them, knowledge about music and the scene is generated, distinctions are made between being

240

inside or outside the scene, and the boundaries of the scene are thus marked. Central locations for interaction between scene participants include record shops and rehearsal and recording studios – most of which are frequented by men who share the jokes, jibes, and jargon, the myths, hype, and bravado surrounding bands and band-related activity. Live performance venues also act as a social hub of the scene, providing a space where musicians and musical styles can interact and where the scene is made more visible, physical, and real. The musicians, audiences, and music business people involved with the scene form various networks, cliques, and factions, and are divided by musical style, social class, feuds, rivalries, and other factors. At the same time, however, they are united by factors such as age and gender, webs of interlinking social networks and a gossip grapevine, and by hurdles and struggles familiar to all involved in the common quest for "success."

Many of the scene's characteristics are shaped by its distinctive local setting, with structural and material conditions in Liverpool providing a specific context for rock music production. The city's role as a port, and local patterns of immigration, particularly Irish immigration, have, for example, encouraged the creation of familiar musical sounds and styles. In this case, that might be described as guitar- and sometimes keyboard-based music of medium tempo, featuring a strong emphasis on song and melody rather than rhythm and dissonance, and a relatively high-pitched male vocal style characterized by thin, reedy, or nasal tones, the distinctiveness of which may be partly attributed to the Liverpool accent and vernacular, with its recognizable styles of intonation, pronunciation, and phrasing. The decline of port activity over recent decades and the poor state of the local economy have contributed to a lack of local music facilities and resources in some areas, and to a sense of vulnerability within the scene. The British recording industry is overwhelmingly concentrated in London, where the major record, publishing, manufacturing, and distribution companies are based. Those involved with the scene are concerned about how to lure London-based record company employees and funds to the city, stop the continual and inevitable "hemorrhage" of local musicians and their earnings from the city, and decrease the spending of local music businesses on services and resources located outside the city.

However, the scene is not just a social and material entity. It is also a meaningful concept defined and interpreted in a variety of ways. Some suggest that rock culture in Liverpool can be labeled a "scene" only if "something is happening" – if local bands are being signed up by record companies and there is coverage of the local scene in the national music press, if a good local performance venue exists that can stimulate music activity and act as the scene's "heart" or "core," if the production of local rock music can be characterized as communal and collaborative rather than fragmented and factional, or if there exists an identifiable and distinctive local musical sound or style. The notion of a local rock scene can thus be related to a romantic ideology familiar to rock culture, and linked with issues of authenticity, difference, and community.

Will Straw has similarly pointed to what he calls the "musical localism" of alternative North American rock scenes of the late 1980s, where, as in Liverpool, an organic relationship between musical sounds and styles and the places in which they were produced and consumed was emphasized. Scenes were associated with notions of community, heritage, and local identity, implying geographical and historical stability and rootedness. The participatory nature of much music-making encourages this sense of community, which is why Barry Shank described scenes as "embryonic signifying communities." Shank explored the development and dynamics of the rock 'n' roll scene in Austin, Texas, beginning with its roots in cowboy song and tracing the way in which the scene formed through interaction between groups of local musicians, students, and policy-makers, and between different musical styles and scenes within and outside of Austin. Shank thus highlighted the changeable nature and life cycles of scenes and the way in which they rise and fall, fragment and disperse. He also portrayed scenes as kinetic entities involving strong sentiments, a sense of excitement or "buzz," a context for exploration and performance of new identities, a focus for collective action, and a strong sense of identification and belonging. For Shank, a scene can thus be empowering and progressive.

Local music scenes certainly have their own distinctive characteristics, conventions, and identities. There are obvious differences, for example, between Liverpool's rock and contemporary dance scenes of the late 1990s in the styles of music involved and the businesses that help to produce and promote them, the audiences they attract, the spaces those audiences occupy and the styles of dress they prefer, and the ideas about music, musicians, and performance that they promote. The scenes also tend to be clearly distinguished by their participants. Some of those involved in the dance scene, for example, describe it as new and inventive, entrepreneurial and forward-looking, in contrast to the rock scene, which they describe as "old school," with "dinosaur" bands that require heavy investment or subsidy in order to develop. Such ideas about scenes, and the boundaries drawn around and between them, are not fixed but change over time and according to situation and circumstance. Ruth Finnegan has also highlighted contrasts between different musical "worlds" (country and western, jazz, classical, brass bands, music theater, folk, rock, pop) in the English town of Milton Keynes, noting how each world could be distinguished not only by its music but by social conventions, such as shared ways of learning, composing, or performing music, structuring and organizing music-making, and conceptualizing and valuing it.

At the same time, however, there are many similarities and overlaps between Liverpool's rock and dance scenes, including a sharing of local facilities and resources and a crossover of musicians, audiences, sounds, and ideologies. Notions of authenticity, for example, are also prevalent in contemporary dance scenes and are apparent in the familiar distinction between underground and mainstream music and clubs. Finnegan has also emphasized overlaps and relationships between local musical worlds and common ways in which all local music-making is supported and funded. Studies of local music scenes or worlds within specific geographical places, such as the studies of Liverpool, Milton Keynes, and Austin I have been describing, can thus highlight ways in which the scenes reflect social, cultural, and economic characteristics of those places. More recently, however, efforts have been made to reconceptualize scenes in order to shift emphasis from music as local culture to music as global, mobile culture.

MUSIC SCENES AS GLOBAL, MOBILE CULTURE

Shank (1993, p. 207) has described the considerable impact that a live performance by the Sex Pistols had on Austin's rock scene. He also refers to the bitterness and regret expressed in Austin over the departure of Janis Joplin and other local musicians to pursue success elsewhere. In the UK, live performances by the Sex Pistols had a similar impact on the rock scenes of cities like Liverpool and Manchester, and the scenes of Liverpool and Sheffield reveal a similar concern with musicians who leave those cities to work elsewhere. Consequently, as in Austin, musicians in Liverpool and Sheffield lobbied their city governments to develop strategies aimed at protecting and promoting local rock scenes and developing their business infrastructure in order to encourage musicians to stay and invest in them.

These and other examples point to connections between scenes of different places and suggest that local music scenes need to be understood in relation to broader transnational processes, and they draw our attention to the existence of translocal or transnational scenes. Liverpool's rock scene does not exist in isolation but has always reflected non-local musical influences. During the 1950s and 1960s, for example, local sailors brought to Liverpool records and instruments purchased in the USA and elsewhere. US servicemen posted at a nearby airbase regularly visited the city's clubs and dance halls and introduced American musical influences to the scene, such as jazz, country, rhythm and blues, soul, and rock 'n' roll. Various immigrant groups have also shaped the scene, such as the Jews, who established many of the music businesses that supported bands like The Beatles during the 1960s, and the Irish, whose emphasis on song and melody is often linked with the so-called "Liverpool Sound." Scenes can thus be linked to diasporas and to the movement of people, music products, and sounds. This has intensified an intermingling of musical cultures, scenes, and sounds, and processes of musical hybridization, cross-fertilization, syncretism, and so on.

Liverpool rock musicians have, of course, always taken inspiration from international mass-mediated music. In this and many other ways, Liverpool's rock scene is connected to rock scenes elsewhere. The scene's musicians have continually toured and performed outside Liverpool, where they have mixed with other musicians and audiences. The scene's audiences also travel from place to place to visit musical sites and attend concerts and music festivals, where they meet with other music fans. Contacts and information between scenes are also established and disseminated through the media, as well as through word of mouth and face-to-face contact. This may involve radio and television broadcasts, nationally and internationally distributed fanzines, newsletters, and other music publications, or on-line computer discussion forums. Such connections between musicians and audiences have promoted the exchange and distribution of music commodities and products and involved a circulation and exchange of money, capital, and music meanings, images, and ideologies. They illustrate some of the possibilities that exist for the development of popular music scenes that have a geographically dispersed membership and are not reliant upon or organized around a particular locality.

Different scenes, however, forge different kinds of connections. Liverpool's contemporary dance scene, for example, like the North American dance scene that Straw discusses, has a sense of affinity with scenes in other places and a cosmopolitan outlook that makes it attentive to music activity elsewhere. The successful Liverpool nightclub Cream, for example, promotes Cream events abroad, attracts audiences from outside the region on a regular basis, and acts as an agency for an international group of DJs. It thus describes itself as an international club that happens to be based in Liverpool. Meanwhile, a major local rock venue such as The Lomax is much more closely linked with debates about the local scene and the responsibility of local venues to promote that scene by offering performance opportunities to local bands. A local venue named Eric's has achieved legendary status within Liverpool's rock scene because of the way in which it acted as a focus for Liverpool's early 1980s rock or post-punk culture and inspired the formation of local bands such as Echo and the Bunnymen, The Icicle Works, and The Mighty Wah!, which went on to achieve national success and become an established part of the scene's heritage or lineage.

THE PRODUCTION OF SCENES: POWER AND CONSTRAINT

The notion of a music "scene" has thus been redefined by Straw to emphasize the fluid, loose, cosmopolitan, transitory, and geographically dispersed nature of local music activity. Rather than linking scenes with notions of a clearly defined and place-bound community or subculture with a relatively fixed population, Straw draws attention to the way in which scenes are created or produced through heterogeneous "coalitions" and "alliances" based on musical preferences, thus linking scene with cultural change and interaction. The production of scenes is, however, constrained or enabled by relations of power that shape the nature of the scene and the way in which it is thought about or imagined.

Since the early 1980s, for example, those who participate in Liverpool's rock scene have continually bemoaned its lack of resources and facilities and commonly described it as insular. At the same time, Liverpool's economic position within Europe has become increasingly peripheral, and its political status and image within the UK has declined. This may help to explain the symbolic significance and value attached in the scene during the 1980s to notions of music as a "way out" of the city, and the preoccupation with musicians who stay or leave. If the latter had achieved success, they were more likely to be perceived as somehow lost to the city or indebted to it. Their relationship with the city became intensely scrutinized, and lines of debt and accountability were more tightly drawn. Those who remained were often perceived as relatively immobile and tied to the city. This rhetoric of leaving and loss suggests a local identity that is strong but also defensive and parochial, and a notion of a scene that is bounded and inward-looking rather than open to dialogue and collaboration. Liverpool's rock scene is thus closely bound up with the local but at the same time related to national and transnational or "global" relations and movements, instabilities, and inequalities.

In addition, the music media strongly influence definitions and interpretations of scenes, and to some extent create or constrain them. Particular music journals, for example, often associate rock musicians and their music with the places they have come from. This practice varies according to musical style and genre, but some rock journals clearly do so in order to link musicians with a sense of local origins and roots and thus authenticate both them and their music. In their coverage of local rock scenes, such journals often stereotype them in certain ways or distinguish them from scenes elsewhere in a way that can exaggerate local rivalries and differences. Some Liverpool musicians thus criticize the music press for inventing or misinterpreting the local rock scene and therefore inhibiting its natural development.

Like the music media, the music industry has also played a significant role in creating and constraining scenes. Shank, for example, shows how the role of Austin's 1980s post-punk scene as a "signifying community," and the desire to construct identity through music, are contested or threatened by the simultaneous struggle to affirm the value of that practice within the commercial marketplace. The Austin scene was transformed, for example, during the mid-1980s when it became more closely linked with the requirements and values of the national recording industry. As the notion of a local music "industry" emerged, the scene became increasingly commodified and redefined to mean the commercial activity surrounding successful musicians who had attracted industry and media attention or were believed to be on the verge of doing so. Shank's argument is that such developments constrained the powerful progressive possibilities of the scene, an argument that, as Jason Toynbee points out, ignores the progressive possibilities within even the most commercial or mainstream scenes.

However, while scenes may be produced by the music industry and the media in order to sustain and extend a market for music industry commodities, scenes are also productive in their own right. For example, Liverpool's rock scene does not just reflect and express its local context: there is also a sense in which it "produces" the local. The activities and sounds of Liverpool's rock scene contribute to and shape Liverpool's social, cultural, and economic life. The scene has, for example, inspired

246

people from all over the world to visit or even move to Liverpool. The success of The Beatles in the 1960s, the city's vibrant rock scene of the 1970s, and its dance scene of the 1990s have all attracted music fans, "tourists" or "pilgrims," music journalists and clubbers, musicians, and students to the city. Hence Mark Olson links scenes with migrancy and permanent motion in order to highlight musical mobility and travel, musical "routes" as opposed to "roots." The scene has thus influenced Liverpool's image outside the city, affecting the way in which the city is thought about or imagined by people all over the world. Meanwhile, within Liverpool, the scene has often been a focus for debates over the marketing and re-imaging of the city and has thus influenced people's sense of local identity and belonging.

For example, the linking of Liverpool's rock scenes with a distinctive local sound by musicians, music fans, music journalists, and business people is quite common, but the relationship between sound and the local is not straightforward. As John Street (1995, p. 259) has argued, while the local matters as a distinctive structural and political setting for the scene, it does not necessarily "follow from this . . . that what is heard and played is itself understood in terms of the local" ("(Dis)located"). Different cities might "make different noises," but music cannot be connected to a city as if it directly mirrored it, reflecting through sound the city's social, cultural, economic, and geographical characteristics. Rather, the "rhetoric of the local" indicates the ways in which place and the local are shaped, produced, or imagined by the scene and through musical discourse, with musicians "placing" themselves and their music through the ways in which they have learned to hear, interpret, and talk about music. Thus, as Olson points out, scenes should not be taken for granted or treated as inert *scenery* or settings for music activity. Rather, attention should be paid to the peculiar characteristics and dynamics of scenes and to their relative autonomy and productive qualities.

CONCLUSION

"Scene" is a familiar term in popular music studies, but it has generally been used uncritically or interchangeably with terms like subculture or community. More recently there have been attempts to use the term as a theoretical tool in order to reconceptualize local popular music culture. Notions of musical "subcultures" or "communities" as groups that are homogeneous, bounded, rooted, and locally confined have been chal-

247

lenged. Scenes have been linked with debates on relations between local and global and with notions of local culture as dynamic, shifting, geographically mobile, and globally interconnected. The concept of "scene" is in some ways particularly pertinent to popular music. Popular music scenes develop because local amateur music-making is cheaper and more accessible and extensive than many other types of local cultural production, such as film and television, and they are also particularly geographically mobile. Musicians and audiences travel and tour on a regular basis, music products are widely distributed in the form of CDs, tapes, fanzines, and so on, and music sounds and discussions are broadcast on radio and television and via the Internet.

Over the past fifteen years or so, European and American policy-makers have become increasingly interested in local music (particularly rock and pop) scenes. Like Austin's alternative rock scene, for example, those of Liverpool and Manchester came to be referred to as local "industries" during the 1980s, and to be increasingly valued by the city governments in terms of their potential to promote new, youthful, and vibrant local images that could help attract visitors and investment. They are valued as well for their glamorous public relations potential, and for their potential to generate business, jobs, and income and thus to improve the local economy. Further research on local scenes could help to explain their global, mobile character, illuminating how scenes emerge; the conditions and circumstances in which they might flourish creatively; whether policy initiatives can help or hinder their economic development; why some scenes travel better than others; how different types of scenes vary in terms of their local, national, and international relationships, and their economic potential and policy needs.

Some academic accounts of music scenes tend to be too abstract and generalized to adequately address such questions, which is why research of an ethnographic, comparative nature could prove particularly helpful in illuminating the nature of local scenes, their life cycles and geographical routes. Ethnographic studies of local music scenes such as those by Shank and Finnegan have been accused of being parochial for focusing exclusively on one particular scene or place and for suggesting that the scene is unique and confined to and determined by that place, thus overlooking complex and important relationships between scenes of different places. However, Shank highlighted the international travels and geographical dispersal of a scene like punk, while also pointing out how punk took on a specifically local form in Austin, shaped by the city's history and contemporary socio-economic characteristics. Similarly, although Finnegan

248

studied musical worlds in Milton Keynes, she also pointed to complex relationships that linked local musical worlds with music institutions and patterns outside of Milton Keynes.

This led Finnegan to reassess the notion of a musical "world," which implies separateness and boundedness, and to consider alternative and more appropriate terms. She rejected the term music "community," which presents local music-making as too stable and close-knit, and she also rejected the idea of a musical "network," because it presents local music-making as too disparate and fragmented. In an attempt to move away from notions of local music-making as enclosed, rooted, and static, and to use a metaphor that conveys a sense of music-making as a more active, open, and dynamic process, she eventually settled upon the notion of musical "pathways." This is in some ways indicative of the way in which "scene" has since been reconceptualized in popular music studies in order to shift emphasis from music as local culture to music as global, mobile culture. Further ethnographies of scenes could help to illustrate the way in which scenes are lived, experienced, and imagined by particular groups within particular situations, and to explore their local, national, and transnational connections. Such ethnographies would not study scenes simply as local culture in particular places, but attend to the ways in which scenes both produce the local and move across and connect disparate places.

Resources

Cohen, Sara (1991) *Rock Culture in Liverpool: Popular Music in the Making.* Oxford: Oxford University Press.

Finnegan, Ruth (1989) *The Hidden Musicians: Music-making in an English Town.* Cambridge: Cambridge University Press.

Kirschner, Tony (1998) Studying rock: towards a materialist ethnography. In Thomas Swiss, John Sloop, and Andrew Herman (eds), *Mapping the Beat: Popular Music and Contemporary Theory.* Malden, MA and Oxford: Blackwell, pp. 247–68.

Kruse, Holly (1993) Subcultural identity in alternative music culture. *Popular Music*, 12(1), 33–43.

Olson, Mark J. V. (1998) Everybody loves our town: scenes, spatiality, migrancy. In Thomas Swiss, John Sloop, and Andrew Herman (eds), *Mapping the Beat: Popular Music and Contemporary Theory.* Malden, MA and Oxford: Blackwell, pp. 269–90.

Shank, Barry (1993) *Dissonant Identities: the Rock 'n' Roll Scene in Austin, Texas.*

249

Hanover, NH and London: Wesleyan University Press.

Straw, Will (1991) Systems of articulation, logics of change: communities and scenes in popular music. *Cultural Studies*, 5, 368–88.

Street, John (1993) Local differences? popular music and the local state. *Popular Music*, 12, 43–56.

Street, John (1995) (Dis)located? Rhetoric, politics, meaning and the locality. In Will Straw, Stacey Johnson, Rebecca Sullivan, and Paul Friedlander (eds), *Popular Music: Style and Identity*. Montreal: Centre for Research on Canadian Cultural Industries and Institutions/International Association for the Study of Popular Music.

Swiss, Thomas, Sloop, John, and Herman, Andrew (eds) (1998) *Mapping the Beat: Popular Music and Contemporary Theory*. Malden, MA and Oxford: Blackwell.

Toynbee, Jason (1995) Review of *Dissonant Identities: the Rock 'n' Roll Scene in Austin, Texas*, by Barry Shank. *Popular Music*, 14, 377–9.

Index